THE CONCISE DICTIONARY
OF EARLY CHRISTIANITY

The Concise Dictionary of Early Christianity

Joseph F. Kelly

A Michael Glazier Book
THE LITURGICAL PRESS
Collegeville, Minnesota

A Michael Glazier Book published by The Liturgical Press

Cover design by David Manahan, O.S.B.

1   2   3   4   5   6   7   8   9

Library of Congress Cataloging-in-Publication Data

Kelly, Joseph F. (Joseph Francis), 1945–
    The concise dictionary of early Christianity / Joseph F. Kelly.
        p.   cm.
    "A Michael Glazier book."
    Includes bibliographical references.
    ISBN 0-8146-5527-0
    1. Church history—Primitive and early church, ca. 30–600–Dictionaries.   I. Title.
BR95.K395   1992
270.1'03—dc20   92-491
                                                                                 CIP

Roberto filio meo dilecto:
Adulescenti scientia et intellectus (Proverbia 1:4)

Contents

Introduction

Although I hope that scholars may find this book a handy ready-reference tool, I have written it primarily for undergraduate and graduate students, seminarians, religious educators, people in ministry, and those who are simply interested, in a nonprofessional way, in early Christianity.

The book is intentionally brief to make it more usable. I have concentrated on people, movements, and terms that will probably be of most interest to the reader. This is something of a value judgment, but one that must be made. Inevitably there are topics and persons on the borderline between fame and obscurity; in dubious cases I have included an entry. In general, I have avoided geography, leaving that to the map, and I have equally avoided dealing with the development of Christianity in a particular place, such as Rome or Constantinople, simply because this would require articles far too long for this book. I have also avoided those topics that necessitate detailed treatment, for example, God and grace. Topics like these and the geography can be found in larger, more encyclopedic works.

This book deals with Christianity from the first to the sixth century. The end point is somewhat artificial, especially for the East, where there was not the sharp break that there was in the West. In the West, however, the seventh and later centuries clearly belong to the Middle Ages, and so, for the sake of balance, I have stopped with the sixth century. As for the starting point, I have not included material from the New Testament. There are several fine New Testament dictionaries, and there is no need for this volume to repeat what they do.

In general, I have followed the consensus of scholars for the entries. To be sure, many people and events of early Christianity continue to be sources of great debates, but a work such as this is not the place to engage in those debates.

Traditionally the study of early Christianity has centered around the study of theologians, but in recent years scholars have emphasized the social background of the period as well as the contributions of people hitherto unstudied, such as

1

women, to use the most conspicuous example. A concise dictionary cannot deal extensively with complex social movements, but I have included entries about all the prominent women of early Christianity. I have also included many saints of the period. While many of them are the products of legend, such as Saint George and Saint Catherine of Alexandria, many Christians grew up hearing about the saints and would probably be interested to know what scholars currently think about them.

Two other groups are covered in this book. Although off to the side of the great developments in early Christianity, the British Isles were converted in that period. There is no way that Patrick and Gildas will ever rival Origen and Augustine, but the early history of Christianity in Britain and Ireland will presumably interest English-speaking readers. Therefore all figures from those countries with a claim to historicity are included.

Much of early Christianity has passed irrevocably into history, but one institution has survived and flourished even to this century—the papacy. The bishops of Rome do not become major figures in Church history much before the fourth century, but the early development of the papacy has had an impact on Christianity ever since. Therefore, there are entries on every pope.

(N.B. The word "pope" was not used exclusively of the bishop of Rome until the ninth century, and it is likely that in the earliest Roman community a college of presbyters rather than a single bishop provided the leadership. For the sake of clarity, however, all those whom the popes have reckoned to be their antecedents, with Saint Peter excepted, are referred to as pope.)

The Christians interacted with the Jews, Greeks, and Romans during this period, and there are references in the text to Jewish writings, Greek philosophy, and Roman emperors, but, in general, I have not included material specifically on non-Christian individuals or groups. The same is true for later, that is, medieval, writers who preserved early Christian material.

The three appendices provide a brief survey of early Christian history, a list of the ancient popes, and a list of the Roman emperors in this period.

In the opening paragraph, I explained for whom this book was intended and why. But there is another reason I wrote it. Like all dictionaries, this one has tried to make its entries self-sufficient, but, inevitably, some entries will cause the reader to look up other ones; for example, going from Cyril of Alexandria to Nestorius of Constantinople to the First Council of Ephesus. This will, equally inevitably, increase the reader's knowledge of early Christianity and, I hope, increase the reader's interest. I love the study of early Christianity and always find myself surprised and disappointed when others find it uninteresting or, even worse, irrelevant to their more modern concerns. I hope that perusal of some entries in this book will lead the reader to learn more and more about this truly fascinating and enormously formative period in Church history. (The brief bibliography at the end of the book can start as a guide.)

It is now my pleasure to thank the people who aided me in writing this book. First and foremost, thanks to Mr. Michael Glazier, who suggested this to me and whose interest has sustained my work. Thanks also to the many early Christian scholars, including my friends and colleagues in the North American Patristic Society, whose tireless research has illuminated this period; particular thanks to Rev. Robert Eno, S. S., of The Catholic University of America and to Prof. W. H. C. Frend, now emeritus from the University of Glasgow, who both read drafts of this manuscript and made many helpful and, indeed, valuable suggestions. My gratitude to Dean Frederick Travis and former Dean William Ryan of the College of Arts and Sciences of John Carroll University, who kindly agreed to give me a reduced load so I could pursue this work, as well as to Dr. Sally Wertheim, dean of the Graduate School at JCU and coordinator of research, who arranged for financial assistance for this project. My gratitude likewise to my graduate assistants at JCU, Mrs. Suzanne Kozub and Ms. Debra Marsey, who helped with the proofreading, and my secretary, Mrs. Pamela Waldschmidt, who took care of many minor details. When this book passed from Michael Glazier, Inc., to The Liturgical Press, Mr. Mark Twomey took considerable interest in the work and smoothed the transition of publishers. Also, Ms. Bette Montgomery read the book for The Liturgical Press and provided numerous editorial suggestions and helped to make this a better book. Finally, my thanks always to my wife, Ellen, for her understanding and encouragement.

This book is dedicated to my son Robert, whose intellectual interests would make any parent proud.

The deficiencies of the book are attributable only to the author.

Joseph F. Kelly
John Carroll University
Cleveland, Ohio

Abbreviations

*   An asterisk before a word means that there is an entry on that person or subject elsewhere in the volume.

ca.   From the Latin *circa,* meaning "around" or "about"; scholars use this when they are uncertain of the exact dates, for example, Telesphorus was pope from ca. 125 to ca. 136.

d.   Before a date, this means the person died in that year.

fl.   From the Latin *floruit,* meaning "flourished"; scholars use this when they do not know a person's birth or death dates but do know when she or he was prominent, for example, the reference for Optatus of Milevis (fl. ca. 370–380) means that he wrote his important book probably between 370 and 380.

Dictionary of Early Christianity

A

AARON AND JULIUS (d. ca. 304)

British *martyrs who died near Caerleon, probably in the *persecution of Diocletian but possibly in that of Decius in 250; they are mentioned by *Gildas and by the Anglo-Saxon Church historian Bede (d. 735).

ABERCIUS (fl. ca. 170)

*Bishop of Hierapolis in Asia Minor in the late second century; his epitaph survives, indicating that he had traveled to Rome and that he opposed *Montanism.

ABGAR OF EDESSA

Historically, King Abgar V of Edessa (4 B.C. to A.D. 46); in legend, according to *Eusebius of Caesarea, he exchanged letters with Jesus, offered him safety from his enemies, and welcomed the Apostle Thaddeus (*Addai) to his court after Jesus' death.

ACACIAN SCHISM

Roman name for the *schism between Rome and Constantinople that began in 482 during the pontificate of the patriarch *Acacius (471–489) and lasted until 519 because the popes perceived Constantinopolitan patriarchs to be temporizing on *Monophysitism and to be deceiving the popes about their relations with *Peter Mongos, anti-*Chalcedonian patriarch of Alexandria.

ACACIUS OF CAESAREA (d. 365)

Disciple and successor of *Eusebius of Caesarea and leader of a moderate *Arian *Homoian party in the East.

ACACIUS OF CONSTANTINOPLE (d. 489)

*Patriarch of Constantinople from 471; he inherited the confused aftermath of the Council of *Chalcedon, particularly the anti-Chalcedonian tide of opposition; the emperor *Zeno (474–491) wanted the *schism ended, and so Acacius and possibly *Peter Mongos of Alexandria drew up a document called the *Henoticon in 482 in an attempt to find a common ground; the defenders of Chalcedon immediately condemned it, and Rome went into schism from Constantinople.

ACEMETAE

Literally, in Greek, "the sleepless ones"; name given to a group of monks who supported the Council of *Chalcedon against the *Monophysites in the late fifth and early sixth centuries, although they were actually established around 400 by an abbot named Alexander, who stressed poverty, withdrawal, and perpetual liturgical adoration (hence, eventually, the name "the sleepless," although the work was done in shifts). In 428 the monks were persecuted by *Nestorius, *bishop of Constantinople, and in 534 some were excommunicated by Pope *John II for, ironically, holding *Nestorian theological views. In the sixth century they opposed the emperor *Justinian's condemnation of the *Three Chapters.

ACHILLEUS

See **Nereus and Achilleus.**

ACTS, APOCRYPHAL

Name given to a collection of books claiming to tell the stories of biblical figures such as Nicodemus and Pilate as well as Peter, Paul, and other apostles such as Thomas; these are often more legendary than theological.

ADAMANTIUS (fl. ca. 300–310)

Greek anti-*Gnostic writer, author of a *Dialogue*; he is sometimes confused with *Origen, who was occasionally called by this name.

ADDAI (fl. ca. 150–170)

In Syriac tradition, one of the seventy-two disciples mentioned in Luke 10; traditional founder of the Church at Edessa; the book *Doctrine of Addai* is a version of the story of *Abgar, dating approximately 400 and from Syria; in the earlier version Jesus replies to Abgar with a letter, but in this version he replies orally; another change is that Abgar's messenger to Jesus paints a portrait of him to take back to the king.

ADOPTIONISM, ADOPTIONISTS

Name given to the theory that Christ was inspired at his baptism by the Holy Spirit and as a result of his perfect human life was adopted after his resurrection into the Godhead; this theory was popular with the *Monarchians and *Paul of Samosata.

AENEAS OF GAZA (d. 518)

Christian philosopher and friend of the historian *Procopius, he wrote a defense of the immortality of the soul and an attack on the notion of pre-existence.

AETIUS (d. ca. 366)

Radical *Arian from Antioch; he studied Aristotelian philosophy at Alexandria and applied logic rigorously to doctrinal problems; he tried to demonstrate the difference between God the Father, who is ungenerated, and the Son, who is generated; he did not take scriptural proofs into account here. Leader of the *Anomoeans, he was consecrated a *bishop during the reign of *Julian the Apostate (361–363), although he never had a see.

AGAPE

Literally, in Greek, "love," but for early Christians, a "love feast"; this was the communal meal of the early Church, modeled after meals of pagan religious fraternities, which often but not always included the *Eucharist; agape appears in the New Testament, for example, in Jude 12, and again in *Ignatius of Antioch, who refers to it aside from the Eucharist, so it is quite ancient. *Tertullian talks of an agape held to alleviate the distress of the poor, and other sources speak of an agape as a funeral meal for those too poor to afford one; by the end of the fourth century this had largely died out in favor of the Eucharistic celebration.

AGAPETUS I (d. 536)

Pope from 535; name sometimes spelled Agapitus; he opposed *Monophysitism and the emperor *Justinian's Italian campaign on a visit to Constantinople, but he managed the deposition of Anthimus, *bishop of the capital, for being a Monophysite; the pope died in Constantinople. Six of his letters are extant.

AGNES

Fourth-century virgin and *martyr known largely from legends centering on her refusal to give up her consecrated virginity and thus incurring martyrdom; since the Latin for "lamb" is agnus, that animal has often been her symbol.

AGRAPHA

Literally, "the unwritten," but in scholarly circles a name given to sayings of Jesus that appear outside the canonical Gospels and are preserved by early Christian writers; the authenticity of an occasional saying is a possibility but unprovable; the agrapha testify to the widespread citation of dominical sayings outside the New Testament; the largest number of "unwritten" sayings appear in a written work, the Gospel of *Thomas.

AGRIPPA CASTOR

Second-century anti-*Gnostic writer who wrote against *Basilides.

ALBAN

Proto*martyr of Britain, he is mentioned by later sources such as *Gildas; the Anglo-Saxon historian Bede places his death during the *persecution of Diocletian (303–305), although modern scholars think it may have occurred during an earlier persecution.

ALEXANDER I (d. ca. 116)

Pope from about 109; Roman tradition says he was a Roman; nothing firm is known of him beyond his name.

ALEXANDER OF ALEXANDRIA
(d. 328)

*Bishop of Alexandria from 313, he is best known as the earliest opponent of *Arius, whom he condemned at an Alexandrian synod of one hundred Egyptian bishops; although most of his writings have been lost, the two letters and one sermon that survive show that he believed in the eternal sonship of the second person of the Trinity and thus could not accept Arius' teaching; he worked with *Hosius of Cordova and with his deacon and successor at Alexandria, *Athanasius, to combat the spread of *Arianism; the First Council of *Nicea supported his stand.

ALEXANDRIAN THEOLOGY AND EXEGESIS

Along with the *Antiochene school, the Alexandrian writers were the most important group of ancient Christian intellectuals; their contributions fall into many areas, but two stand out. First, on the incarnation they emphasized the unity of the divine and human in Christ; this produced some brilliant theology under *Athanasius and *Cyril, but under *Dioscorus it produced *Monophysitism. Second, in exegesis they favored the *allegorical approach, considering the historical and literal senses of the text to be pointers to a higher truth.

ALLEGORY

Literary device in which a story is told on one level but with its meaning on another level. Because of the many difficulties with the literal meaning of epics such as the *Iliad* and the *Odyssey,* Greek literary critics took to allegorizing the text. An Alexandrian Jewish writer named *Philo (d. ca. 50), who was much taken with Greek culture, applied allegory to parts of the Old Testament. Christian biblical exegetes also took up this method, applying it not only to the Old Testament but also to the New. Although discounted by modern scholars, this was the primary instrument for most *Fathers, including *Origen, who did not initiate it but did popularize it among Christians, and *Augustine, whose influence guaranteed that medieval exegetes would use this method, at least to the time of Thomas Aquinas. This method allowed the Fathers to deal with the apparent crudities of the Old Testament, both moral (Joshua's massacre of the entire population of Jericho) and theological (divine anthropomorphism in Gen 1–11).

ALOGI

Second-century sect from western Asia Minor that opposed *Montanism but that also was wary of the Gospel and Revelation of John, which they attributed to the *Gnostic *Cerinthus; their name comes from their denial of the divinity of the *Logos, possibly to protect the divine oneness.

AMBROSE OF MILAN (ca. 339–397)

*Bishop of Milan from 374, when the populace demanded his appointment to halt the strife between Catholics and *Arians; born to a noble Roman family and well educated (one of the few Westerners of his day fluent in Greek), he is known as the teacher of *Augustine and as the supposed composer of *Ambrosian chant, but his real achievement was in establishing the moral authority of the Church in civic affairs. He did not intend to be a bishop; a lawyer by training, in 370 he was appointed as imperial *praeses* (superintendant) in Milan. In 373, when *Auxentius, Arian bishop of Milan, died, there were fierce disputes in the city between the Arians and Catholics as to who would succeed him. Ambrose intervened to keep the peace, but soon the contending factions decided that he should be the bishop, although he was then only a *catechumen. Ambrose accepted episcopal consecration and soon proved himself an able administrator and concerned pastor. He also exercised considerable influence over the Roman emperor Gratian (375–383), whom he convinced to pass anti*heretical and antipagan legislation. In 382 Gratian removed from the senate chamber the statue of victory, to the pagans a symbol of Roman greatness, and Quintus Aurelius Symmachus, one of the most influential Roman senators of the day, rose in defense of the statue. Ambrose and Symmachus debated the issue in a famous exchange, which is extant; the statue was not replaced. In 386 he forcefully prevented the Arians from gaining control of a Milanese cathedral by literally standing in their way in the cathedral; aided by the presence of Augustine's mother, *Monica, he had his staff do some digging on the cathedral grounds, where they discovered two bodies, which Ambrose proclaimed to be the remains of Saints *Gervasius and Protasius, thus convincing the populace that a miracle had occurred

and God was on his side. The Arians and their imperial supporters withdrew from the fray. When *Theodosius I was emperor (379–395), Ambrose twice rebuked him, once for trying to force Christians of Callinicum in Syria to replace a synagogue that an anti-Semitic mob had burned down (an act in which the emperor was clearly in the right), and he even forced the emperor to do *penance (388), and another time for a massacre of civilians in Thessalonica (391). His view, stated during the Arian imbroglio of 386, was that "the emperor is within the Church, not above the Church." Ambrose was also a theologian of some note and introduced much Greek theology into the West; his writings on the *sacraments are particularly important, as are his main works of Old Tesament exegesis and his commentary on Luke. He was also the author of moral and spiritual works, including several on virginity. Ambrose was the most important Italian bishop of his day, and his tireless efforts to weaken paganism and Arianism resulted in the serious decline of both in Italy.

AMBROSIAN CHANT

The chant of the Church of Milan, dating to the *patristic period and associated with Milan's most famous *bishop; it is a form of plainsong.

AMBROSIASTER (fl. ca. 365–385)

Literally, "*Pseudo-Ambrose," the name given by Erasmus (ca. 1469–1536) to the anonymous author of a Latin commentary on the Pauline epistles, written in Rome during the pontificate of *Damasus I (366–384); the commentary relates the epistles to their historical background; scholars have yet to identify him, although many theories have been proposed.

AMMON (d. ca. 360)

Also called Ammonas or Amun; Egyptian monk and abbot; disciple and successor of *Antony at the monastery of Pispir; seven of his letters are extant.

AMMONIUS

Third-century Alexandrian who wrote biblical commentaries extant only in fragments; marginal markings in Gospel *manuscripts to indicate parallel passages are called Ammonian sections, but they appear to be the work of *Eusebius of Caesarea.

AMPHILOCHIUS OF ICONIUM (ca. 340–395)

Friend of the *Cappadocians, *bishop of Iconium in Asia Minor from 373, stong opponent of *Arianism and of sects practicing fanatical *asceticism; fragments of his writings survive.

ANACLETUS (d. ca. 91)

Pope from approximately 79; name also spelled Anencletus or just Cletus; *Irenaeus mentions him as Peter's second successor; nothing is known about him beyond his name.

ANAPHORA

In Greek, the "lifting up," used liturgically to mean the second part of the early Christian liturgy, specifically, the consecration of the *Eucharist and the prayers associated with it; several *anaphoras* survive, attributed to individual Church *Fathers.

ANASTASIA (d. ca. 304)

*Martyr from Pannonia, modern Croatia; her name was included in the old Roman Canon of the Mass.

ANASTASIUS I (d. 401)

Pope from 399; his brief pontificate had to deal with the *Origenist controversy, about which he was poorly informed; he struggled to keep the see of Thessalonica in the orbit of Rome rather than Constantinople.

ANASTASIUS II (d. 498)

Pope from 496; he tried to end the *Acacian schism and maintain Roman primacy by diplomacy, only to be criticized in Rome for weakness and leniency; he also worked for the Byzantine recognition of Theodoric the Ostrogothic king as the de facto ruler of Italy; four of his letters are extant.

ANATOLIUS (d. ca. 282)

A native of Alexandria, he founded a school of Aristotelian philosophy; *bishop of Caesarea in Palestine around 264; bishop of Laodicea in 268; only fragments of his writings survive.

ANCHORITE

A monk who was a hermit; normally used of *eremitic monks but also of *cenobitic monks if they lived in individual cells.

ANDREW, ACTS OF

Nonextant second-century *apocryphon that described Andrew's life and miracles and expressed *Encratite values; these facts can be gathered from surviving fragments in Coptic and Latin.

ANDREW OF CAESAREA

Fifth-century *bishop of Caesarea and author of the earliest Greek commentary on the Book of Revelation, which he explains in spiritual rather than literal terms.

ANICETUS (d. ca. 166)

Pope from about 155; a Syrian; the only event known from his episcopate is a visit by *Polycarp in an attempt to settle the *Quartodeciman controversy; the two *bishops agreed to disagree.

ANOMOEANS

Fourth-century sect that claimed that the Father cannot be divided and thus the Son is a creature who is unlike (*anomoios* in Greek) the Father in essence; traditionally understood as a form of *Arianism, although few Arians were that radical; *Aetius of Antioch and *Eunomius of Cyzicus were its leaders.

ANTERUS (d. 236)

Pope from 235; virtually nothing is known of him beyond his Greek name,

proof that the non-Latin element continued to be strong in the Roman Church into the third century.

ANTI-MARCIONITE PROLOGUES

A set of short prologues to the Gospels of Mark, Luke, and John (the one for Matthew is apparently missing), thought earlier in this century to have been composed against *Marcion of Pontus but actually from the fourth century and possibly not composed as a group; they were widely popular in the Middle Ages and appear in many *manuscripts of the *Vulgate.

ANTIOCHENE THEOLOGY AND EXEGESIS

Along with the *Alexandrian school, the Antiochene writers were the most important group of ancient Christian intellectuals; their contributions fall into many areas, but two stand out. First, on the incarnation they emphasized the distinction between the divine and human in Christ, occasionally to the point of separating the two and thus resulting in *Nestorianism. Second, as exegetes they stressed the historical and literal meanings of the scriptural text, very much the type of exegesis done by contemporary scholars.

ANTIPOPE

A person who claimed to be pope but who is not recognized by later popes as one of their predecessors; *Hippolytus was the first antipope.

ANTONY (251-356)

Long-lived founder of Egyptian *asceticism, he was eighteen when he gave his goods to the poor and went to the desert to live as a *hermit, but his life attracted many followers and he was forced to head a community; he became a hermit again around 310 but stayed in contact with the outside world and supported *Athanasius in the *Arian controversy; Athanasius' vivid *Life of Saint Antony* was widely read and helped spread both knowledge and acceptance of desert *monasticism and its values. This *vita does not provide many historical details about Antony—indeed, since Antony was a hermit, much would be known only to him—but it does stress his battles with demons and his enormous effect on those with whom he came in contact. Antony was apparently a man of great spiritual power and presence whose influence on monasticism was enormous and long lasting, since even lifelong *cenobites often felt the summit of their career was to become a hermit like the great Antony.

APELLES

Second-century *Gnostic and one-time disciple of *Marcion of Pontus; he taught at both Alexandria and Rome; he defended the necessity of good works for salvation, denied Marcion's dualism, and accepted Christ's coming in the flesh; he was important enough to merit an attack by *Tertullian.

APHRAATES (fl. 330-350)

The earliest Syriac Church *Father; he grew up within the Persian Empire during a period of *persecution of Christians; he apparently held a hierarchical post, but of what kind is unknown; his writings deal largely with *asceticism and show no influence of either Greek philosophy or *Nicene theology.

APHTHARTODOCETAE

A *Monophysite sect of the sixth century that claimed that Christ's human preresurrection body was not subject to corruption, in contrast to the more common belief of Monophysites and *Chalcedonians alike that only the resurrected body could enjoy such a state.

APIARIUS (fl. ca. 415-425)

African *priest who was deposed for misconduct in office; his appeal to *Bishop *Zosimus of Rome (417-418) provoked a crisis between Rome and Africa when the pope insisted on his reinstatement; astonishingly the same thing occurred in 423, but then Apiarius confessed his guilt; after this case the African hierarchy forbade African clerics to appeal "beyond the sea."

APOCALYPSES, APOCRYPHAL

Visionary treatises claiming to have been written by biblical figures such as Peter and Paul and to describe either the end of the world or the worlds to come; some date as early as the second century, others as late as the fifth.

APOCRYPHA, APOCRYPHON

A term for all writings which claim to be by or about biblical figures but which are not included in the Old or New Testament canon; there are many of these; some may contain historical reminiscences, but the real value of this literature is the picture it provides of popular religious life; apocryphal works emerged from both orthodox and *heterodox circles from the late first century to the end of the *patristic period; many apocryphal works, especially those about Jesus, influenced Christian artists. The singular form of the word is "apocryphon."

APOLLINARIS (ca. 310–ca. 390); APOLLINARIANISM

*Bishop of Laodicea in Asia Minor from 361, Apollinaris was a strong opponent of the *Arians and a strong supporter of *Athanasius. In his youth, his father and he rewrote sections of the Old and New Testaments in classical rhetorical forms (hexameters and dialogues) to provide literature for Christians who were forbidden by the emperor *Julian the Apostate (361–363) to teach the classics. As bishop, Apollinaris argued for the divinity of the Son against the Arians, but his teaching eventually denied the full humanity of Christ, saying that the rational soul in him had been replaced by the divine *Logos, a rather widely accepted idea, which now came under scrutiny. Soon his teaching was attacked by several leading *Nicene theologians and finally condemned, first by a Roman synod in 379 and then by the First Council of *Constantinople in 381. His extant writings are few, but because some of his works were later thought to be by Athana-

sius, his influence survived to the mid-fifth century.

APOLLINARIS, CLAUDIUS (fl. ca. 170)

*Bishop of Hierapolis and *apologist who wrote now nonextant defenses of Christianity against the pagans during the reign of Marcus Aurelius (161–180) as well as a critique of the *Montanists.

APOLOGETICS; APOLOGISTS

Apologetics is the art of rational self-defense, especially of one's intellectual position or belief. In the second century a group of theologians known as the apologists defended Christianity against slanders by (1) refuting the slanders of pagans, (2) recounting the true beliefs and practices of the Christians, and (3) attacking the beliefs of their opponents. Christian apologetics began with *Quadratus in the early second century and flourished for the rest of that century, for example, in the careers of *Justin Martyr and *Athenagoras; it continued through *Origen and down to *Augustine; it had a long post-*patristic history, for example, against Islam in the Middle Ages and among Christian denominations in the Reformation. In historical context, the apologetic movement is very important, representing the first attempt by Christians to win over the wider world with the first Christian books written for non-Christians; this concern for living in peace with pagans and Jews also indicates that *eschatology was dying out in the Church at large.

APONIUS (fl. 405–415)

Italian writer of an *allegorical commentary on the Song of Songs, much used in the early Middle Ages.

APOPHTHEGMATA PATRUM

Greek for the *Sayings of the Fathers,* an anonymous collection of stories and especially edifying sayings attributed to the great Egyptian monks; this collection probably originated orally in Coptic but was written in Greek by the end of the fourth century; the collection gives a colorful, lively picture of the monks as well as passing on the folk wisdom of rural Egypt; it was known in Latin no later than the sixth century; it exercised enormous influence in popularizing *monastic values.

APOSTLES' CREED

A Western Latin *creed first mentioned by *Ambrose about 390 and commented upon by *Rufinus of Aquileia; although in its current form it apparently was composed in France in the eighth century, an earlier form was known and widely used in the sixth century. Ultimately, however, this creed looks back to the questions asked of *baptismal candidates in Rome in the second century; a Greek version probably came into use in the third century. Later tradition claimed its twelve individual parts were each composed by an apostle. At the *Council of Ferrara in 1438 the Latins were surprised to learn that the Greeks knew nothing of this creed.

APOSTOLIC CHURCH ORDER

An Egyptian work of the early fourth century, this claims to give the teachings of the apostles after the resurrection on such topics as Church order and morality.

APOSTOLIC CONSTITUTIONS

A collection of eight books containing ecclesiastical legislation dating from the fourth century and probably emanating from Syria; they draw from a large variety of earlier literature, such as the *Didache and the *Didascalia Apostolorum, and they deal with a wide variety of topics: *martyrdom, widowhood, *sacraments, and Church order. In its current form, this is probably a *Semi-Arian composition.

APOSTOLIC FATHERS

Name given in the seventeenth century to a group of early *Fathers, supposedly immediate successors to the apostles; actually the title is also given to written works about whose author virtually nothing is known. The Apostolic Fathers include *Clement of Rome, *Ignatius of Antioch, *Hermas, *Polycarp, *Papias, the authors of Second *Clement, the Epistle of *Barnabas, the Epistle to *Diognetus, and the *Didache.

APRINGIUS (fl. ca. 550)

*Bishop of Beja in modern Portugal, he wrote an Apocalypse commentary.

AQUARII

Literally, "the water men"; extreme *ascetics, similar to the *Encratites;

mentioned by several fourth-century writers.

ARATOR (fl. 530–545)

A Roman sub*deacon, originally trained as an orator, who wrote in verse an *allegorical commentary on the Acts of the Apostles, the first Latin commentary on that biblical book.

ARIANISM

In letter, the teaching of *Arius, but in actuality, a cover-all name for a variety of fourth-century teachings deriving from his teachings. Arius denied the divinity of the *Logos, asserting it to be the most perfect of creatures but still a creature. His teaching provoked the first *ecumenical council, at *Nicea, at which the *homoousios, a term connoting consubstantiality of the Father and Son, and thus the Son's divinity, was employed to refute him. Despite the condemnation, confusion over the term homoousios and political maneuvering kept Arianism alive in the fourth century although in varying forms (*Semi-Arianism); the efforts of *Ulfilas brought Arianism to the Germanic peoples entering the Roman Empire. Arianism was finally condemned within the empire at the First Council of *Constantinople in 381. The struggle against Arianism engaged the best Greek minds of the fourth century (*Athanasius, *Gregory of Nyssa, *Gregory of Nazianzus, and *Basil of Caesarea), along with *Hilary of Poitiers in the West.

ARIMINUM AND SELEUCIA

Joint synods of 359, held in both West and East to settle the *Arian question.

The *council at Ariminum (modern Rimini) was initially anti-Arian, but the machinations of two Arian *bishops, *Valens and *Ursacius, along with pressure from the Arian emperor, *Constantius II (337–361), got the bishops to agree to a vague *creed susceptible of Arian interpretation.

ARISTIDES

Second-century Athenian *apologist who used Stoic natural philosophy (i.e., science) to argue for God's existence and the misunderstanding of God by pre-Christian peoples; he divided the peoples of the world according to religion, that is, pagans, Jews, and Christians, and argued for the superiority of the last; his apology, put together by scholars from other sources, is the oldest extant Christian apology.

ARISTION

First-century *presbyter mentioned by *Papias as one who preserved reliable traditions about Jesus.

ARISTO OF PELLA (fl. ca. 140)

He wrote the now nonextant *Dialogue Between Jason and Papiscus,* an *apologetic work involving a dialogue between the converted Jew Jason and his friend Papiscus, whom Jason converts by demonstrating that Christianity is the true successor to Judaism.

ARIUS (ca. 260–336)

Alexandrian *priest who initiated *Arianism. He was a student of

*Lucian of Antioch and headed a large parish church in Alexandria, where he won a reputation as a preacher and an *ascetic, but his teaching about Christ (Arianism) caused notoriety. His *bishop, *Alexander of Alexandria, excommunicated him. He went to Palestine, where he received a sympathetic hearing, but in 325 he was condemned for *heresy at the *ecumenical Council of *Nicea. He was banished to Illyria, but through the influence of *Eusebius of Nicomedia he was called back from exile and died shortly before his full rehabilitation. Although routinely damned as a frightful heretic, he did in fact teach a *subordinationist *Christology that others before him had taught; also, toward the end of his life, he had ceased to be a leader of anything and was largely caught up in a movement headed by others.

ARNOBIUS THE ELDER (d. ca. 330)

African rhetorician and convert from paganism, he wrote *Adversus nationes,* literally, "against the peoples" (although pagans are meant), a defense of Christianity and an attack on paganism that preserved some material about ancient mythology. His earnestness outweighed his knowledge of basic Christian teaching; he relied little on Christian sources but heavily on Plato and some Roman writers, as well as more mystical writers such as Pythagoras.

ARNOBIUS THE YOUNGER (fl. ca. 450)

African monk who fled the Vandal invasion to live in Italy, where he wrote against the teaching of *Augustine on grace.

ARTEMON

Third-century teacher at Rome who claimed that Christ had no divine qualities; he was probably a disciple of *Theodotus the Shoemaker and derived his notions from *Adoptionist *Monarchianism.

ASCETICISM

From the Greek *askesis* (athletic training), it came to mean rigorous physical self-denial for religious perfection; it is closely associated with *monasticism but was widely practiced by many people in their own homes or in nonmonastic religious communities in early Christianity; many ascetic values spread to the larger Church in the fourth and fifth centuries.

ASTERIUS OF AMASEA (d. ca. 410)

*Bishop by 390; he wrote homilies praising the *martyrs and condemning paganism. One of his sermons on the martyr Saint Euphemia describes a painting of her death, an important text for art history.

ASTERIUS THE SOPHIST (d. after 341)

Before his conversion he had been a philosopher; he studied with *Lucian of Antioch and apparently was the first supporter of *Arius to use philosophy to support his teaching; he also wrote extant commentaries on the Psalter and lost commentaries on Paul and the Gospels; *Athanasius considered him an important and worthy opponent.

ATHANASIAN CREED

A Western, probably Gallic *creed of the fifth century; it deals with the Trinity and the incarnation, reflecting the doctrinal questions of the period, especially *Nestorianism; it also introduces some anathemas. Medieval tradition linked it to *Athanasius.

ATHANASIUS OF ALEXANDRIA
(ca. 296–373)

The greatest of the fourth-century defenders of the First Council of *Nicea and opponents of *Arius, he was a *deacon at the first *ecumenical council and later *bishop of Alexandria. He was a voluminous writer and skilled politician who advanced the Nicene cause; he was clearly the dominant ecclesiastical figure of the fourth century. He was enormously popular in Alexandria, and although he was driven five times from his see by ecclesiastical and imperial enemies (often working together), he was always able to return; indeed, the unwavering support of his people made much of his career possible. He was deacon to Bishop *Alexander of Alexandria, whom he succeeded in 328. He had to deal initially with the *Melitian schism, which decreased in significance throughout his epsicopate but which never was settled. His greatest challenge was with the *Arians, who, despite their namesake's condemnation at Nicea, persisted and then grew in strength as Eastern bishops had second thoughts about the *homoousios. His doctrinal and ecclesiastical enemies (Athanasius was often high-handed in his dealings with other bishops) engineered his condemnation at a synod at Tyre in 335, and the emperor *Constantine I exiled him to Trier, making him familiar with the Western Churches and the Western Churches familiar with him. He returned upon the emperor's death in 337, only to be exiled again in 339 by the Arianizing emperor *Constantius II. Pope *Julius I welcomed him and favored his cause; thanks to Western ecclesiastical and imperial support, in 346 he was able to return to his see, where he stayed for ten years. Constantius turned against him again, and from 356 to 361 he hid among the monks of the Egyptian desert and governed his diocese in secret. The emperor's death allowed him to return, but in 362 the new emperor, *Julian the Apostate, exiled him again, but Julian soon died and Athanasius returned in 363. Yet another exile awaited him, in 365–366, under another Arianizing emperor, Valens (364–378), but the bishop's great popularity forced the emperor to recant, and Athanasius was in Alexandria again until his death in 373. This remarkable man was the truest of the Nicene theologians, firmly believing in the consubstantiality of the Son, who was begotten, not created, by the Father. He argued as well for the eternity of the Son and, later in his life, for the eternity and divinity of the Holy Spirit. He pressed for the redemptive necessity of the incarnation and was careful to keep the Son's humanity from being swallowed up in the divinity, although Athanasius does not seem to have dealt very clearly with the notion of a human soul for Christ. Although he always promoted the Nicene cause, he worked for reconciliation with the *Semi-Arians, many of whom he realized to be close to Nicea in their doctrines, and his council at Alexandria in 362 furthered these efforts. As *patriarch of Alexandria, he was also patriarch of the monks in the Egyptian desert; his exile among them resulted in his *Life of Saint *Antony,* the work which popularized *monasticism in the East and, via a Latin translation, in the West as well. He has the distinction of being the first Christian to list as his New Testament canon the twenty-seven books accepted by the Church at large, which he did in a festal (for Lent) letter in 367. A considerable body of his writings survives, including theological, *apologetic, exegetical, *ascetical, and pastoral works. Even today Athanasius remains a controversial figure, but the history of the fourth-century Church is literally unthinkable without him.

ATHENAGORAS (fl. 170–180)

Athenian Christian philosopher of the late second century. Around 177 he wrote a defense of Christianity addressed to the emperor Marcus Aurelius (161–180) and his son Commodus (180–192) and a treatise on the resurrection, more from philosophical than from theological considerations, probably to make the work more relevant to the emperor as well as to use his considerable knowledge of Greek literature.

ATTICUS (d. 425)

*Patriarch of Constantinople from 405 to 425, he initially *persecuted the followers of *John Chrysostom but later reconciled himself to them and ac-

knowledged John's place as one of his predecessors; he is not known as a theologian.

AUGUSTINE OF CANTERBURY (d. ca. 605)

A monk at Rome, he was sent to England in 596 to convert the pagan Angles and Saxons by Pope *Gregory the Great; hearing of the barbarities of these pagan tribes, Augustine and his companions prepared to turn back while journeying through Gaul, but Gregory urged them to persevere, which they did, landing in Kent in 597; the Kentish king *Ethelbert had a Christian wife, Bertha, a Frankish princess, who interceded for the missionaries. Augustine returned to Gaul to be consecrated a *bishop at Arles; he established his see at Canterbury, the traditional see of the *primate of England. In 603 Augustine's rudeness to the British bishops in refusing to stand when they arrived for a meeting caused a break with the Celtic Church in Britain, which was not healed for more than century. Although his own work was limited largely to Kent, Augustine established a base for the Christianization of the English and the Romanization of the English Church.

AUGUSTINE OF HIPPO (354–430)

The greatest of the Latin *Fathers and one of the half-dozen or so greatest thinkers in Christian history. Son of a pagan father, Patricius, and a Christian mother, *Monica, he grew up in Africa and, except for a few years in Italy (383–387), remained there for his entire life. His personal Christianity was not strong, and he became a *Manichee for some time. Disillusioned with Manicheism, he migrated to Italy to advance his career. He was originally a teacher of rhetoric, but under the influence of *Ambrose he was *baptized in 386 and decided to devote his life to Christianity. After the death of his mother he lived briefly in a *monastic community at Cassiciacum; he then returned to Africa to become a *priest and later *bishop of Hippo Regius, an office he held until his death in 430 and to which he devoted enormous amounts of time and energy, so much so that anyone familiar with his works wonders how he had time to write. Augustine died in his episcopal city during the Vandal siege. He was a man of enormous versatility; he can be studied as a theologian, philosopher, humanist, rhetorician, exegete, homilist, spiritual writer, *catechist, and mystic. His spiritual and psychological autobiography, the *Confessions,* is the most widely read of *patristic books. His *City of God,* written first to answer pagan charges that the Christian God had allowed the barbarians to sack Rome in 410, ranks with *Origen's *Against *Celsus* as the most important patristic works of *apologetics; its later sections, with the account of the perpetual struggle between the City of God and the City of Man in human history from creation to the second coming, influenced medieval and even Renaissance historiography. His *De Trinitate* was the basic Western handbook on the Trinity down to the age of the Scholastics, taking the concepts of the Greek theologians and putting them in Western dress with Augustine's own insights.

His extensive biblical exegeses, especially on the Gospel of John, the Psalms, and the Book of Genesis—about which he wrote three books—were likewise the standards for the West. His sermons were long considered Latin models for the genre. His numerous letters reveal the everyday life of a patristic bishop, and his writings on Christian education and the spiritual life reveal the depth of his religion. But his most important theological legacy lay with his apologetic writings against three groups and the dogmatic writings these works engendered. The Manichees were dualists who patronized the Old Testament and its God; against them Augustine affirmed the goodness of creation and the validity of the Old Testament. The *Donatists were African rigorists who insisted on the ritual purity of ecclesiastical groups and insisted that they were the only Christians who had not been tainted by cooperation with pagans during *persecutions; against them Augustine wrote about the spiritual nature of the Church. It was also against the Donatists, when they refused in 412 to accept an imperial decision against them, that Augustine defended the use of political force in ecclesiastical matters, a conclusion he had come to only gradually but an argument with a long and unfortunate legacy. The *Pelagians argued for the possibility of natural perfectability of humans, which Augustine took as an attack on the absolute necessity of divine grace. His many and forceful writings against them led him logically and inevitably to a *predestinationist stance, claiming that only an elect few were to be saved. This pessimistic view of God was moderated in the Middle Ages but revived among right-wing Protestant sects during the Reformation. One could legitimately say that a history of Augustine's teachings in the Western Church is a history of Western theology. His literary output was enormous, and most of it survives.

AUSONIUS (ca. 310–ca. 395)

Gallic nobleman and teacher of rhetoric, he taught members of the Christian imperial house, including the emperor Gratian (375–383) as well as *Paulinus of Nola, whom he tried to discourage from *asceticism and with whom he later corresponded. He was an accomplished poet who wrote verses for the emperor Valentinian I

(364–375), but his Christianity, if not a veneer, was not very deep.

AUXENTIUS (ca. 343–373)

*Arian *bishop of Milan from 355, he was a Cappadocian by birth who owed his office to imperial favor; he does not seem to have vigorously tried to have advanced his cause among the *Nicene Italians.

AVITUS OF VIENNE (450–518)

Gallic nobleman who succeeded his father in 490 as *bishop of Vienne, he worked to convert the *Arian Burgundians and succeeded in converting the king, Sigismund; he was a firm supporter of papal claims in Gaul; many letters as well as some poems and homilies are extant.

B

BACHIARIUS (fl. ca. 375–400)

Spanish monk who apparently had *Priscillianist sympathies; he left Spain and emigrated to Rome, where he wrote two minor works.

BAPTISM

The rite of initiation of the early Church and one of four *sacraments known from antiquity; baptism replaced circumcision as the sign of membership in the community; it was originally by immersion to symbolize the dying and rising of the Christian with Christ, although the second-century *Didache indicates that aspersion was permissible if immersion was not feasible; aspersion was common by the fourth century. Baptism was a communal ceremony peformed usually by the local *bishop during Easter or Pentecost; *catechumens were scrutinized for their knowledge of the basics of the Faith, and by at least the third century a confession of faith was an integral part of the rite; baptism of infants was known from the earliest times but became especially common after the *Pelagian controversy, when *Augustine's vivid picture of the terrors of hell awaiting unbaptized infants moved many not to wait for the sacrament considered essential for salvation. Baptism was the initial penitential sacrament of the early Church; for some time it was thought that there could be no postbaptismal *penance, so people frequently put off being baptized until they were ready to make so serious a commitment, for example, the emperor *Constantine I was baptized on his deathbed. Theological emphasis is usually put on the efficacy of baptism as removing original sin and bringing one into the community, but its symbolism was likewise important in the *patristic period, with much attention paid to Old Testament antecedents such as the passing through the Red Sea.

BARDESANES (ca. 154–222)

Greek form of Bar Daisan; native of Edessa and a pagan, converted to Christianity in 179; he was a *Docetist and, ancient sources say, a disciple of *Valentinus; with his son Harmonides he authored 150 Syriac Christian hymns, which *Ephraem says were so popular that he had to write hymns to counterbalance them; Bardesanes tried unsuccessfully to mix his interest in astrology with his Christianity.

BARNABAS, ACTS OF

A fifth- or six-century Greek *apocryphon of no historical value; it purports to give Mark's account of Barnabas' death on Cyprus (Acts 15:39).

BARNABAS, EPISTLE OF

One of the writings of the *Apostolic Fathers and usually dated from around 125 to 135; it emphasizes the figurative interpretation of the Scriptures in opposition to literal Jewish exegesis and finds predictions of Christ in the Old Testament, thus allowing the author to claim that the Old Testament is now a Christian work; the latter part of the book follows the *Didache in its moral teaching, teaching, that is, on the Two Ways of light and darkness and the importance of choosing the former.

BARSANUPHIUS (d. ca. 540)

Palestinian monk whose many (396) letters deal with *ascetical topics; a teacher of *Dorotheus of Gaza.

BARTHOLOMEW, ACTS OF

Fifth-century possibly Latin *apocryphon about the supposed deeds of the Apostle Bartholomew.

BARTHOLOMEW, GOSPEL OF

Third-century *Gnostic work with a detailed account of Christ's descent into hell.

BASILIDES (fl. 125–150)

Alexandrian *Gnostic who wrote a biblical commentary and a gospel of his own; *Irenaeus indicates that he had a strong interest in cosmology and downplayed the role of the body; he considered God beyond description and the material world, created by angels, to be evil; only fragments of his work survive, but he was important enough to be quoted and attacked by several orthodox writers.

BASIL OF ANCYRA (ca. 300–364)

A *Homoiousian and *bishop of Ancyra from 336; he presided over a synod in 358 that condemned the *homoousios but also opposed radical *Arianism; this was the height of his influence, and when he tried to get the emperor *Constantius II (337–361) to support his activities with a larger *council—which turned out to be that of *Ariminum and Seleucia—he found himself politically outmaneuvered by the radical Arians, who had him deposed from his see and exiled.

BASIL OF CAESAREA (ca. 330–379)

One of the *Cappadocian *Fathers, brother of *Gregory of Nyssa and

*Macrina; member of a distinguished Christian household, he received a good education but abandoned the world for the desert (358–364) until he went to Caesarea as a *priest and became *bishop there in 370. He led the effort to defeat *Arianism and to reconcile the various anti-Arian and *Semi-Arian factions to the Council of *Nicea; he defended the divinity of the Holy Spirit against the *Pneumatomachi. During the reign of the Arian emperor Valens (364–378), Basil also labored to free the Church from state domination. During thc pontificatc of *Damasus Basil tried to convince the Westerners to help end the squabbling in the East, particularly the trouble caused by the *Meletian schism in Antioch, but the pope was more interested in furthering Roman primacy in the East, and a great opportunity for unity and cooperation was lost. A man of great personal spirituality, Basil wrote a Rule for monks, still widely used in the Eastern Churches; he had great reservations about *eremitic *monasticism because he believed that the Christian spirit was fundamentally communal, and eremitic monasticism went contrary to that. As a practicing, workaday bishop, he strove tirelessly to help the poor and ill of the diocese, founding hospitals and hospices. He is justly known in the East as Basil the Great; his writings include dogmatic, *ascetic, and pastoral works.

BASIL OF SELEUCIA (d. ca. 468)

A *bishop whose confusion and hesitation about pre-*Chalcedonian *Christology may reflect a general situation; a Chalcedonian after the *council and a prolific homilist.

BENEDICT I (d. 579)

Pope from 575; he had to deal with the brunt of the Lombard invasion of Italy; his negotiations with the Byzantine emperor Justin II (565–578) for help produced few results, and he died during the Lombard siege of Rome. He extended papal influence in Italy, consecrating no fewer than twenty-one *bishops, including John III of Ravenna, a see that had often challenged Roman primacy.

BENEDICT OF NURSIA
(ca. 480–ca. 550)

A Roman who withdrew from the world to become a *hermit, he later attracted disciples and thus established a monastery at Subiaco; local opposition forced him to move to Monte Cassino, his homc until his death. The influence of his *Rule for Monks,* composed over many years and drawing from common sense and spiritual wisdom, was enormous in the Middle Ages and still is today; it emphasized community and Roman *stabilitas* in opposition to the wandering associated with some Eastern monks. Benedict was extraordinarily thorough, trying to anticipate in his *Rule* any problem that might arise, and he attempted to establish a firm ("the word of the superior is the word of God") yet benevolent authority structure. Modern scholarship has determined that he drew from a wide variety of *patristic sources for his *Rule,* as well as from other *monastic legislators, including an anonymous writer called simply "the Master," author of the *Regula Magistri*. Pope *Gregory I wrote a highly thaumaturgical *vita about him.

BISHOP

See **Episkopos.**

BLANDINA (d. 177)

Christian woman *martyred at Lyons after a series of frightful tortures; her endurance proved a model and inspiration to other Christians during what was the worst *persecution then known.

BLASIUS

According to a very popular legend, a fourth-century Armenian *bishop and *martyr who cured a child who was choking on a fish bone; known in English-speaking lands as Saint Blaise.

BOETHIUS (ca. 420–524)

Anicius Manlius Torquatus Boethius Severinus Senator was a noble Roman who attempted to work with the ruling barbarian Ostrogoths in hopes of preserving Roman culture but who was executed after an accusation of treachery; he wrote several philosophical and theological treatises reflecting *Augustinian and *Chalcedonian views as well as his masterpiece, *On the Consolation of Philosophy,* a meditation on evil and justice with no explicit Christian teaching nor any contradiction either;

he greatly influenced medieval humanistic culture.

BONIFACE I (d. 422)

Pope from 418; he condemned the teachings of *Pelagius, and he extended papal power in southern Gaul and the Balkans; he also had to deal with the *antipope *Eulalius, but the support of the emperor Honorius (395–423) enabled Boniface to keep his see.

BONIFACE II (d. 532)

Pope from 530; a Goth and first pope of Germanic background, he was culturally a Roman; he supported the decrees of the Second Council of *Orange and condemned *Semi-Pelagianism; he also worked to maintain papal authority in the Balkans, threatened by the *bishops of Constantinople; for three weeks in 530 he had to deal with the *antipope *Dioscorus, whose early death avoided a potential *schism.

BORDEAUX, PILGRIM OF (ca. 333)

Anonymous Christian from Bordeaux who traveled to Jerusalem, remained in the Holy Land for some months, and then went at least to Milan (where his account of his journey ends); presumably he attempted to return home; his account provides some information about the holy places of Palestine in the *Constantinian period.

C

CAECILIAN OF CARTHAGE
(d. ca. 345)

Elected *bishop of Carthage in 311 but accused of having been consecrated by a *traditor, that is, one who handed over the Scriptures to the pagans; opposition to him resulted in the *Donatist schism, although three non-African synods (Rome, 313; Arles, 314; Milan, 316) all supported his claim to the see.

CAESARIUS OF ARLES
(ca. 470–542)

Son of a noble Gallo-Roman family, he was a monk at *Lérins for some years; he later studied rhetoric and entered the clergy; he became abbot of a monastery near Arles in 499 and *bishop of that city in 502; he established Arles as *primatial see in Gaul, fought *Semi-Pelagianism at the Second Council of *Orange in 529, founded a women's monastery and wrote a Rule for it, and generally worked to improve the state of Christian life in his diocese; famous as a homilist (more than two hundred sermons survive).

CAINITES

A *Gnostic sect dating from the second century; its adherents apparently numbered very few, and their teachings are not always easy to distinguish from those of other groups such as the *Sethians; they praised both Cain and Judas, the first as one of many primordial beings—a concept known in ancient Iran—and the second as superior to the other apostles because he knew the (Gnostic) truth about Christ.

CALLISTUS I (d. 222)

Pope from 217; a former slave and convicted embezzler, he was rescued from the Sardinian penal mines when *Marcia, concubine of the emperor Commodus (180–192) and a Christian, requested from the emperor the release

27

of some Christian prisoners. Callistus was apparently very influential during the pontificate of *Zephyrinus (198–217), with some sources picturing him as the power behind the throne. Not surprisingly, given his background, he had a controversial papacy, accused by rigorists, especially his mortal enemy the *antipope *Hippolytus, of laxity and *heresy, the former charge obviously a value judgment by a right-wing group and the latter unsubstantiated. Despite being the first pope to have to deal with an antipope, Callistus remained firmly in office and took realistic steps to make post*baptismal *penance more accessible and marriage regulations more equitable. The *catacomb of San Callisto in Rome is named after him.

CAPPADOCIANS

Name given to three theologians from Cappadocia, a large and prosperous Roman province in eastern Asia Minor, which was Christianized no later than the second century and possibly earlier; the theologians are *Basil of Caesarea, his brother *Gregory of Nyssa, and their friend *Gregory Nazianzus; the three are linked not only by their geographical origins but also by their common struggle to make the teachings of the First Council of *Nicea acceptable to all Greek-speaking Christians.

CARPOCRATES
(fl. mid–second century)

Alexandrian *Gnostic teacher, founded sect bearing his name, apparently taught the natural birth of Jesus, and

practiced or at least was interested in magic; he and his followers (Carpocratians) also believed in the transmigration of souls, according to *Irenaeus; he was also the father of *Epiphanes.

CASSIAN, JOHN (ca. 360–435)

Possibly from the Balkans, he lived for a decade with the monks of Palestine and Egypt, was ordained a *deacon in Constantinople by *John Chrysostom, and went to Rome (401) to defend his *bishop; he stayed in the West, became friends with the future pope *Leo I, founded two monasteries in southern Gaul (by 415), one for men and one for women, and he wrote in Latin two important books, the *Institutes,* a guide for monastic life, and the *Conferences,* a highly edited account of his conversations with Egyptian *hermits; he opposed *Augustine's *predestinationism and also the teaching of *Nestorius. He was a major figure in the spread of *monasticism in the West, largely because his two books not only contained many valuable passages on monastic life and discipline, such as his list of the eight principal sins (which metamorphosed in the Middle Ages into the seven deadly sins), but also because he eschewed the thaumaturgical and the fantastic so common to other accounts of the Eastern monks, thus reassuring the conservative Western episcopate.

CASSIODORUS (ca. 485–580)

A Roman senator and contemporary of *Boethius, he rose through the Roman governmental ranks and tried to work with the Gothic rulers of Italy, for whom he wrote a history of their people as well as many official letters; he achieved a high position in the Gothic government but had to retire around 540; by 554 he had moved to his estate in southern Italy, Vivarium; there he established a monastery, wrote some scriptural commentaries, a guide to sacred and secular literature, and, most importantly, urged his monks to copy books, thus helping to ensure the preservation of many ancient works. Like Boethius, he greatly influenced medieval culture.

CATACOMBS

Burial places of ancient Christians, mostly in Rome although found elsewhere in Italy and in other areas; these preserve much early Christian art as well as many inscriptions; they are quite large and extend literally for miles underground; Pope *Damasus I first made them places for visiting; burials in the catacombs ceased in the fifth century; the modern understanding and popularity of the catacombs derives from the work of G. B. de Rossi in the nineteenth century. The origin of the name is uncertain, probably deriving from the phrase *ad catachumbas,* that is, "at the ravine."

CATECHETICAL SCHOOL; CATECHESIS

Contrary to much modern practice, ancient catechesis strove to educate adult converts, and the most famous Christian school in antiquity was the catechetical school of Alexandria, founded by *Pantaenus and headed by *Clement and *Origen, then by several Alexandrian *bishops and in the fourth century by *Didymus the Blind; this school fostered much Eastern theology and did attract pagans to the Faith.

CATECHUMEN

Someone who was undergoing training in the rudiments of Christian belief and practice prior to *baptism; catechumens could attend the liturgy but had to leave before the *Eucharist.

CATENA

Literally, "chain," a term used for collections of sayings by various Church *Fathers made by later writers; works of some writers survive only in *catenae.*

CATHERINE OF ALEXANDRIA

According to legend, she was a Christian virgin who refused marriage to a pagan emperor and disputed with fifty philosophers who tried to turn her away from her faith; she was racked on the wheel (thus the name "Catherine's wheel") although the torture instrument broke down before she died, so the emperor had her decapitated.

CECILIA

According to Roman tradition, a third-century Roman woman who converted her husband and his brother; all three were *martyred; her legend says that she sang at her wedding, and this is the probable origin of her patronage of music, a late devotion, known first in the fifteenth century but tremendously popular, for example, Purcell's *Ode for St. Cecilia's Day* (1692).

CELESTINE I (d. 432)

Pope from 422; he opposed the teaching of *Nestorius and supported *Cyril of Alexandria at the First Council of *Ephesus in 431, a rather naive approach, since Cyril bluntly abused the pope's trust; after the council Celestine attempted the reconciliation of the Alexandrian and Antiochene factions; his insistence on Roman primacy at the council did not win over the Easterners, but he was more successful and far more active in the West: he opposed *Semi-Pelagianism in Rome and sent *Germanus of Auxerre to halt *Pelagianism in Britain in 429; he also sent *Palladius to be the first *bishop of the Irish in 431; in Rome he worked to build or rebuild church buildings, including Santa Sabina.

CELESTIUS (fl. 400–430)

A *priest, possibly a Briton, who supported *Pelagius and who was probably more responsible for the more ''*Pelagian'' aspects of his teaching than the master himself; whereas Pelagius stressed the possibility of salvation based upon rigorous disciplining of a free will, Celestius went beyond to deny that *baptism remitted sins or that original sin was transmitted from generation to generation; Celestius accompanied Pelagius to Africa in 410, and he (but not Pelagius) was condemned by the African *Council of Carthage in 411; he then went to the East while the Western condemnations, including one at Rome, continued to mount. In a daring move Celestius went to Rome during the pontificate of *Zosimus in 417 and persuaded the pope to reopen the case, but the protests of the Africans caused the pope to back down; simultaneously, the emperor Honorius denounced Pelagius and Celestius. In 429 Celestius reappeared in Constantinople, where he appealed to the *bishop, *Nestorius, for help, but the First Council of *Ephesus in 431 condemned both of them for *heresy.

CELSUS (fl. ca. 175)

A Greek pagan provincial and a Platonist in his philosophy, he wrote *The True Discourse,* a learned attack on Christianity warning of its threat to the Roman Empire; he knew much of the Bible and the teaching of *Gnostic sects—his work is the only source of information for some of them—and he portrayed Christianity as a religion for the unlearned lower classes; he was a very skilled opponent who made good use of the different accounts of Jesus in the Gospels as well as the divisiveness of the Christian sects; *Origen refuted him in *Contra Celsum,* a large work that preserves approximately 90 percent of Celsus' book, which is otherwise unknown.

CENOBITE;
CENOBITIC MONASTICISM

The practice of monks' sharing a common (Greek: *koinos*) life (Greek: *bios*), a way of life traditionally founded by *Pachomius.

CERDO

A second-century Syrian *Gnostic who, *Irenaeus claimed, taught the existence of two Gods, one of the Old Testament and the other the Father of

Jesus; Irenaeus also says he was the teacher of *Marcion of Pontus.

CERINTHUS

An early second-century Asian *Gnostic who separated the God of the Old Testament (whom he called a *Demiurge) from the supreme God; he also taught *Docetism and *asceticism, possibly in a gospel; *Irenaeus says the Apostle John wrote his Gospel in opposition to Cerinthus, while the *Alogi considered him to be the author of the Gospel and of Revelation.

CHALCEDON

*Ecumenical council held in 451 at a city in Asia Minor to determine the person and nature of Christ, partly in response to the Second Council of *Ephesus in 449; the council declared Christ to be one person with two natures, human and divine, united but not mixed; due to the difficulties of Greek theological terminology the *Monophysites were convinced the teaching was *Nestorian, and they eventually went into *schism; this council rejected the theology of *Eutyches and affirmed that of *Leo I of Rome, the only pope whose views played a significant role in an ancient ecumenical council, largely because the Eastern *bishops believed that Leo's *Tome (the writing he sent to the council) was in accord with that of *Cyril of Alexandria, whose theology dominated the proceedings. Chalcedon was a watershed; the divisions it caused in the East were never healed and actually persist today; in the West, Chalcedon was always readily accepted.

CHARITON (fl. 340–350)

Traditional founder of Palestinian *monasticism, known from an anonymous *vita of the sixth century.

CHILIASM

Belief in the earthly return of Christ, who will then reign for a thousand years (in Greek, chilias) before the end of the world, a widespread belief in earliest Christianity, for example, *Papias of Hierapolis; also called *millenarianism.

CHOREPISCOPUS

A *bishop, usually of a rural area, who, though fully ordained, could exercise only limited powers; in order to prevent the excessive multiplication of bishoprics, the *Council of Laodicea in 357 declared that visiting *priests, representing the local ordinary, should replace chorepiscopi; modern arch-*deacons are their descendants.

CHRISTOLOGY

The theology of Christ; this begins in the New Testament with the Pauline epistles and continues throughout all of Christian history; it is an involved theological matter and one that has constantly developed. This was a major theological concern for the early Church; although the Christological councils of *Ephesus in 431 and *Chalcedon in 451 embodied later *patristic Christology, virtually every major Christian had a personal theology of Christ. In general, one can speak of a low Christology which emphasized the human in Christ, and a high Christology which emphasized the divine. In addition to the two councils, *see also* **Docetism, Modalism, Monarchianism,** as well as the theological terms associated with the ecumenical councils, for example, **Homoios, Homoiousios, Homoousios, Hypostasis.**

CHROMATIUS OF AQUILEIA
(d. 407)

Native of Aquileia in northeastern Italy, *presbyter by 368, took part in the *Council of Aquileia in 381 (under *Ambrose) to combat *Arianism, he was *bishop of Aquileia in 388 and proved a hardworking, effective ordinary; at the end of his life he had to deal with the invading Germanic barbarians; his writings include a Matthean commentary and forty-five homilies.

CHRONOGRAPHER OF 354

Name given to anonymous chronicler (possibly Dionysius Philocalus, the calligrapher of Pope *Damasus I) who preserved a melange of historical material including a chronicle of the city of Rome to A.D. 354, an Easter table, and a list of the Roman *bishops and their obits as well as a *martyrology; the list of the popes and *martyrs is also known as the *Liberian Catalogue,* after Pope *Liberius.

CHRYSIPPUS (ca. 405–479)

Rhetorician and *priest from Cappadocia, became a monk about 428 in Jerusalem; wrote panegyrics on Mary, John the Baptist, the Archangel Michael, and Saint Theodore Teron.

CIARAN OF CLONMACNOISE
(ca. 512–ca. 555)

Irish abbot and founder of the important monastery of Clonmacnoise, today the site of some important ruins; little is known historically of his life, although tradition makes him a pupil of *Finnian of Clonard.

CIARAN OF SAIGHIR (fl. 600)

Irish monk from West Cork who lived first as a *hermit and then as an abbot of the large monastery of Saighir, possibly once a pre-Christian site.

CIRCUMCELLIONS

Rural peasants who combined their social grievances with their *Donatist allegiance and attacked North African Catholics, especially wealthy ones; they carried clubs, which they called Israels and with which they intimidated or even killed landowners and debt collectors; their name comes from *circum cellas,* that is, those who lived around the *cellas,* or shrines, of the Donatist *marytrs; *Optatus and *Augustine reproached the Donatists for the circumcellions, but their exact relation to the Donatist hierarchy is uncertain.

CLAUDIANUS MAMERTUS
(ca. 425–ca. 474)

Gallic philosopher and *priest, brother of *Mamertus, arch*bishop of Vienne, friend of several leading Gallic figures, including *Sidonius Apollinaris and *Eucherius of Lyons; he wrote *De statu animae* to defend the *Augustinian notion of the immateriality of the soul.

CLAUDIUS CLAUDIANUS
(d. ca. 404)

Alexandrian pagan poet who arrived in Italy in 394 and became court poet to the Christian emperor Honorius (395–423); his Christianity was at best nominal, but he wrote some Christian poetry, including *De salvatore,* a brief *Christology.

CLEMENTINE HOMILIES

Collection of missionary homilies of the Apostle Peter, supposedly excerpted by *Clement of Rome and sent to James of Jerusalem, who is lavishly praised in them; they present an *ascetic and very Jewish Christianity; they probably date to the third century.

CLEMENTINE RECOGNITIONS

Romantic novel tracing the adventures of *Clement and his sons, who are separated and years later come together and recognize (hence the title) one another through the assistance of Saint Peter; this third-century Greek work, which survives only in a Latin translation of *Rufinus of Aquileia (ca. 400), follows standard literary techniques; its historical value is not great, except to show the popularity of such a work among Christians and also the Christian missionary method; doctrinally it treats Judaism as a preparation for Christianity.

CLEMENT OF ALEXANDRIA
(ca. 150–ca. 220)

Probably a native Athenian, he wandered about in his studies before settling in Alexandria with *Pantaenus, founder and head of the *catechetical school there; Clement apparently succeeded his teacher in 190 but fled in 202 during a *persecution; his subsequent life is unknown. Clement held to the traditional faith against the *Gnostics but believed that a Christian gnosis was possible. A broad-minded man, he believed Greek learning had prepared the Greeks for Christianity as the Old Testament had for the Jews; indeed, he cited Greek pagan writers more than he cited the Scriptures in his writings. His diverse, often meandering works show a man of great learning and liberal attitudes. He had a strong concern for ethics and education, reflected in his famous trilogy. His *Protreptikos* (exhortation) was aimed at the unbaptized who were getting their first training; the *Paidagogos* (teacher) was for the baptized and dealt with ethical behavior; *Stromateis* (literally, "carpets," implying miscellaneous items) guides Christians toward gnosis and more demanding ethics. In back of this was his *Logos doctrine, since the Logos exhorts and teaches and is the goal of our gnosis.

CLEMENT OF ROME (d. ca. 100)

Pope from about 91 and one of the *Apostolic Fathers; representative of the Roman community but probably not *bishop, he wrote a conciliatory letter (*1 Clement*) to Corinth to heal a *schism there; this very early noncanonical work is of great historical value for the early history of Roman Christianity. Clement did not write in his own name but in that of the community, leading some scholars to posit a collegial form of government in Rome; a letter of *Dionysius of Corinth identifies Clement as the author of the letter. The document itself is clearly Christian but also suggests the Jewish background of the author; the Old Testament, Paul, and the Gospels are cited to show the harm conflict can do to the community and how good people have suffered from this in the past. Furthermore, the letter has several pagan elements, such as the stress on the importance of harmony, possibly reflecting the Stoic notion of a harmonious cosmos; the praise of the Roman army's organization; and the comparison of Christ's resurrection to the phoenix, a mythical bird that died and then arose anew from its own ashes.

CLEMENT OF ROME, SECOND LETTER OF

Erroneous name given to a mid-second-century homily; this brief text provides information about some liturgical practices, including *baptism, as well as an intriguing reference to the "spiritual" Church, which existed from the Creation, for example, in Genesis 1:27, the male is Christ and the female is the Church.

CLOTILDA (ca. 470–545)

Burgundian Christian princess who in 492 married *Clovis, king of the pagan Franks; she worked successfully for his conversion (496); when he died in 511, she went to a convent, where she established a reputation for piety and charity.

CLOVIS (ca. 466–511)

Pagan king of the Franks who converted upon the urging of his Christian wife, *Clotilda; Clovis rose quickly to power, often at the expense of the Christian Gallo-Romans but just as often at the expense of other pagan or *Arian barbarians; his conversion in 496 took great pressure off the Church, and his continued conquests helped to spread the Faith, albeit by unconventional means. His story is told by *Gregory of Tours, who makes it plain that few people have personally been as little affected by their conversion as Clovis; from being a bloodthirsty pagan barbarian, he went to being a bloodthirsty Christian barbarian; nonetheless, there can be no gainsaying the tremendous importance of his conversion for the history of Christianity in Western Europe.

CODEX

From the Latin *caudex,* the name for a book in which the pages are bound at one end like modern books; very popular with Christians, the codex replaced the older roll; several important early Christian *manuscripts of the Bible are known as the *Codex* (title), such as the fourth-century *Codex Vaticanus* and the fifth-century *Codex Alexandrinus.*

COLUMBA (ca. 521–597)

Also known as Columcille (Dove of the Church; *columba* means "dove" in Latin); he came from an aristocratic Irish family, became a monk under *Finnian, and founded some monasteries in Ireland, but in 563 he left Ireland, possibly because of a political dispute, and two years later settled on the island of *Iona in southwest Scotland, where he founded a monastery; Iona was the chief religious foundation in the area; a later abbot, Adamnan, wrote the *vita of Columba.

COLUMBANUS (ca. 540–615)

Irish monk who migrated to Gaul in 590, where he established several Celtic monasteries; his great learning and piety made him popular with the Franks, but his independence and his Celtic observation of the date of Easter angered some Frankish *bishops, who worked for his exile; he left Gaul in 610 to do missionary work on Lake Constance; expelled in 612 by the Frankish king of Burgundy, he crossed the Alps into Italy, where he founded the monastery of Bobbio and opposed the papacy on the question of the *Three Chapters; his extant writings include a *monastic rule, a *penitential, some letters, and poetry.

COMMODIAN

Latin poet who lived either in the third or fifth century; scholars are divided over the point with most favoring the third; he was a *chiliast and apparently a *Patripassianist as well as the first Christian Latin poet; if the third-century date is correct, he knew Christian writings but apparently not the pagan classics.

CONFESSOR

Title given in early Christianity to one who suffered for the Faith but did not die; in North Africa in the third century there was a popular belief that confessors could forgive sins; *Cyprian of Carthage, who admired the confessors, had to limit their power vis-à-vis that of *bishops.

CONFIRMATION

One of four *sacraments known in the early Church; there are New Testament references, such as Acts 19:1-7, to the imposition of hands upon converts, indicating a second gift of the Spirit apart from *baptism; *Tertullian and *Cyprian of Carthage both witness to a second rite, complementary to baptism, which involved the imposition of hands, while *Hippolytus speaks of an anointing given after baptism in which the Christian received the Spirit in a fuller way than from baptism alone; by the fourth and fifth centuries in both East and West it was still part of the baptismal rite but distinct from the actual baptism; Pope *Innocent I (401–417) limited the performance of this rite of anointing to the *bishop— he called it "consignation"—and this appears to make the initial break with baptism; in the Middle Ages the theology and ritual of confirmation developed significantly.

CONSTANTINE I THE GREAT
(b. 274 or 288; d. 337)

Son of the emperor Constantius I (305–306) and his wife, *Helena, he led his late father's armies in the civil wars at the opening of the fourth century, emerging victorious with his colleague Licinius (whom he defeated in 324, and thus he became sole ruler); a vision prior to the battle of the Milvian

Bridge convinced him to put the Chi-Rho (X and P), or labarum, on his soldiers' shields; after his victory he issued the Edict of *Milan, which gave the Christians freedom of worship; by 319 he had become a Christian himself. He effectively ended the *persecutions and gave the Christians freedom to evangelize, which they did with great success; at the same time, as emperor and thus responsible for the welfare of the empire before the deity, he took it upon himself to intervene in Church affairs, beginning with *Donatism in 313 and continuing through the *Arian controversy; he called the first *ecumenical council at *Nicea in 325; he built several great churches in Italy and Palestine; he also rebuilt Byzantium and renamed it in 330 the City of Constantine, that is, Constantinople, a city that played a great role in Eastern Christian life; he made a conscious effort to bring Christian values into Roman law, sometimes helping the downtrodden, at other times raising the civil rank of the clergy; toward the end of his life he was favorable to the Arian cause and hostile to *Athanasius, but he never gave the Arians formal support; he was the friend of *Eusebius of Caesarea, had *Hosius of Cordova as his theological advisor, and employed *Lactantius as tutor to his son; venerated as a saint in the Eastern Church, he influenced early Christianity as much as any Church *Father, and his view of Church-state relations, that is, of the emperor's important if not dominant role in the Church, affected much medieval thinking and actually survived into the twentieth century in Russia (czar = caesar).

CONSTANTINOPLE, FIRST COUNCIL OF

In 381 the emperor *Theodosius I (379–395) summoned a *council to end the *Arian controversy; under the presidency of *Meletius of Antioch, the 150 *bishops affirmed the teaching of *Nicea, affirmed the humanity of Christ by condemning the teaching of *Apollinaris, and asserted the divinity of the Holy Spirit; it also gave the bishop of Constantinople the second place of honor in the Church after the bishop of Rome, a recognition of the importance of the bishop of the capital; the bishop of Rome, *Damasus I, took no part in the council, either personally or via legates, but accepted its dogmatic decisions in a Roman council in 382; Constantinople I is now a universally accepted *ecumenical council.

CONSTANTINOPLE, SECOND COUNCIL OF

Called by the emperor *Justinian in 553, this *council dealt with the so-called *Three Chapters, that is, writings taken from three authors loathed by the *Monophysites, whom Justinian was trying to win over; it was not a popular idea to condemn as *heretics three men who had died in the peace of the Church, and Justinian and his agents used threats and actual violence to get some *bishops, especially Western ones, to attend. The emperor brutalized *Vigilius of Rome into signing the council's decrees, and this caused a *schism in the West that lasted into the seventh century; although the Three Chapters were condemned, Justinian failed to win back the Monophysites.

CONSTANTIUS II (317–361)

Third son of *Constantine I and co-emperor (ruling in the East) with his father from 337, he eventually (353) followed his father as sole ruler of the Roman Empire; he fervently supported the objections of the Eastern episcopate against *Athanasius and believed in a *Semi-Arian understanding of the Trinity, which would bring the greatest unity to the empire; thanks to Constantius the teaching condemned at *Nicea flourished throughout the middle of the fourth century. This emperor sponsored a series of *Arianizing *councils in the East and tried the same in the West; he also exiled *bishops, such as *Liberius of Rome and *Hilary of Poitiers, who opposed him; but he was not ungenerous to his supporters and often gave tax exemptions to the clergy. Whereas as Constantine had to fight for his empire, Constantius grew up in the imperial household; both men planned to control the Church in order to govern more effectively, but Constantius clearly saw no limit to his authority in religious matters, the first example of what came to be called Caesaropapism, the domination of the Church by the secular monarch.

COPTIC CHURCH

The name for those Egyptian Christians who lived outside Alexandria and who continued the older, pre-Greek traditions of Egypt; many of the great Egyptian monks such as *Pachomius were Copts; the Copts, heavily *Monophysite, broke off from the larger Church after the Council of *Chalcedon and established a separate, independent hierarchy in 537; many great Coptic Christians wrote in their own language, partially as a protest against the Greek Christianity of Alexandria.

CORINTHIANS, THIRD EPISTLE TO

Part of the second-century *Acts of *Paul*, its emphasis on Christ's birth from Mary and the resurrection of the body suggests it opposed *Gnostic or at least *Docetic theology; it was for a time in Syria and Armenia thought to be authentically Pauline.

CORNELIUS (d. 253)

Pope from 251; the see of Rome had been vacant since the *martyr's death of *Fabian in 249 and under the governance of the *priest *Novatian, who expected to be elected *bishop; Cornelius, a priest who had advanced through the ecclesiastical grades at Rome, was chosen, probably because of his moderate and merciful approach toward those who had *lapsed and denied the Faith in a *persecution; with the support of *Cyprian of Carthage, Cornelius gained the upper hand in Rome and excommunicated Novatian at a synod of sixty bishops; exiled by the emperor Gallus (251–253), he died at Civitavecchia.

COSMAS INDICOPLEUSTES (fl. ca. 550)

Literally, "Cosmas the Indian navigator," he was a geographer who had traveled to Ceylon and wrote an account of the world that preserves much geographical information and recounts the spread of Christianity; he also opposed the prevailing Ptolemaic notion of the universe; in addition to his geography, he wrote some exegesis; he was apparently a *Nestorian.

COUNCIL

A meeting of *bishops to discuss problems facing the Church; these problems can be theological or disciplinary or both; councils in the early Chuch were local, regional, provincial, or *ecumenical; in some places, like North Africa, they were frequently held and were an essential instrument of ecclesiastical government.

CREATIONISM

Despite its modern association with the literal interpretation of the Genesis Creation account, this term meant for the early Church the belief that God created a new soul for every person; this technical point was closely involved with the question of original sin, that is, how could sin be transmitted if every soul were newly created; it stood in opposition to *traducianism.

CREED

A brief formulation of Christian beliefs and popular in the later *patristic period; the various creeds developed from *baptismal formulae and from *Christological statements; many personal creeds have survived, but the most important creeds are those associated with the founders of Chris-

tianity (*Apostles' Creed) or with a famous *council (*Nicene Creed).

CYPRIAN (ca. 205–258)

A pagan rhetorician, he converted to Christianity around 246, becoming *bishop of Carthage only two years later; when the emperor Decius (249–251) launched a *persecution in 250, Cyprian fled, not returning until 251, when he found his Church in a shambles—many had *lapsed and others had bribed their way out of the persecution, while still others who had suffered (*confessors) were claiming spiritual authority equal to that of the bishop; Cyprian worked out a formula for readmitting the lapsed and asserted his authority over the confessors. He also became involved in the *schism in Rome, favoring *Cornelius over *Novatian, albeit after some hesitation. When some schismatic Christians wished to join his communion, Cyprian, following African custom and supported by *councils of African bishops, insisted they be rebaptized, or, for him, baptized, since he did not recognize *heretical or schismatic *baptism; this went contrary to Roman practice, and Cyprian became involved in a bitter struggle with *Stephen of Rome, which ended unsettled with Stephen's death in 257; when the emperor Valerian (253–260) initiated a persecution, Cyprian was arrested, tried, and executed. Many of his letters survive and provide valuable witness to African Church life, the Novatianist schism in Rome, the controversy with Stephen, and the functioning of early Church councils. His book on the lapsed (*De lapsis*) explains his views on that difficult question, and his *De unitate Ecclesiae (On the Unity of the Church)*, although narrow and legalistic in its view, is the first formal Christian ecclesiology. Very much an African, Cyprian was heavily influenced by *Tertullian, and he himself heavily influenced the *Donatists.

CYPRIAN OF GAUL
(fl. ca. 420–440)

Poet whose major work is the *Heptateuchos*, a metrical retelling of the first six books of the Old Testament; he knew classical works as well as Scripture.

CYPRIAN OF TOULON (d. 549)

Gallic *bishop, friend of *Caesarius of Arles and opponent of *Semi-Pelagianism at the Second Council of *Orange in 529; he composed a *vita of Caesarius.

CYRIL OF ALEXANDRIA (d. 444)

An Alexandrian by birth and nephew of the *patriarch *Theophilus, he succeeded his uncle in 412; a harsh, combative man who had joined his uncle in the persecution of *John Chrysostom, Cyril used intimidation and even violence against Jews, *Novatianists, and pagans in Alexandria. In 428 *Nestorius became *bishop of Constantinople and soon denied Mary the title *Theotokos*, that is, Mother of God, a traditional title. Cyril insisted that the unity of divine and human in Christ made the title permissible and attacked Nestorius; both appealed to

Pope *Celestine I, who sided with Cyril. At Nestorius' urging, the emperor *Theodosius II (408–450) called an *ecumenical council at *Ephesus, where Cyril, using devious and political methods, managed to make himself the spokesman for Rome and incited the local populace against Nestorius; he presided at the Council of Ephesus (431), which affirmed his theology: divine and human were united in Christ and *Theotokos* was a theologically valid title. The party from Antioch protested against Cyril's methods and his theology, thinking it to be *Monarchian, but in 433, he worked out a Formula of *Union with them. Cyril was a brilliant theologian who drew from his predecessors; he worked to emphasize the unity of human and divine in Christ, although he used the term *mono physis* when he meant "one person," whereas the term could also mean "one nature," and the *Monophysites claimed his support for their teaching. Although best known as a dogmatic theologian, he was also an exegete and homilist.

CYRIL OF JERUSALEM
(ca. 315–368)

*Bishop of Jerusalem from 349, he opposed radical *Arianism, although he had been consecrated by the Arian bishop *Acacius of Caesarea, and he was banished three times (357–358, 360–362, 367–378) from his see when the Arians were in control; ironically, his own views about *Nicea were somewhat suspect and, no less than *Gregory of Nyssa, had to vouch for his orthodoxy. Cyril's twenty-four *catechetical homilies stress the significance of what the *catechumens were about; numbers 19–23 are known as the *Mystagogical Catecheses* and deal with the significance of the *sacraments of *Eucharist, *baptism, and *confirmation; he affirms the Real Presence in the Eucharist. To this day some doubts remain about his authorship of the *Catecheses,* although most scholars accept it.

CYRIL OF SCYTHOPOLIS
(ca. 524–ca. 558)

Palestinian monk who as a child came under the influence of the abbot *Sabas, he first lived as a *hermit, then joined a monastery in 544 and joined the community of Sabas in 555; he wrote in Greek the biographies of several famous Palestinian monks, including Sabas.

D

DAMASUS I (ca. 305–384)

Pope from 366; native Roman and son of a *priest, he accompanied *Liberius in his exile of 355 but soon returned to serve the *antipope *Felix II. When Liberius died in 366, Damasus won a bitter election contest against *Ursinus, a contest in which Damasus' followers killed 137 opponents. This bloody beginning as well as lingering charges of immorality weakened the pope's prestige but did not keep him from ruling his see effectively. A vigorous promoter of the Roman primacy and the first pope regularly to refer to Rome as the Apostolic See, he strengthened Rome's authority by vigorous anti*heretical measures, by getting the secular government to recognize the Roman see as a court of appeal for the Western *bishops, and by intervening in the *Meletian schism in Antioch to the consternation of many Greek bishops. Damasus had the popular touch, and he turned Rome into the City of Apostles and Martyrs by building churches, making the *catacombs into tourist attractions, and replacing the pagan founders of Rome, Romulus and Remus, with Peter and Paul as the founders of Christian Rome. He also engaged the scholar *Jerome as his secretary and encouraged him to revise the Latin Bible. His controversial episcopate marked a turning point in the history of the papacy.

DAVID (d. ca. 601)

Patron of Wales, he is known only from a late *vita that contains much legendary material; he apparently led a life of strict *asceticism, attended an episcopal synod in 560, and founded several monasteries. A *penitential is falsely attributed to him.

DEACON

See **Diakonos.**

DEACONESS

See **Diakonos.**

DECRETALS

Papal letters, usually in reponse to a question of discipline or doctrine and carrying the pope's jurisdictional authority; the earliest extant decretal is that of *Siricius in 385; *Dionysius Exiguus first compiled papal decretals in the sixth century for a canon-law collection.

DECRETUM GELASIANUM

Actually the *Decretum Gelasianum de libris recipiendis et non recipiendis* (The Gelasian Decree About Which Books Are to Be Received and Not Received [into the canon of Scriptures]), an unofficial sixth-century canon list from Gaul attributed to Pope *Gelasius I; it lists a goodly number of *apocrypha; its influence is debated among scholars; the widespread use of apocrypha in the Middle Ages suggests its influence was at best limited.

DEMETRIUS OF ALEXANDRIA
(d. 231)

*Bishop of Alexandria from 189, he is best known for his opposition to *Origen, whom he eventually banished from Alexandria in 231; *Eusebius of Caesarea suggests the cause was the bishop's jealousy of the brilliant *catechist.

DEMIURGE

A word with significant meaning in Platonic philosophy, usually translated as "craftsman," but, in early Christian circles, used of the *Gnostic Demiurge, a lesser divine being who created the material world and whom many believers mistook for the supreme Deity; many Gnostics considered the God of the Old Testament to be merely a Demiurge.

DER BALYZEH PAPYRUS

Discovered in 1907, fragments of a Greek liturgical document dating to the sixth century that illustrate some points about the early Greek liturgy in Egypt.

DIADOCHUS OF PHOTICE
(d. ca. 468)

His life is largely unknown; he opposed the *Monophysites at *Chalcedon; otherwise, he is known primarily as the author of *One Hundred Chapters on Spiritual Perfection,* a guide to the spiritual life that emphasizes *asceticism; a thorough work, it enjoyed popularity in the East for centuries, especially in the Russian Church.

DIAKONOS

Literally, "one who serves"; it came to mean a particular office in the Church; the New Testament is not clear as to the relation of the *diakonos* to the *episkopos and the *presbyteros,* but in the writings of *Ignatius of Antioch the offices are quite distinct, with the *episkopos* as the chief officer, the *presbyteros* beneath him, and *diakonos* still further down; in the New Testament there is no separate term for deaconess; in Romans 16:1 the word used of Phoebe is the same as that for men, namely, *diakonos;* deaconesses were common in the Eastern Church into the fourth century, less so in the West; the deaconess was usually limited to ministry to women and the needy; deacons in both East and West were usually minor figures liturgically, limited to assisting the priest; they also had the important job of collecting alms for the needy; in Rome, however, deacons were routinely used to carry out papal business and became trusted advisors to the popes; in the sixth century it was common to choose a deacon and not a priest to be pope; the diminution of the diaconate to an office on the road to priesthood is a later development.

DIATESSERON

Literally, "through the four," this is a gospel harmony of the mid-second century put together by the *apologist *Tatian, which became the standard "gospel" for the Syriac Churches down to the fifth century; the original language is uncertain—the main contenders are Greek and Syriac—and it survives in fragments in several languages; it demonstrates that although the traditional four Gospels were widely accepted in the second century, Christian scholars did not hesitate to combine them into a unique narrative; this was also the first example of a very popular literary genre.

DIDACHE

The full title is *The Teaching* [in Greek, *didache*] *of the Lord Through the Twelve Apostles to the Nations;* one of the works of the *Apostolic Fathers, this is a brief manual of discipline that dates to the mid-second century, although its primitive character (wandering prophets are a regular feature of the community) suggests that its origin may be much earlier; it apparently came from a Syrian Church, apparently something of a backwater and not in contact with the new movements in Antioch; its early date makes its liturgical content of considerable value. Its moral teaching deals with the antithetical Way of Life and Way of Death; its liturgical section deals with instructions for community services and for ministry.

DIDASCALIA APOSTOLORUM

Literally, "the teaching of the apostles"; this Syriac Church order dates to the third century and contains moral instruction for Christians in all walks of life; among other things, it deals with *deaconesses and widows and provides an insight into the roles of women at this time; an episcopal-centered community is presumed. The author apparently was a converted Jew (and possibly a physician, since he knew quite a bit about medicine) who polemicized against Jews and Jewish worship.

DIDYMUS THE BLIND
(ca. 313–398)

An Alexandrian who lost his sight at age four, Didymus gained such a wide knowledge of theology that *Athanasius appointed him head of the *catechetical school of Alexandria; he was an orthodox *Nicene who wrote anti-*Arian treatises and advocated the divinity of the Holy Spirit; he also defended his great predecessor *Origen against charges of *heresy, which resulted in his own posthumous condemnation at the Second Council of *Constantinople in 553; Didymus exercised considerable influence on Western thought via his two pupils *Rufinus of Aquileia and *Jerome; his book *On the Holy Spirit* survives in the Latin translation by Jerome.

DIODORE OF TARSUS (d. ca. 392)

A native of Antioch, he taught there until his banishment to Armenia in 372 by the *Arianizing emperor Valens (364–378); after the emperor's death in 378, he became *bishop of Tarsus in Asia Minor and attended the First Council of *Constantinople in 381; a man of some courage, he opposed the pagan emperor *Julian the Apostate (361–363) when he tried to restore the old religion in Antioch in 362. Diodore's reputation rests on his exegesis, which stressed the literal and historical understanding of the text, a method usually termed *Antiochene and which he passed on to his two great pupils, *John Chrysostom and *Theodore of Mopsuestia. He also had a great interest in astronomy and chronology.

DIOGNETUS, LETTER TO

A work included among the *Apostolic Fathers, this early second-century *apology of unknown provenance is addressed to a noble pagan who wishes to know God (the meaning of "Diognetus"); the anonymous author attacks paganism and Judaism and presents an attractive if idealized picture of Christian life, summed up in a famous line, "What the soul is in the body, that the Christians are in the world" (ch. 6).

DIONYSIUS EXIGUUS (d. 545)

A monk from the Romanized Balkans, he lived in Rome from about 500 to 545; a man of great learning, he compiled documents such as papal *decretals and conciliar records for canon law, and he propagated Greek learning in increasingly barbarized Rome by translating some Greek works into Latin. Invited by the Romans to compose an Easter table to settle the constant difficulties in computing the date of that feast, he compiled a new calendar, dating the birth of Christ (wrongly) from the 754th year from the founding of Rome. His system is still used today and is the origin of the B.C. and A.D. dating.

DIONYSIUS OF ALEXANDRIA (fl. 233–264)

An Alexandrian and pupil of *Origen who became head of the *catechetical school and later *bishop of Alexandria; having escaped capture by one *persecuting emperor (250) and having been banished by another (257), he returned to his see to deal with the post-persecution problems; his efforts against his attackers and on behalf of his diocese earned him the epithet "the Great." Fragments of his writings survive; he opposed *Sabellianism and wrote a brief but perceptive analysis of the literary styles of the Gospel of John and the Book of Revelation, demonstrating that the same author could not have written both. In his dealings with Rome he supported *Cornelius against *Novatian, but he had a run-in of sorts about his theology with *Dionysius of Rome but had little trouble explaining that his opposition to Sabellianism did not mean *Tritheism, that is, the belief in three gods.

DIONYSIUS OF CORINTH

*Bishop of Corinth in the late second century; he wrote several letters preserved by *Eusebius of Caesarea, including one to the Roman community, which acknowledges Roman charity and mentions the earlier letter to Corinth by *Clement, thus providing the name of the author of the earlier letter.

DIONYSIUS OF ROME (d. 268)

Pope from 260; he worked to reorganize the Roman Church after the *persecution of Valerian (258), the severity of which had prevented the Romans from electing a *bishop for two years; in addition to straightening out affairs in Rome, he also helped the barbarian-ravaged Church of Caesarea in Asia Minor; he had doubts about the *Origenist theology of his namesake in Alexandria, who had little trouble in allaying the pope's misgivings.

DIONYSIUS THE PSEUDO-AREOPAGITE

A late fifth-century Syrian Neoplatonist Christian, he wrote under the name of Dionysius the Areopagite, the fellow converted by Paul on the hill of the Areopagus in Athens in Acts 17:34; this clever forgery worked, and his writings were accepted as authentic until the Renaissance; since then *Pseudo- has been added to his name. He wrote four books dealing with heavenly things, such as divine names, the nature of angels, the soul's mystic union with God, and the spiritual nature of the Church, whose hierarchy is related to the angelic one; some letters also survive. "Dionysius" emphasized the soul's union with God and the series of beings through which God deals with humans, since God is per se unknowable. He was the first to suggest that there are nine choirs of angels. In medieval tradition, Dionysius, which in French is Denis, became confused with the patron saint of France.

DIOSCORUS

*Antipope for three weeks in 530; Pope *Felix III (IV) designated his *deacon *Boniface as his successor to continue the pope's pro-Gothic policy, but the senate and people rejected this and chose the pro-Byzantine Dioscorus; a smaller group chose Boniface II, thus beginning a *schism that ended quickly with Dioscorus' death; although considered an antipope, he was probably legitimately elected according to the practice of the time.

DIOSCORUS OF ALEXANDRIA (d. 454)

*Bishop of Alexandria from 444 and successor of *Cyril, he supported the teachings of *Eutyches and used his presidency at the Second Council of *Ephesus in 449 to enforce his views as well as to depose his ecclesiastical rival, *Flavian of Constantinople; his high-handed treatment of his opponents (Flavian eventually died from a beating given to him by Dioscorus' supporters) and his rejection of the views of Pope *Leo I led to his own condemnation at the Council of *Chalcedon in 451, called after the death of the emperor *Theodosius II (408–450), who had been his imperial protector. Deposed from his see, he went into exile. Alexandrian *Monophysites considered him a *martyr to their cause.

DISCIPLINA ARCANI

Latin term for the discipline or (better) the rule of secrecy, that is, the belief that some elements of religion should not be made available to the uninitiated, a common practice among some pagan religions and from the second century a practice of Christianity, specifically, keeping the not-yet *baptized from the *Eucharist and even from discussion of the *sacraments in their presence; the mass conversions of the fourth and fifth centuries made this practice necessary.

DISMAS

According to the *apocryphal *Gospel According to *Nicodemus,* this is the name of the Good Thief of Luke 23:39-43.

DOCETISM

Name given to the belief that Jesus did not really have a body but only ''seemed'' to have one (in Greek, *dokeo*); its adherents probably wanted to protect the divine Son of God from the corruptibility of the flesh, but a Christ with a phantom body could not suffer, die, or rise, and so Docetism compromised the redemption; it apparently dates to the first century (John 1:1-18; 1 John 4:1-3; 2 John 7); if the scriptural references are not to Docetism, certainly *Ignatius of Antioch (ca. 115) had to deal with it; several *Gnostic groups were also Docetic, and Docetic notions appear in some *apocryphal *gospels and *apocalypses.

DOMITILLA, FLAVIA (d. ca. 100)

Roman woman of the imperial Flavian family, wife of Titus Flavius Clemens; the emperor Domitian (81–96) executed her husband in about 95, possibly for being a Christian; Domitilla was herself a Christian and suffered exile to the prison island of Pandateria; the *catacomb of Domitilla bears her name.

DONATISM; DONATUS

After the Great *Persecution of 303–305, a *schism developed in Africa over who had been a *traditor,* that is, one who had handed over the sacred books to the pagans; several accused *Caecilian of Carthage of this, and a dissident group broke off communion with him in 311. The original head of the dissident group, Majorinus, died and was replaced by Donatus of Casae Nigrae in 313, after whom the group and the movement are named. The Donatists appealed to the emperor *Constantine I (306–337), but the Synod of Arles (314) and then the imperial court declared for Caecilian. When the emperor used force (316–321), the Donatists portrayed themselves, not unjustly, as upholders of African traditions against outside oppressors; by the middle of the fourth century the majority of North African Christians were Donatist. Donatus ruled much of the African Church and around 336 called a synod of 270 *bishops, the largest *council anywhere till that time. When imperial commissioners arrived in Africa in 346 to try to settle the dispute, some radical Donatists, the *Circumcellions, attacked them; this resulted in a second persecution in 347 and the exile of Donatus and some of his chief supporters to Gaul, where Donatus died in 355. In Africa, however, the persecution only hardened Donatist resolve, and by the end of the century they had resorted to violence, employing the Circumcellions against Catholics. Because the Donatists could justify their isolation from the rest of the Christian world only by claiming that they were the sole uncorrupted Christian body (the rest having chosen to keep communion with Caecilian and his successors and thus sharing the taint of the *traditores*), the Catholic *apologists *Optatus of Milevis and *Augustine of Hippo attacked their rigorist and provincial theology. The Donatist movement itself split up after Donatus' death, and the internecine warfare weakened its organization but not its hold on the people. The moderation of the only great Donatist theologian, *Tyconius, likewise hurt the cause. But to Augustine goes the credit for Donatism's downfall. He argued mercilessly against their theological weaknesses and, more importantly, convinced the imperial government to move against them, especially after some prominent Donatists had supported the revolt of Count Gildo (397) against the emperor. The Council of Carthage in 411 brought Catholics and Donatists together under the presidency of a somewhat biased imperial commissioner, who declared for the Catholic position. After that, the Roman government persecuted the Donatists, and many abandoned the movement. But it did not die out until the Moslem conquest of North Africa in the seventh century. It was a thoroughly African movement, and that contributed to its success: its rigorism, fidelity to tradition as represented by *Cyprian of Carthage, and moralizing criticism of the Constantinian state derived from *Perpetua and *Tertullian and represented the African Christian conscience.

DOROTHEUS OF ANTIOCH

Third-century *presbyter of Antioch known only from a reference by *Eusebius of Caesarea, who praises his learning, especially his knowledge of Hebrew, and says he was a eunuch "by nature," possibly implying a birth defect; Eusebius does not say that he wrote anything but he did practice scriptural exegesis.

DOROTHEUS OF GAZA

Sixth-century monk and *ascetic writer; his *Spiritual Colloquies* drew from earlier writers and thus preserved some that were otherwise unknown; he emphasized humility above all other virtues, and he attacked the teachings of *Origen and *Evagrius Ponticus.

DOROTHY

According to the *Hieronymian Martyrology, she was a fourth-century virgin and *martyr who probably died in Asia during the *persecution of Diocletian (303–305) or that of his successor, Galerius (311–312); this is all that is known of her life, but a highly legendary *vita was popular in the Middle Ages.

DOSITHEUS

Second-century *Gnostic from Samaria who, says *Origen, claimed to be the Messiah foretold by Moses; a treatise of one Dositheus was found at *Nag Hammadi; he also appears in the Ecclesiastical History of *Eusebius of Caesarea and in the *Clementine Recognitions, but he probably was not a Christian but rather a Jewish Gnostic.

DOXOLOGY

In Greek, "words of praise" but in actuality a prayer; these are common in both the Old and New Testaments as well as in early Christianity, especially for liturgies; a doxology could be as simple as the Gloria ("Glory be to the Father and to the Son and to the Holy Spirit") or as long as the early Roman doxology at the end of *Clement of Rome's Letter to the Corinthians (ca. 95); doxologies are still common in modern vernacular liturgies.

DRACONTIUS (fl. 480–490)

Blossius Aemilius Dracontius was a lawyer in Carthage during the Vandal occupation and was imprisoned for his pro-Roman sympathies; he wrote De laudibus Dei (On the Praises of God) and some other poetry.

DUBRICIUS

Sixth-century South Welsh saint known primarily via legendary material; he was apparently Romano-British and a *monastic founder; a seventh-century tradition names him a *bishop.

DURA EUROPOS

Roman garrison town in Syria in which was found the earliest known Christian church, a simple building built from two houses; it had a baptistery and apparently an altar; it dates from about 240. The considerable artistic remains include wall paintings. Dura also contains the oldest extant Jewish synagogue.

DYOPHYSITES

*Monophysite term for the supporters of *Chalcedon; literally, "believers in two natures" of Christ.

E

EBIONITES

Name derives from a Hebrew word meaning "poor men." They were a Jewish Christian group that had a very low *Christology, considering Jesus the son of Joseph and Mary, and they stressed *asceticism; *Irenaeus said they rejected Paul and accepted only the Gospel of Matthew, the most Jewish of the Gospels, but *Eusebius of Caesarea said their gospel was the *Gospel According to *Hebrews.* *Ephiphanius speaks of the *Gospel of the Ebionites,* and he preserves some fragments of it; *Jerome identified this gospel with that of the Hebrews, but scholars generally reject the identification. The gospel does not contain an infancy narrative but otherwise relates to the Synoptics. Some *Fathers used the term in a general way for Jewish Christians.

ECUMENICAL COUNCIL

Name given to a meeting of all the *bishops of the inhabited world (in Greek, *oikumene*); the first four ecumenical councils are recognized by most Christian denominations as representing the faith of the early Church, although most denominations also accept the next three (*Constantinople II, Constantinople III in 680, and Nicea II in 787). The Roman Catholic Church accepts fourteen more, from Constantinople IV (869–870) to Vatican II (1962–1965).

EDESSENE CHRONICLE

Sixth-century Syriac chronicle giving an account of Christianity in Edessa from the early second century to the author's own day.

EGERIA (fl. 380–390)

Sometimes spelled Etheria; a Gallic or Spanish noblewoman and nun who went on pilgrimage to the Holy Land and Egypt; she wrote an account of this journey, the *Itinerarium ad loca sancta,* (Journey to the Holy Places), often called simply the *Pilgrimage,* in which she insightfully described the lives of the Eastern *ascetics, the condition of the holy places, and several Eastern liturgies; her account is crucial for liturgical historians, especially for the determination of feast days; her work also demonstrates what educated Western Christians thought of the Holy Land.

EGERTON PAPYRUS 2

Fragment of a second-century gospel with Johannine characteristics but also elements of the Synoptics, suggesting the anonymous author knew all four canonical Gospels; it also includes a miracle story not known elsewhere.

EGYPTIANS, GOSPEL OF THE

Second-century gospel written to justify the doctrines of the *Encratites; it was known to *Clement and *Origen of Alexandria, who quoted some fragments of it.

ELEUTHERIUS (d. 189)

Pope from about 174; name sometimes spelled Eleutherus; a *deacon to *Anicetus, he was the pope whom *Irenaeus of Lyons visited in Rome to discuss *Montanism, then a source of great concern in the West, but Eleutherius apparently did nothing about it; according to legend, the British king *Lucius asked him to send a mission to his country.

ELKESAITES

Jewish Christian sect of the second century that rejected Paul, stressed obedience to the Mosaic Law, understood Christ *Docetically, and practiced *asceticism; they are known primarily through references in *Hippolytus and *Epiphanius, but their doctrines probably influenced the *Clementine Recognitions; Hippolytus traced their teaching to an Elkesai, whose revelations were spread in second-century Rome by a Syrian named Alcibiades.

ENCRATITES

Literally, "those who abstain"; an *ascetical sect most likely founded by the Syrian *apologist *Tatian; the Encratites rejected marriage, sexual relations, and the eating of meat and the drinking of wine, which they replaced in the *Eucharistic service with water, thus earning themselves the name *Aquarii (the water drinkers). This sect produced a number of *apocryphal *gospels and *acts, such as the *Acts of *Andrew* and the *Acts of *Thomas.*

ENNODIUS (ca. 473–521)

Magnus Felix Ennodius was a noble Gaul who moved to northern Italy, becoming *bishop of Pavia around 511; a defender of the papacy's freedom from intervention by civil authorities, he represented the papacy on two legations (515, 517) to Constantinople to end the *Acacian schism; his writings include almost three hundred letters, some poems and epigrams, and some spiritual and educational treatises.

EPARCH

Head of an ecclesiastical province, an office somewhat similar to that of *metropolitan; this office is recognized as early as the Council of *Nicea.

EPHESUS, FIRST COUNCIL OF

Third *ecumenical council, held in 431; the background is complicated, involving the rival theologies of *Alexandria, represented by its *patriarch, *Cyril, and of *Antioch, represented by *Nestorius, *bishop of Constantinople but formerly an Antiochene monk; it also reflects the opposition by Alexandria to the growing importance of Constantinople as the imperial see of the East. Nestorius taught that the title *Theotokos (God-bearer) could not be used of Mary; rather she was Christotokos. Cyril feared that this represented a strict separation of the human and divine in Christ and thus destroyed the unity; since the title Theotokos was an old and widely used one, Nestorius found himself in popular difficulty as well. Both sides appealed to Pope *Celestine I, who sided with Rome's traditional ally, Alexandria. The emperor *Theodosius II (408–450) called an ecumenical council at Ephesus to settle the matter. Celestine appointed Cyril to be his representative at the council; armed with Roman support and accompanied by dozens of his suffragan bishops, Cyril went to Ephesus, effectively turned the local populace against Nestorius, and opened the council without the presence of Nestorius or the bishops still journeying from Antioch or the papal legates or the permission of the emperor's agent. The council quickly approved Cyril's theology as consonant with that of *Nicea and condemned Nestorius as "the new Judas." When the Antiochenes, led by *John of Antioch, arrived, they called their own meeting and condemned Cyril. Next to arrive were the Roman legates who supported Cyril. The emperor had both Nestorius and Cyril arrested; he deposed Nestorius and would probably have done the same to Cyril, but he escaped and, depleting the treasury of the see of Alexandria, bribed his way back into the emperor's favor. Nestorius was banished. A *schism seemed likely, but Cyril and the Antiochenes worked out the *Union of 433 to settle their differences, which turned out to be largely terminological. Ephesus was a scandal and Cyril's conduct despicable, but the council did affirm the unity of Christ by allowing the title Theotokos and by furthering the *Christological discussion that eventually led to *Chalcedon. It also demonstrated that Nicea had become the touchstone of orthodoxy, thus putting to rest all the *Arian controversies of the fourth century.

EPHESUS, SECOND COUNCIL OF

Not recognized in Christian tradition as an *ecumenical council, this was called by the emperor *Theodosius II in 449 to settle the dispute caused by the condemnation of *Eutyches' theology by *Flavian of Constantinople; Eutyches' strongest supporter, the autocratic *Dioscorus of Alexandria, presided at the council, rehabilitated Eutyches, and deposed Flavian; the council declared for *Monophysitism in the belief that this was the theology of *Cyril of Alexandria. The papal legates, bearing the *Tome of *Leo I, were denied a hearing at the council;

this insulting rebuff along with Dioscorus' general behavior caused Leo to give this council its nickname of *latrocinium (robber council). The Council of *Chalcedon in 451 reversed the decisions of Ephesus II.

EPHRAEM THE SYRIAN
(ca. 306–373)

Native of Nisibis and a *priest there; when the Roman Empire ceded his province to the Persians in 363, Ephraem moved to Edessa, where he established a theological school; known as "the lyre of the Holy Spirit" for his poetry, he was an exegete, homilist, and a polemicist, although even much of that was written in verse; a great stylist, he influenced the development of Syriac literature; his Marian devotion strongly influenced Eastern piety, and his efforts against the *Marcionites, *Manicheans, *Gnostics, and *Arians kept the Syriac Church for *Nicene orthodoxy; he stressed the wonder of the incarnation and the value of the natural world.

EPIGONUS

Early third-century Roman *Monarchian known only from a reference in *Hippolytus.

EPIPHANES

*Gnostic teacher, the son of *Carpocrates, he wrote a treatise, On Justice, which advocated the community of property and wives; he died at the age of seventeen.

EPIPHANIUS OF SALAMIS
(ca. 315–403)

*Bishop of Salamis in Cyprus from 367 and a self-appointed *Nicene *heresy hunter; he was active in the campaigns against *Apollinaris and *Origenism, but he apparently considered heresy whatever he could not personally understand. In 392 he attacked the Origenism of Bishop *John of Jerusalem in Palestine itself—working with the Latin *presbyter *Jerome—and in 400 the unscrupulous *Theophilus of Alexandria used him in Alexandria's campaign against *John Chrysostom, bishop of Constantinople. Realizing he was being used, Epiphanius took sail for Cyprus but died along the way. His claim to fame rests on his Panarion (medicine box) for heresies, which lists many heresies and quotes from them; in many cases the Panarion is the only source available for some of these groups, for example, only he preserves several *Montanist oracles.

EPISKOPOS; EPISKOPOI

Originally the words meant "overseer" in Greek; it eventually evolved into "bishop"; the term was not originally distinguished from *presbyteros, and *Clement of Rome (ca. 95) uses the terms equivalently; *Ignatius of Antioch (ca. 110–115) clearly uses the term to mean the head of a local Church, and throughout the second century, bishops of that type became more and more frequent; evidence from Egypt, Rome, and Africa makes it clear that by the end of the second century bishops were clearly in charge of churches, a situation that continued through early Christianity; *Irenaeus of Lyons saw the bishops as successors of the apostles, a notion the bishops did not discourage; despite *Cyprian's attempts to say that all bishops were equal, the bishops of the larger sees (including Cyprian's Carthage) soon dominated the provinces, while some, such as the *episkopoi* of Alexandria and Rome, became major figures in the Church as a whole. Indeed, the *ecumenical Council of *Nicea in 325 recognized the superior status of the bishops of those two cities and of Antioch, and in 381 another ecumenical council, the First Council of *Constantinople, tried to elevate the status of Constantinople. Nicea also forbade the translations of bishops from one see to another. Ancient bishops were originally expected to preach frequently and to be with the people, but as time went on these duties were more frequently handled by priests, although many bishops, such as *John Chrysostom, *Augustine, and *Caesarius of Arles, were famous preachers. Ancient bishops were also expected to be competent theologians; the names of the participants in the great theological controversies prove how true that was.

EPISTOLA APOSTOLORUM

Also called *Dialogues of Jesus with His Disciples After the Resurrection,* this *apocryphon was composed (ca. 160–170) in Egypt or Asia Minor; it claims to preserve postresurrection conversations between Jesus and his disciples; drawing from the canonical Gospels, it emphasizes the resurrection of the body against the *Gnostics, and it preserves a brief *creed that discusses *baptism and the *Eucharist.

EREMITE; EREMITIC MONASTICISM

Eremites lived as hermits, a common form of early *monasticism that maintained itself well into the Middle Ages; they usually withdrew to deserts or forests or, in Britain and Ireland, offshore islands; those in popular areas sometimes lived in private residences, or some, the *stylite saints, lived on pillars.

ESCHATOLOGY

Literally, "the doctrine of the last things"; in fact, a belief in the imminent end of the world; very popular in early Christianity (Matt 24; 1 Thess 4:13-18), by the early second century it was fading and had to be propped up (2 Pet 3:8-10); the writings of the *apologists, who attempted to reconcile the Roman world to the Christians, prove that by the mid-second century most Christians had given up eschatological hopes; since then eschatology has appeared only in fringe movements.

ETHELBERT (d. 616)

Pagan Anglo-Saxon king of Kent, whose Christian wife, the Frankish princess Bertha, induced him to allow the mission of *Augustine of Canterbury; Ethelbert became the first Christian Anglo-Saxon king and a strong supporter of the Christian mission.

ETHERIA

See Egeria.

EUCHARIST

One of the four *sacraments of the early Church; the word means thanksgiving but soon came to mean exclusively the remembrance of Jesus' Last Supper; the eating of the bread and the drinking of the wine made Jesus present to the community; although the detailed theologies of the Real Presence awaited the Middle Ages, most of the *Fathers testify to the belief in a Real Presence—this is as early as *Ignatius of Antioch and *Justin Martyr in the second century; there was equally strong evidence for belief in the sacrificial nature of the Eucharist; as with *baptism, the symbolic nature of the Eucharist played a great role in the early Church; sacred banquets were known in both paganism and Judaism, and the strong imagery of eating and drinking made vivid the notion of the life-sustaining sacrament; the Eucharistic meal often coincided with but was never identical to the *agape, but by the end of the fourth century the agape had largely died out; later theology, which stressed the Real Presence and the efficacy of the sacrament in the individual, has obscured the strong communal notion of the early Church.

EUCHERIUS OF LYONS (d. ca. 450)

Gallic nobleman who, along with his wife, Galla, chose a life of *asceticism; they moved to the island monastery of *Lérins; around 432 he became *bishop of Lyons, an office he held until his death; he was an avid letter writer and a confidant of all the major figures of the Gallic Church: *Hilary of Arles, John *Cassian, and *Paulinus of Nola. His influence was extended in a personal way when his two sons, *Salonius and Veranus, both became bishops. His two major writings are guides to the interpretation of Scripture: the *Formulae spiritalis intelligentiae,* which discusses *allegorical exegesis, and the *Instructiones,* which deals largely with the interpretation of words; he also wrote some ascetical treatises.

EUDOXIA (ca. 400–455)

Born of pagan parents probably in Athens and given the name Athenais, she became a Christian when she met *Pulcheria, sister of the emperor *Theodosius II (408–450), whom she married in 421; she went to Jerusalem in 437 and brought back the relics of Saint Stephen (Acts 6–7) to Constantinople; she went permanently to Jerusalem in 440, apparently banished by her husband but for what reason is unknown; there she was a great supporter of the anti-*Chalcedonian monks in their conflict with *Bishop *Juvenal of Jerusalem. She was one of few famous Christian women writers of this age, author of several poems on the Bible and the *Martyrdom of Saint Cyprian,* a supposed bishop of Antioch but whose historicity is questioned by modern scholars.

EUDOXIUS (ca. 300–ca. 368)

*Anomoean leader, *bishop of Antioch in 358 but soon expelled by the *Nicenes, bishop of Constantinople in 360; only fragments of his writings survive.

EUGIPPIUS (d. ca. 533)

Abbot of Lucullanum near Naples and disciple of *Severinus, he wrote the saint's *vita as well as a collection of excerpts from the writings of *Augustine and a rule for monks; a friend of *Cassiodorus, he also had his monks copy *manuscripts, thus aiding the eventual preservation of much ancient literature.

EULALIUS (d. 423)

*Antipope from December 418 to April 419; an archdeacon of *Zosimus, he was elected pope by the Roman *deacons, but the *presbyters elected *Boniface I; the matter was referred to the emperor Honorius (395–423), who decided to call a *council at Spoleto to settle the matter; he ordered the two contestants to stay out of Rome in the meantime; Boniface obeyed but Eulalius did not, so the emperor cancelled the council and installed Boniface; Eulalius accepted the verdict and caused no trouble, even when Boniface died in 422.

EULOGIUS (d. 608)

*Bishop of Alexandria from 580, he attacked the *Novatianists and *Monophysites; fragments of his writings survive.

EUNOMIUS OF CYZICUS (d. 394); EUNOMIANS

Pupil and secretary of *Aetius of Antioch, Eunomius became *bishop of Cyzicus in Asia Minor in 360, appointed by *Eudoxius; a great dialectician, he worked out much of the theology of the *Anomoeans, although his logic-filled homilies bored his congregation, who expelled him after only a few months; he took refuge with Eudoxius and later retired to a country estate only to be exiled twice, by Emperor Valens around 369 and by Emperor *Theodosius I around 384; he died in exile; he led the Anomoean cause, arguing that God is simple and unique, incapable of division or even distinction—he thus had to deny the divine sonship of Christ; although his views did not win wide support, they challenged many theologians, such as *Basil of Caesarea, *Didymus the Blind, *Apollinaris of Laodicea, *Gregory of Nyssa, and *Theodore of Mopsuestia, to reply; his followers were called Eunomians.

EUSEBIAN CANONS

A set of canon tables, that is, tables that demonstrate parallel passages in the Gospels, prepared by *Eusebius of Caesarea; these were enormously popular and are found in most Greek and Latin Bibles down to the late Middle Ages.

EUSEBIUS OF CAESAREA (ca. 260–ca. 340)

Apparently a native of Palestine, he studied with *Pamphilus and thus became an admirer of *Origen; around 309 he fled to Egypt to avoid *persecution but spent some months in prison there; he became *bishop of Caesarea in Palestine in 315; when the *Arian controversy broke out, he sympathized with *Arius and was condemned by an Antiochene synod in 325; he rebounded at *Nicea, however, even to the extent of proposing a *creed to the council, although after Nicea he worked against it; he was an avid partisan of *Constantine I, seeing in him the savior of the Church as well as the empire. Although he wrote some exegesis and polemics, his reputation rests on his historical works such as his *Life of Constantine* and his *Chronicle,* but his masterpiece is his *Ecclesiastical History,* an invaluable narrative of Christianity from the New Testament to the fourth century; Eusebius was a great preserver and quoter of documents, and his *Ecclesiastical History* has literally hundreds of citations from now nonextant works—often his citations are all that survive from an author. He also established Christian historiography, that is, an understanding of how history should be written; he portrays the Church as a model of holiness and orthodoxy moving through history, attacked from outside by wicked emperors, gnawed at from within by *heretics, but maintaining its integrity via a succession of orthodox bishops and the courage of the *martyrs; all this leads up to the new, golden age of Constantine. He wrote a brief *vita of his hero Origen into his history, but he routinely omitted mention of people he did not care for, such as *Methodius of Olympus, and he did not refrain from harsh criticism; for example, *Papias of Hierapolis was "not very intelligent." He was a great storyteller; given the considerable range of subjects he had to cover, his narrative flows well. The value of this work is incalculable; on so many issues the history of the early Church is what Eusebius tells us it is.

EUSEBIUS OF DORYLAEUM
(fl. 425–450)

Anti-*Nestorian *bishop who led the attack on *Eutyches, he was deposed by the Second Council of *Ephesus in 449 and restored by *Chalcedon in 451.

EUSEBIUS OF EMESA (d. ca. 359)

Disciple of *Eusebius of Caesarea, this native of Caesarea was an anti-*Nicene but refrained from becoming an *Arian, even turning down the offer of an Arian synod in 340 to become *bishop of Alexandria; he took the bishopric of Emesa in Syria but could not occupy his office because the townspeople did not want an intellectual as a bishop. He fled to Antioch but was eventually able to return. At best a *Semi-Arian, he left behind few writings, mostly sermons and some exegetical fragments.

EUSEBIUS OF NICOMEDIA
(d. ca. 342)

*Bishop of Berytus (modern Beirut) and then of Nicomedia near Constantinople from 317, he supported the *Arian cause only to be rebuffed at the First Council of *Nicea, where he signed the *creed but opposed *Arius' condemnation, for which *Constantine I deposed him. Soon after Nicea, however, he began working against the council, using his reestablished influence with Constantine and his family; a remarkable politician, he soon engineered the removal from their sees of three great Nicenes, *Eustathius of Antioch (330), *Athanasius of Alexandria (335), and *Marcellus of Ancyra

(336). He *baptized the first Christian emperor on his deathbed in 337, and he received the see of Constantinople from Constantine II in 338. He converted *Ulfilas to Arianism in 340 and consecrated him bishop of the Goths, thus (unknowingly) guaranteeing the survival of Arianism among the Germanic barbarians long after its demise in the Roman Empire. Only a few of his letters survive, but his greatness lay in his political acumen, not in his theology.

EUSEBIUS OF ROME (d. ca. 309)

Pope for six months in 309 (or possibly 310); he had to deal with the consequences of *schism produced by his predecessor, *Marcellus I, and his stern treatment of the *lapsed, but his attempt to readmit the lapsed after *penance did not stop the ecclesiastical infighting. The schism worsened, and the dissident group elected its own pope, *Heraclius. The continuing strife forced the emperor Maxentius (306–312) to intervene; he exiled both Eusebius and Heraclius to Sicily, where the pope died.

EUSEBIUS OF SAMOSATA
(d. 380)

*Bishop of Samosata in Syria from 361, he fought the *Arians and suffered exile for his faith in 374 under the Arianizing emperor Valens (364–378), only to be recalled in 378 by the *Nicene Gratian (375–383); an Arian woman killed him, perhaps inadvertently, by throwing a brick at his head.

EUSEBIUS OF VERCELLI
(d. ca. 370)

A Sardinian by birth and a cleric at Rome, he became the first *bishop of the see of Vercelli in about 344; he strongly opposed the Italian *Arians and suffered exile in 355 as a result; freed in 362, he journeyed in the East before returning to Italy; in a significant innovation, he required his clergy to live under a rule, a practice later adopted or attempted by many Western bishops, including *Augustine. Only three letters of his survive; some exegetical works have been attributed but none reliably.

EUSTATHIUS OF ANTIOCH
(d. ca. 335)

*Bishop of Antioch from 324, he played a major role at *Nicea but earned the enmity of *Eusebius of Caesarea and *Eusebius of Nicomedia, who worked for his deposition from the see of Antioch in 330; *Constantine I banished Eustathius to an exile from which he never returned; like many Antiochenes, he worried about *Sabellianism and *Origenism, and he thus offered a theology that emphasized the distinction of human and divine in Christ; only fragments of his writings survive.

EUSTATHIUS OF SEBASTE
(ca. 300–ca. 378)

*Bishop of Sebaste in Asia Minor from 354, he supported *Arius early in his career but moved to a *Homoiousian position; he was, however, more interested in *monasticism than in theology, and his friendship with *Basil of Caesarea enabled him to influence Basil in the organization of his monastic rules; he did, however, break with Basil over the question of the divinity of the Holy Spirit, which Eustathius denied.

EUSTOCHIUM (370–ca. 419)

Roman noblewoman and disciple of *Jerome, upon whose advice she led a life of *asceticism in her home. When the Roman clergy and populace drove Jerome from the city in 385, she accompanied him to Bethlehem, where her mother *Paula used her fortune to establish four monasteries, one of which she headed until her death in 404; Eustochium then succeeded her mother as head of the monastery. Jerome portrays her as a pious and very learned woman.

EUTHYMIUS (377–473)

Armenian *priest who went to Palestine to live as a *hermit, he established a *lavra around 425; unlike most Palestinian monks, he supported *Chalcedon; he was an influential abbot, and *Sabas was his disciple.

EUTROPIUS (fl. 390–410)

A *priest either in Spain or in southern Gaul; a friend of *Paulinus of Nola, he wrote four extant letters, which betray considerable education in the pagan classics as well as an *ascetical Christian spirituality.

EUTROPIUS OF VALENCIA (fl. 590–600)

Spanish *bishop and *ascetical writer.

EUTYCHES (ca. 378–454)

Archimandrite, or superior, of a monastery in Constantinople and with powerful influence at the imperial court, he maintained, against *Nestorius, that there were "two natures in Christ before the incarnation, one afterward," a doctrine that became known as *Monophysitism. *Flavian, arch*bishop of Constantinople, deposed him in 448, so he appealed to *Leo I of Rome and *Dioscorus of Alexandria, claiming that his theology followed that of *Cyril of Alexandria. Leo rejected the appeal but Dioscorus supported him. At the Second Council of *Ephesus in 449, Eutyches was vindicated, Flavian deposed, and Leo's legates sent away; but two years later the Council of *Chalcedon reversed this decision, deposing and exiling Eutyches, who died soon afterward.

EUTYCHIAN (d. 283)

Pope from 275; nothing historically reliable is known of him beyond his name; his episcopate fell between two *persecutions.

EVAGRIUS PONTICUS (346–399)

From Pontus in Asia Minor, he was a confidant of *Basil of Caesarea and *Gregory of Nazianzus, and after the First Council of *Constantinople in 381, he stayed in the capital. But the city's threats to his morals sent him to *Melania in Jerusalem, and by 383 he was in the Egyptian desert, first as a *hermit and then as a disciple of the *Macarii. He was among the most learned of the monks; *Palladius of Helenopolis was his disciple, and

*Theophilus of Alexandria offered him a *bishopric, which he refused. A follower of *Origen, he interpreted the *monastic life mystically, placing less emphasis on feats of physical *asceticism than on the abandoning the body to achieve oneness with God. He was the first monk to write extensively, and although the later anti-Origenist reactions made his works suspect, he still influenced many later Eastern writers and, via John *Cassian, many Westerners as well. His writings emphasize the psychological progress toward unity and play down the thaumaturgic, until then the traditional sign of monastic sanctity. Most of his surviving writings are spiritual in character; his *Antirrhetikos* refers to the eight principal vices, which became metamorphosed in the West into the seven deadly sins.

EVAGRIUS SCHOLASTICUS (ca. 536–600)

A Syrian and a lawyer in Antioch who wrote a *Church History* covering the years 431 to 594, which provides much information about the *Nestorian and *Monophysite controversies; he cited several earlier historians whose works are now lost.

EVARISTUS (d. ca. 109)

Pope from about 100; nothing reliable is known of him besides his name.

EVE, GOSPEL OF

*Gnostic gospel quoted by *Epiphanius; the brief passage preserved indicates the gospel was revelatory in orientation and dealt with the need to save one's self from the world.

EXUPERIUS OF TOULOUSE (fl. 400–410)

Gallic *bishop who led resistance to the invading Visigoths; also known for his kindness to the poor.

EZNIK OF KOLB (fl. ca. 430)

Armenian *bishop and student of *Mesrob, Eznik wrote *Against the False Doctrines,* that is, of pagans, both Greek and Persian, classical philosophers, and the Marcionites, proof that followers of *Marcion of Pontus were still a factor in Christian life in the fifth century; he visited Edessa and Constantinople to learn about the larger Church outside Armenia, and upon returning to his homeland, Eznik aided the *patriarch *Sahak in the Armenian translation of the Bible.

F

FABIAN (d. 250)

Pope from 236; legend says that when the Romans were trying to choose a new pope, a dove settled on Fabian's head, and this was taken as a sign from the Holy Spirit; Fabian was a good administrator who rearranged the structure of the Roman Church, specifically by dividing it into seven districts, each with a *deacon and subdeacon to govern it; he was sufficiently influential with the government to arrange for the return and burial of the bodies of *Pontian and *Hippolytus; when the Decian *persecution erupted in 250, Fabian was one of its first victims.

FABIOLA (d. 399)

Noble Roman who, after an uncanonical divorce and remarriage, did *penance, gave her fortune to the poor, led a life of austerity, and stayed for a while in Bethlehem with *Jerome's community, although she eventually returned to Rome.

FACUNDUS (fl. ca. 550)

*Bishop of Hermiane in North Africa who opposed the emperor *Justinian (527–565) on the *Three Chapters, partly theologically and partly because he opposed secular interference in Church affairs; he fought for his cause by writing and by a journey to Constantinople itself; after the Second Council of *Constantinople, he maintained his position and was excommunicated by Pope *Vigilius.

FASTIDIUS

Early fifth-century British *bishop; he is historically very obscure; possibly he traveled to Italy; two *Pelagian works are attributed to him.

**FATHER;
FATHERS OF THE CHURCH**

Title originally reserved for *bishops, in the fourth century the word had been widely used of all orthodox writers, whether or not they were bishops; the Latin word for "father," *pater,* gives us the word *"patristics" for the study of the early Christian writers outside the New Testament; since the term now includes writers later generations considered *heretical, such as *Gnostics and Pelagians, as well as women Christian writers, the term is now rather inaccurate but is still widely used.

FAUSTINUS (fl. ca. 360–380)

Roman *presbyter; a theologically competent if unoriginal anti-*Arian writer who composed a treatise on the Trinity; he belonged to the sect of *Lucifer of Cagliari.

FAUSTINUS OF BRESCIA

According to tradition, he was *martyred in the early second century with his brother Jovita; this is probably a legend.

FAUSTUS OF BYZANTIUM (fl. ca. 400)

First historian of Christianity in Armenia, although his work deals with the fourth century, not with the earliest appearance of the Faith there.

FAUSTUS OF MILEVIS (fl. ca. 380–410)

African *Manichean *bishop who had a considerable reputation as a scholar but whom *Augustine found (and portrayed in the *Confessions*) to be a poorly educated bumbler; this disappointment helped Augustine's aban-

donment of Manicheism; Faustus may have been more important or at least more competent than Augustine portrayed him, because Augustine felt it necessary to write a *Contra Faustum* (Against Faustus) in about 397 to refute him.

FAUSTUS OF RIEZ (ca. 408–ca. 495)

A Briton who entered the monastery of *Lérins around 433; *bishop of Riez in Provence around 458; exiled from his see from 478 to 485 by Euric, king of the barbarian Visigoths and an *Arian; he was a strong anti-Arian writer but also a *Semi-Pelagian who opposed *Augustinian *predestinationism and argued for the human will's cooperation with God's grace in the process of salvation.

FELICISSIMUS

Mid-third-century African *presbyter who favored immediate readmittance to communion of the *lapsed and who went into *schism from *Cyprian of Carthage on this issue.

FELICITY (d. 203)

In Latin, Felicitas; an African *martyr and a companion of *Perpetua; her death is recounted in the *Passion of Saints Perpetua and Felicity,* written shortly after the event; she was a young and pregnant slave at the time of her arrest; she gave birth to a girl shortly before her heroic death; widely venerated in Christian Africa.

FELICITY OF ROME

Mentioned in the *Liberian Catalogue* as a second-century *martyr.

FELIX I (d. 274)

Pope from 269; little is known of him; he probably was the pope to whom the emperor Aurelian (270–275) referred the case of *Paul of Samosata.

FELIX II (d. 365)

*Antipope from 355; when *Constantius II (337–361) banished Pope *Liberius in 355, the Roman clergy swore allegiance to their exiled leader, but under imperial pressure they chose the arch*deacon Felix as pope. The clergy and people, however, never really accepted him, and when Constantius allowed Liberius to return, Felix had to retire to the suburbs. Ironically, he did get into official Roman lists of popes, and the numbering of his accepted successors must always allow for this (*see* **Felix II (III)**).

FELIX II (III) (d. 492)

Pope from 483; a Roman widower with two children, he was originally styled Felix III because of the prevailing confusion over the first *Felix II; this Felix II had to deal with the *Henoticon, a credal statement by the Byzantines trying to win back the *Monophysites; Felix saw a threat to *Chalcedon, demanded that the emperor *Zeno (474–491) depose the Monophysite bishop *Peter Mongos of Alexandria, and when *Acacius of Constantinople accepted Peter, Felix broke off communication with him, stressing his disciplinary differences and thus initiating what the West calls the *Acacian schism. Felix did not recognize or possibly did not care about the extent of the Monophysite

problem for the East, and his stern personality probably prolonged the schism unnecessarily. He was also the first pope to send the emperor the news of his election, a practice that continued well into the High Middle Ages.

FELIX III (IV) (d. 530)

Pope from 526; like his predecessor of this name he also has a confusing number because of the career of the first *Felix II; he was very pro-Gothic and received the support and cooperation of the Gothic court in Italy; he supported the efforts of *Caesarius of Arles against the Gallic *Semi-Pelagians and sent a series of propositions on grace to the Second Council of *Orange in 529.

FELIX OF NOLA (fl. 240–258)

Italian *priest who was *martyred sometime between 250 and 258; a popular cult grew up around him in his hometown; when *Paulinus of Nola moved there and eventually became *bishop, he promoted the cult of Felix with a series of annual poems for the saint's feast day (January 14).

FERRANDUS (fl. 520–547)

Carthaginian *deacon who wrote the *vita of *Fulgentius of Ruspe and who made a collection of early Greek and African *councils.

FILASTER OF BRESCIA (d. ca. 397)

Italian *bishop and antiheretical writer whose *Liber de haeresibus (Book of Heresies)* catalogued and refuted more than 150 *heresies; he probably drew from *Hippolytus and definitely from *Epiphanius of Salamis; he influenced *Augustine in the preparation of his catalogue of heresies; Filaster's book was popular in antiquity.

FINNIAN OF CLONARD (d. 549)

Abbot and founder of the monastery of Clonard, he supposedly had connections with *David and the Welsh Church; he was also a famous teacher whose chief disciples are known as the Twelve Apostles of Ireland; he is the likely author of the earliest extant Irish *penitential.

FINNIAN OF MOVILLE (ca. 495–579)

He apparently is the one who introduced the *Vulgate into Ireland; he was a famous abbot and much venerated in northern Ireland, but little is known of him historically.

FIRMICUS MATERNUS (d. ca. 365)

A pagan Sicilian by birth, he was a well educated aristocrat who wrote *Mathesis,* a manual for astrologers that also contains moral ruminations and a description of the Deity; after his conversion, he wrote *On the Errors of the Pagan Religions,* which vigorously defends Christianity and urges intolerance of paganism upon the Christian emperors, including the destruction of pagan shrines.

FIRMILIAN OF CAESAREA (d. ca. 268)

*Bishop from about 230 of Caesarea in Asia Minor and a pupil of *Origen;

he is known only from his letter to *Cyprian of Carthage, in which he criticizes the arrogant behavior of Pope *Stephen I, and by his presidency of the Antiochene synod of 264, dealing with *Paul of Samosata.

FISH

See Ichthus.

FLAVIAN OF CONSTANTINOPLE (d. 449)

*Patriarch of Constantinople from 446; he excommunicated *Eutyches for his *Monophysite teaching only to find himself condemned and deposed at the Second Council of *Ephesus in 449, called by Eutyches' supporter, the emperor *Theodosius II (408–450), and presided over by Flavian's rival, *Dioscorus of Alexandria; he died a few days after the council, possibly because of the harsh treatment he received there; he was rehabilitated at the Council of *Chalcedon in 451.

FLORILEGIUM; FLORILEGIA

Literally, "a collection of flowers"; toward the end of the *patristic period some writers made collections of excerpts from the *Fathers, and these were called *florilegia;* this was done for various reasons, for example, selections from several Fathers on a particular point, such as the spiritual life, or sometimes a collection from one Father on a dogmatic point to prove his orthodoxy; this practice continued well into the Middle Ages. Some patristic works are known only from *florilegia,* such as the *Philocalia.*

FORTUNATIANUS OF AQUILEIA

African who became *bishop of Aquileia in Italy in the mid-fourth century; originally a *Nicene, he gave in to imperial pressure and condemned *Athanasius and helped to persuade Pope *Liberius to sign the *Semi-Arian *creed of *Sirmium; his commentary on the Gospels survives in fragmentary form and was largely preserved by early medieval Irish monks.

FRONTO OF CIRTA

Pagan of the second century and tutor to the Roman emperor Marcus Aurelius, he made a famous anti-Christian speech that helped to provoke the response of the *apologists.

FRUCTUOSUS (d. 259)

*Bishop of Tarragona in Spain who was burned at the stake during the *persecution of the emperor Valerian (253–260).

FRUMENTIUS (ca. 300–ca. 380)

A native of Tyre in Palestine, he was sold as a slave in Ethiopia (then called Abyssinia); he converted his master and his family, then the royal Ethiopian house; he went to Alexandria and met *Athanasius, who consecrated him *bishop and sent him back to Ethiopia; revered by the Ethiopians as *Abuna* (Our Father), he was the Apostle to the Abyssinians.

FULGENTIUS OF RUSPE (467–533)

African noble who had a solid education that included knowledge of Greek (rare in Africa in that day), he first pursued a civil career, later lived as a monk, and in 507 became *bishop of Ruspe during the Vandal occupation of Africa; exiled to Sardinia from 508 to 515 and again from 517 to 523 because of his opposition to the *Arianism of the Vandals; he wrote several anti-Arian treatises as well as several against *Semi-Pelagianism; some letters and sermons survive.

G

GAIUS (fl. 200–220)

Possibly a Roman, he debated with a prominent *Montanist named Proclus during the pontificate of *Zephyrinus; an anti-*Gnostic writer as well, he rejected the authority of the Gospel of John and the Book of Revelation because he believed their author to have been the Gnostic *Cerinthus; he also spoke of the (burial) monuments of Peter and Paul in Rome; Gaius was the apparent leader of the *Alogi.

GAIUS (d. 296)

Pope from 283; nothing reliable is known of his papacy; legend associates him with the *martyrdom of Saint *Sebastian, whom he encouraged to stand firm; his Greek epitaph is the last papal epitaph in that language.

GALLA PLACIDIA (ca. 390–450)

Daughter of the Roman emperor *Theodosius I (379–395), she led an adventurous life, having been kidnapped by one Gothic king in 410 and becoming wife to another in 414, she returned to Rome after her husband's murder in 415; in 417 she married the future Constantius III; upon his death in 421 she was regent for her son, Valentinian III; she was a strong supporter of *Leo I in his struggle against *Eutyches and his supporters; she also supported anti-*Pelagian and anti-*Manichean measures. She built several churches in Ravenna as well as her own magnificent mausoleum there, the latter containing some of the most famous and beautiful mosaics of the ancient world.

GANGRA, COUNCIL OF

Held in 343 to condemn the excessive *asceticism of *Eustathius of Sebaste, which opposed marriage and devalued ordinary Christian devotions.

GAUDENTIUS OF BRESCIA

*Bishop of Brescia from 397; the dates of his birth and death are uncertain;

he was known in Italy as a homilist, although few of his works survive; in 404 or 405, at the request of Pope *Innocent I, he went to Constantinople to try to save *John Chrysostom from deposition.

GELASIUS I (d. 496)

Pope from 492; he was an arch*deacon to *Felix II (III) and inherited from him the *Acacian schism, which he only made worse. He distrusted the speculative theology of the Greeks, which he thought led to *heresy, and he resented the political power of the emperor at Constantinople. He refused all overtures of reconciliation, instead emphasizing the power of the Roman see. The first pope to be hailed as the Vicar of Christ, he claimed that only the popes could ratify the decisions of *councils and, further, that there were two powers, a spiritual one residing with the papacy and a political one residing with the emperor, but the spiritual was the superior (called in the Middle Ages the Doctrine of the Two Swords; cf. Luke 22:38); these claims advanced Roman primacy in the West but angered the Greeks and laid the foundation for the eventual *schism of 1054. Gelasius was popular in Rome itself for his personal sanctity and concern for the poor. Approximately one hundred of his letters survive.

GELASIUS OF CAESAREA (d. 395)

Second successor to *Eusebius, he also continued his great predecessor's *Ecclesiastical History,* which does not survive, although portions of it may have been incorporated into the history of *Rufinus of Aquileia; *bishop of Caesarea in 367, his support of *Nicea cost him his see under the *Arian emperor Valens (364–378), but he returned in 379 under *Theodosius I.

GELASIUS OF CYZICUS (fl. 475)

Anti-*Monophysite writer who collected the acts of *Nicea to prove that the Monophysites were not in harmony with that council.

GEMELLUS

Supposed disciple of *Simon Magus and the continuator of his teachings at Rome; a group called the Gemellites taught a strict *asceticism in the fourth century; *Amphilochius of Iconium wrote against them.

GENEVIEVE (ca. 422–ca. 500)

According to tradition, a Gallic consecrated virgin whose prayers deterred Attila the Hun from attacking Paris; she is the patroness of that city, and her statue stands behind the Cathedral of Notre Dame.

GENNADIUS OF CONSTANTINOPLE (d. 471)

*Bishop of Constantinople from 458; contemporaries call him a man of great learning, but except for one letter none of his writings survive; he opposed the *Monophysites and tried to reform his clergy.

GENNADIUS OF MARSEILLES (fl. 480–500)

*Priest of Marseilles and continuator of *Jerome's *On Famous Men,* a collection of brief biographies of important Christians; much of what he wrote deals with Gaul; a *Semi-Pelagian, he wrote against *Pelagius and also against *Nestorius and *Eutyches, but these works do not survive.

GEORGE

Palestinian *martyr in the late third or early fourth century; apparently he was a Roman soldier; his existence is not doubted, but no reliable historical material survives except his name; Lydda, in Palestine, the place of his martyrdom, was reputedly the place where the Greek hero Perseus rescued Andromeda from a dragon; scholars think that a mixing of the two heroes in the popular mind led to the legend of George's having killed the dragon. The legend of George was very popular in the Middle Ages, especially in England, where he eventually became the national patron saint.

GEORGE OF CAPPADOCIA
(d. 361)

*Arian *bishop forced on Alexandria in 357 by the emperor *Constantius II; a violent man, he was resented by the populace, who wanted their beloved *Athanasius back; a mob murdered George, and Athanasius returned the following year.

GEORGE OF LAODICEA
(fl. ca. 350–365)

Moderate *Arian and leader of the *Homoiousian party; he worked with *Basil of Ancyra.

GERMANUS OF AUXERRE
(ca. 378–448)

Gallic nobleman; he had a civil career and was married before becoming *bishop of Auxerre in 418, he twice visited Britain (429, 447) to combat *Pelagianism there; his mission was apparently successful; he died in Ravenna in 448 interceding for some Gallic rebels against the emperor; British legend also had him routing a barbarian invasion, a combined force of Picts and Saxons, from the province.

GERMANUS OF PARIS
(ca. 496–576)

*Bishop of Paris from 555, he tried to civilize the newly converted but still very barbarous Frankish royal house; buried beneath the church of Saint-Germain-des-Pres.

GERVASIUS AND PROTASIUS

Proto*martyrs of the Church of Milan, whose bodies *Ambrose claimed to have discovered in 386; nothing is known of the two saints; Ambrose's clever use of their posthumous miraculous powers against the Milanese *Arians is their greatest claim to fame.

GILDAS (ca. 500–ca. 570)

British monk who traveled considerably, including a pilgrimage to Rome, several visits to Ireland, and the establishment of a monastery in Britanny; of his *monastic activity in his native Wales, little is known; around 540 he wrote *On the Ruin and Conquest of Britain,* an account of the pagan Saxon invasion of Britain, brought on, so Gildas thought, by the immorality of the British clergy and aristocracy; this is a valuable history of Britain in an otherwise very obscure period. He mentions the battle of Badon Hill but not King Arthur. A letter and a *penitential are ascribed to him, but they are probably inauthentic.

GNOSTIC; GNOSTICISM

These names derive from *gnosis,* Greek for "knowledge," although this was a particular kind of knowledge, not merely that gained from study but rather a knowledge of God and often some cosmology as well. Although the term "Gnosticism" implies a belief system, there was no formal organized Gnostic teaching but rather a variety of individual teachers and sects; scholars are generally cautious about assigning particular traits or teachings to Gnostics in general. Still, some traits were widespread, particularly the notion that humans who achieve divine gnosis would redeem their spiritual beings from the imprisonment of the flesh. It seems clear now that there were both pre-Christian and Jewish varieties of Gnosticism, but Christian Gnosticism represents the largest group. Many Gnostic teachers claimed that their teachings derived from secret traditions handed down from Jesus and his followers, although these supposedly apostolic—and thus Jewish— traditions were routinely mixed with speculative, scientific, astrological, and mythological elements. Many Gnostics taught the existence of two Gods, a good God who sent Jesus as the re-

vealer of the world of the spirit, and a lesser God, the *Demiurge, who created the material world and who was often identified with the God of the Old Testament. This Demiurge ruled the world, but some people possessed a spiritual spark of the knowledge of the true God, and the proper gnosis could rescue this spark from the flesh. Gnostic teachers devised methods by which this could be done, but it could not be done by all. Spiritual persons, called *pneumatikoi,* would achieve this knowledge, but others, the *psykikoi,* or people of the soul, were capable of illumination, while the fleshly or *sarkikoi* would remain enslaved to matter and thus to eventual oblivion. Jesus did not come to die for humans or to demand faith of them; rather he came as the ambassador of the true God to impart knowledge of that being to humans. These ideas were heavily propagated in the second century, especially by means of (now) apocryphal *gospels, *acts, and epistles. Several Gnostic teachers, such as *Valentinus, *Basilides, and *Marcion of Pontus, whose Gnosticism is less intense than the others, became prominent figures in the Church, and in Egypt in the second century the Gnostics possibly outnumbered those who came to be called the "orthodox." Many orthodox writers, such as *Irenaeus and *Tertullian, attacked Gnosticism, and it largely died out in the third century. In 1945 a large collection of fourth-century Gnostic documents was discovered at *Nag Hammadi in Egypt, proof that it survived there until then; it is also likely that some Gnostic ideas influenced Egyptian monks in this period. No one doubts the enormous importance of Gnosticism for understanding early Christianity, and many of its tenets appeal to moderns, for example, its emphasis upon knowledge instead of simple belief, its openness to the individual rather than an insistence on obedience to authority, and its rather positive attitude toward women (although no founder or head of a Gnostic sect was a woman); however, its elitism and anti-Semitism would never have permitted Christianity to become a universal religion or to keep the Old Testament.

GOSPELS, APOCRYPHAL

Term given to all gospels not included in the canon of the New Testament; many of these are *Gnostic and further Gnostic ideas; many reflect the attitudes of the Christians who produced them and thus are of value historically; possibly the *Gospel of *Thomas* is of the first century.

GREGORY OF AGRIGENTUM
(d. ca. 592)

Sicilian *bishop, correspondent of *Gregory the Great, and possible author of a commentary on Ecclesiastes.

GREGORY OF ELVIRA
(d. after 392)

Spanish *Nicene *bishop who attacked *Arianism and who joined the *Luciferians and even became their leader after *Lucifer's death; he also opposed *Priscillianism. He wrote some *allegorical exegesis of the Old Testament and some dogmatic works.

GREGORY OF NAZIANZUS
(329–389)

One of the three *Cappadocians, he was the son of the *bishop of Nazianzus; he became great friends with his fellow student *Basil of Caesarea; he wished to become a monk, but at the wishes of his father and the local populace, he reluctantly became a *priest in 362; bishop of the small town of Sasima in 371, he never visited the place; in 379 the Nicenes at Constantinople convinced him to accept the bishopric there, but the feuding and politicking surrounding the First Council of *Constantinople in 381 discouraged him so much that he resigned; he spent much of the rest of his life writing. His *Theological Orations* represent his best work. He defended and clarified the teaching of *Nicea on the Trinity, and he won over many of the *Semi-Arians to the Nicene cause. He defended the unity of the Trinity and also the divinity of the Holy Spirit; he also wrote of the duality of natures in Christ, including a defense of Christ's human soul against the teaching of *Apollinaris. Poems and letters of his also survive.

GREGORY OF NYSSA
(ca. 335–ca. 395)

One of the three *Cappadocians, he was the younger brother of *Basil of Caesarea; he entered a monastery his brother had founded, but when Basil got him appointed to the see of Nyssa in 371, he dutifully went there and tried to be an administrator but with little success; the local *Arians deposed him in 376, although he returned in 378; he took an active part in the First

Council of *Constantinople in 381; he preached in the capital a few times after that, but otherwise his later life is obscure. He was an original thinker and a prolific writer. He defended the *Nicene teaching on the Trinity and two natures of Christ, including the fullness of the human nature; he emphasized the unity of the Trinity and the separation of Christ's natures. He made extensive use of the prevailing philosophy, Neoplatonism, and he argued that the human mind could be elevated to an immediate knowledge of God; this fit his own mystical bent as well as the mystical side of Neoplatonism. Gregory wrote exegesis, *apologetics, *ascetical and mystical treatises, and many sermons and letters.

GREGORY OF TOURS (ca. 540–594)

He came from a noble Gallo-Roman family, and he worked for much of his life to Christianize the supposedly Christian Frankish kings; *bishop of Tours from 573, he wrote many *vitae of the saints, but his great work is his *History of the Franks,* an enormously valuable account of that people from their arrival in Gaul to the year 591. The superstitious Gregory filled his narrative with references to demonic and saintly interventions—indeed, one of the major characters is the long-deceased *Martin of Tours, whose spiritual presence fills the narrative—but Gregory's overall story of the bloody, retrograde Christianization of the barbarians, much of which he witnessed, makes exciting and invaluable reading.

GREGORY THAUMATURGUS (ca. 213–ca. 260)

The Apostle of Cappadocia was born a pagan and went to Beirut to study law, but instead he studied with *Origen at Caesarea (233–238) and there became a Christian; when he parted from his teacher, he wrote a farewell address, a panegyric in which he praised Origen's teaching; this has provided scholars with an important look at the great theologian's pedagogical methods. Gregory returned to his native country and became a *bishop around 243; he worked long and successfully to convert the local pagans, and he led his diocese through the terrors of the barbarian invasion (ca. 254). His reputation was such that many miraculous legends became attached to it, thus his name, "Thaumaturgus" (Wonder-Worker).

GREGORY I THE GREAT (ca. 540–604)

Pope from 590; Gregory came of a noble Roman family; he held a secular position, prefect of the city of Rome from 572 to 574, but became a monk upon his parents' deaths, turning his house into a monastery; the popes, however, denied him his solitude; *Benedict I appointed him a *deacon in 578, and in 579 *Pelagius II sent him as legate to Constantinople to try to get imperial help for Italy against the ravages of the Lombards; Gregory had little success and returned to Rome—and his monastery—in 586 only to be called to the papal throne, under protest, four years later. Although never in good health, Gregory was a man of enormous energy; he worked tirelessly to keep the Lombards at bay and then to convert them; he tried to reform the Italian clergy and to wipe out the vestiges of paganism found in Sardinia and in some rural areas of Italy itself; he asserted Roman primacy against what he considered the pretensions of the see of Constantinople, which had the support of the emperor Maurice (582–602); when Phocas (602–610) murdered Maurice and his family and seized the throne, Gregory's unseemly rejoicing hurt the image of his see. Gregory's real legacy lay in the lands of the West. He worked with the Spanish *bishops and especially his old friend *Leander of Seville to convert the barbarian Visigoths to Catholicism; he urged the Africans to check the rising strength of *Donatism; most important for the English-speaking world, he dispatched the monk *Augustine (later to be known as Augustine of Canterbury) to the pagan Saxons in 596, and he always kept in close contact with the English mission. Gregory was the first monk to become pope, and he actively promoted *monasticism, including writing the first *vita of Saint *Benedict of Nursia. Amazingly, he also found time to write. His *Dialogues*

portray the lives of many Italian saints; his *Pastoral Care* explains his understanding of the bishop's office; his heavily *allegorical and moralizing exegetical writings on Job, Ezekiel, the Song of Songs, and the Gospels were enormously popular in the Middle Ages. He was first pope to style himself *servus servorum Dei* (servant of the servants of God).

GREGORY THE ILLUMINATOR (ca. 240–332)

The Apostle of Armenia, he was an Armenian by birth, possibly of royal blood; he converted to Christianity while in exile in Cappadocia; he returned home as a missionary and succeeded in converting King Tiridates, a former persecutor; in 302 Tiridates made Christianity the official religion of Armenia, the first country to take such a step. The Christian *bishop of Caesarea in Cappadocia consecrated Gregory the head of the Armenian Church, a task Gregory took seriously, even to the point of destroying one famous pagan shrine and converting another into a church. No writings of his survive.

H

HAGIOGRAPHY

Literally, "writing about the holy"; specifically, it means writing the life of a saint; the actual life itself is usually called a *vita.

HALO

In Christian art, a circle of light floating above the head of God, an angel, or some sacred person; this should be distinguished from a *nimbus, although such a distinction may not have been the case for the earliest Christian art.

HEBREWS, GOSPEL ACCORDING TO

*Jerome refers to a copy of this work at the library of Caesarea in Palestine; he said it was used by the *Ebionites and *Nazarenes and that it was written in Aramaic; surviving fragments indicate a relationship to the Gospel of Matthew; this gospel presents a Jewish but not *heretical view of Christianity; it probably dates to the second century.

HEGEMONIUS

A fourth-century writer who attacked *Manicheism and some other *heresies in a work called the *Acta Archelai,* a supposed debate between a Christian *bishop named Archelaus and Manes himself.

HEGESIPPUS (fl. 150–180)

A (probably) Jewish Christian anti-*Gnostic writer who came to Rome during the pontificate of *Anicetus; he was convinced that the surest guide to the true faith was that passed on from the apostles by a succession of *bishops, a conclusion he reached from his journey when he found bishops in many cities teaching the same doctrine, and so he drew up a list of the bishops of Rome down to Anicetus, although the main purpose of his *Memoirs* was to combat the

Gnostics; his works do not survive, but *Eusebius of Caesarea preserves some fragments.

HELENA (ca. 225–330)

Around 270 this innkeeper's daughter married the Roman general Constantius, who divorced her in 293 after he became emperor (292); her son, *Constantine I, however, always gave her a place of honor; she became a Christian around 312 and soon became famous for her works of charity; she encouraged her son's building projects in the Holy Land, where she died while on a pilgrimage; later tradition, which may have a historical basis, associated her with the finding of the True Cross.

HELVIDIUS (fl. ca. 380–390)

Latin writer known only through *Jerome's vicious attack on him in *Against Helvidius;* offended by the *ascetics' contempt for marriage, he apparently denied the virginity of Mary, Christ's mother, by claiming that the brothers of the Lord in the Gospels were indeed children of Joseph and Mary; Jerome vigorously defended Mary's perpetual virginity.

HENOTICON

A document drawn up in 482 at the encouragement of the emperor *Zeno by *Acacius of Constantinople and addressed to the *bishops, monks, and laity of Alexandria and areas dominated ecclesiastically by Alexandria to find a common ground to reconcile the see of Constantinople with the anti-*Chalcedonians in Egypt. It enabled the preservation of communion between the major sees of the East during the reigns of Zeno and his successor Anastasius; it was not aimed at Rome but it did precipitate what Rome called the *Acacian schism. Basically, it condemned *Nestorius and *Eutyches and praised *Cyril of Alexandria, but it avoided the real question of the natures in the person of Christ.

HERACLAS (fl. 232–247)

Student of *Origen and *bishop of Alexandria from 232; his predecessor, *Demetrius, had excommunicated Origen from Alexandria, and the great theologian hoped for better treatment from Heraclas, who, however, maintained the excommunication.

HERACLEON (fl. ca. 150)

*Gnostic disciple of *Valentinus, he wrote a now nonextant commentary on John's Gospel; *Origen has preserved fragments of it in his own Johannine commentary; Heracleon favored *allegorical exegesis.

HERACLIUS

*Antipope in 309; he is known only from an epitaph, which Pope *Damasus I prepared for Pope *Eusebius; Heraclius apparently represented a Roman faction that favored a lenient treatment of the *lapsed; he was exiled with Eusebius to Sicily by the pagan emperor Maxentius (306–312) when the ecclesiastical factionalism caused public disturbances.

HERESIARCH

Title given to the head of a *heretical sect.

HERESY

This often misused technical term means conscious deviation from a formally and publicly declared tenet of the Faith; the word *hairesis* originally meant "sect," and by the second century Christian writers such as *Irenaeus used the term to distinguish the teachings of those who belonged to small sects as opposed to the teachings of the larger or Catholic Church, which were preserved in the Scriptures and by a succession of *bishops; the term "heresy" has little relevance before the fourth century, when *ecumenical councils formally defined points of the Faith; for pre-*Nicene teaching that deviated from the norm, the term "*heterodoxy" is more appropriate.

HERMAS (fl. ca. 140–150)

One of the *Apostolic Fathers and author of *The Shepherd,* an *apocalyptic and visionary work; the *Muratorian Fragment says he was the brother of *Pius I of Rome, where the work is set; Hermas was apparently a Jewish Christian. *The Shepherd* tells of apparitions to Hermas by the Church, personified by an old woman who gets progressively younger and also by an angel of *penance who appears in the garb of a shepherd, hence the book's name; this work testifies to the continuation of apocalyptic notions in the Church and also to the possibility if not the actual practice of a second penance after *baptism, something opposed by Christian rigorists.

HERMIAS

An author known only from his book, the *Satire of Hermias,* probably written around 200; the work is not mentioned by any other early Christian author; it attacks, often with sarcasm, the futile attempts of pagan philosophers to know God.

HERMIT

See **Eremite.**

HESYCHASM

An Eastern tradition of inner prayer often leading to mysticism; it is a post-*patristic phenomenon that, however, traces its origins to several early Christian spiritual writers, such as *Gregory of Nyssa and *Evagrius Ponticus.

HESYCHIUS (fl. ca. 300–310)

Alexandrian biblical critic who revised the text of the *Septuagint, according to *Jerome.

HESYCHIUS OF JERUSALEM (d. ca. 455)

A monk and later a *priest, he supposedly—and possibly—commented on the entire Bible; he also wrote sermons and a *Church History* dealing with fifth-century events. His surviving works, on the Old Testament, show him to have been a genuine biblicist, eschewing philosophy and even current theological terminology that had a philosophical tinge; he attacked several *heretical groups, such as the *Arians and *Apollinarians, but may himself have had *Monophysite leanings.

HETERODOXY

A deviation from the widely accepted standard (e.g., the *Docetic rejection of Christ's physicality) but not yet from an established, formal teaching, which would be *heresy; before the age of the *ecumenical councils, heterodoxy is a more accurate term that heresy for those doctrines that differed from those held by the larger Church.

HEXAPLA

Literally, "the sixfold [Bible]," an edition of the Old Testament made by *Origen in six parallel columns and running to six thousand handwritten pages; it contains the Hebrew text, a Greek transliteration of that text (i.e., the Hebrew letters sounded out in Greek letters), the *Septuagint, and three revisions of the Septuagint. Clearly so monumental a work could not be copied easily, and probably no copy was ever made; *Jerome claimed to have used the original at Caesarea in Palestine. Fragments of this great work have survived.

HIERONYMIAN MARTYROLOGY

Fifth-century Italian *martyrology that provides in addition to the names and dates of saints to be honored the places of their burial.

HILARION (ca. 291–371)

Known largely from his *vita by *Jerome, Hilarion was a pagan from Gaza in Palestine who became a Christian at Alexandria; he visited the famous *Antony but did not then decide to be a monk; when he returned to Palestine and learned that his parents had died, he gave away his inheritance and became a *hermit, around 306; his rigorous life attracted disciples, and he was soon forced to purchase a house and goods for them; this was contrary to his own desires, so he fled first to Egypt, then to Sicily, then to Dalmatia (modern Croatia), and finally to Cyprus, where he died.

HILARUS (d. 468)

Pope from 461; he was one of *Leo I's legates to the Second Council of *Ephesus in 449, and his description of the violent events, from which he barely escaped, provided the basis for Leo's branding of that council as *latrocinium* (robber council); Hilarus showed little initiative but instead followed Leo's conservative path with the East, condemning *heresies and asserting Roman primacy wherever possible; in the West he fought a losing battle against Gothic *Arianism in Italy but managed to extend Roman primacy in Gaul. He also intervened in Spain but with little controversy, since the Spanish episcopate was already looking to Rome.

HILARY OF ARLES (401–449)

Gallic nobleman, disciple and relative of *Honoratus, founder of the Gallic island monastery of *Lérins. Hilary had a brief civil career, became a monk at Lérins, and tried to reject the see of Arles on Honoratus' death (ca. 430), but the people insisted. As a *bishop, Hilary was a great preacher who called and presided over several Gallic *councils, although when he tried to establish himself as *metropolitan of Gaul, another bishop, Celidon, appealed to Rome to *Leo I, who limited the authority of Arles. Hilary was a *Semi-Pelagian in his theology.

HILARY OF POITIERS (ca. 315–367)

A pagan by birth and a married man, he became *bishop of Poitiers from 350 and one of the strongest defenders of *Nicea in the West; he suffered exile to Asia Minor by the emperor *Constantius II in 356; the exile was surprisingly fruitful because Hilary came into firsthand contact with Greek Nicene theology; he also so vigorously opposed the local *Arians that they asked the emperor to return him to Gaul; he arrived home in 360. He wrote a fine commentary on Matthew's Gospel and some Old Testament exegesis as well as some works against the Arians and a treatise, *De Synodis,* about the *creeds of various synods both Catholic and Arian, but his *De Trinitate,* written while he was in exile, stands as his most important book, a staunch defense of the divinity and consubstantiality of the Son of God. His efforts earned him the title "the *Athanasius of the West." He was also the first Latin Christian to write hymns.

HIPPOLYTUS OF ROME (ca. 170–235)

Known as the first *antipope, he probably migrated to Rome from the East, because in addition to the Greek phi-losophy that many educated Romans learned, he knew about the various Greek religious sects; he was, in fact, the last great Roman writer to write in Greek. He accepted the *Logos theology of the Alexandrians and thus opposed the *Monarchianism and *Sabellianism current in Rome. He was a rigorist in morals, and when, about 217, Pope *Callistus relaxed the penitential requirements for serious sin (*see* **Penance**), Hippolytus broke relations with him and headed a small group of dissidents. He remained in *schism through the pontificates of two more popes, until both he and Pope *Pontian were exiled to Sardinia in 235 by the emperor Maximinus Thrax (235–238). His community apparently reconciled itself to the larger group, and Hippolytus and Pontian were personally reconciled and both died soon afterward. Pope *Fabian brough back both bodies for honorable burial, and the Roman Church commemorates Hippolytus as a *martyr. Hippolytus was a wide-ranging scholar who wrote exegesis, homilies, and a world history, but his most valuable book is his *Refutation of All Heresies,* by which he meant mostly *Gnostics, whom he accuses of taking their doctrines from the pagans and thirty-three of whose sect he lists and discusses, thus providing a valuable source book on Gnosticism. He is also the author of the *Apostolic Tradition,* an account of Christian worship as well as a set of rules for the ordination and functions of various ministers as well as the administration of *sacraments, particularly *baptism and the *Eucharist. This work was preserved primarily in Egypt, and only in this century was it proven to be a Roman Church order.

HOMOIOS; HOMOIANS

Also spelled Homoeans; *homoios* was a term used by *Semi-Arians who could accept neither *Arianism nor the *Nicene *homoousios; homoios* means simply "like," and the Homoians asserted that the Son was simply like the Father in the Trinity; the vagueness of the term prevented its widespread adoption, although the emperor *Constantius II favored this term because it avoided the troublesome word "substance" (*ousia* in Greek).

HOMOIOUSIOS; HOMOIOUSIANS

A *Semi-Arian term asserting that the Son is like to the Father in substance but not of the same substance, as claimed by the *Nicene *homoousios*; the Homoiousians formed a large party in the Eastern Church, and it was the achievement of the *Cappadocians to realize how close they were to the Nicenes and to work to close that gap. The mission of *Ulfilas to the Goths kept *homoiousios* alive for some centuries after matters were settled in the East.

HOMOOUSIOS

Literally, "of one substance," a term used by the Council of *Nicea to assert the oneness of the Father and Son in the Trinity, but unfortunately the term, which had a checkered history before the council (having been used by *Origen and by *Paul of Samosata), could be interpreted as "of one person" and, thus, to many Eastern ears smacked of *Sabellianism. The term translates as "consubstantial" in Latin, and many scholars attributed it to *Hosius of Cordova, the emperor *Constantine I's theological advisor at Nicea. This term became the touchstone of Nicene orthodoxy, and *Athanasius, the *Cappadocians, and *Hilary of Poitiers strove to make it acceptable to those adherents of *homoiousios* who had reservations about the Nicene term.

HONORATUS OF LÉRINS
(ca. 350–ca. 430)

Noble Gallic convert who decided to become a monk at *Lérins, where he founded a monastery that attracted the leading Christian figures of Gaul, such as *Salvian, *Eucherius, and *Hilary of Arles. He became *bishop of Arles in 428 but died soon after. His life is known primarily from a sermon in his honor by Hilary of Arles.

HORMISDAS (d. 523)

Pope from 514; he ended the *schism of the *antipope *Laurence at Rome and, most importantly, the *Acacian schism with the East, although that was achieved more because the Latin-speaking Justin I, guided often by his nephew and successor, *Justinian, ascended to the Byzantine throne in 518; the emperor abandoned the *Henoticon* and acknowledged Roman orthodoxy in matters of faith but was careful not to acknowledge jurisdictional authority for Rome over Constantinople. In the West, Hormisdas got along well with Italy's Gothic rulers, and in his extensive correspondence he maintained a strong Roman presence in Gaul and Spain.

HORSIESI

See Orsisius.

HOSIUS OF CORDOVA
(ca. 257–357)

Sometimes spelled Ossius; Spanish *bishop who became, how is unknown, the theological advisor to the emperor *Constantine I (306–337); his report of the *Arian controversy apparently prompted Constantine to call the First Council of *Nicea, at which Hosius suggested the term *homoousios* for the relationship between Father and Son in the Trinity; he worked for the Nicene cause but suffered for it under *Constantius II; in spite of his very advanced age he was banished in 355 and, under pressure, signed the socalled Blasphemy of *Sirmium in 357 acknowledging Arian teaching, although he repudiated this action just before his death.

HYGINUS (d. ca. 142)

Pope from about 136; several ancient sources say Hyginus was pope for six years, but little else is known of his pontificate, which must have been a lively one, since several prominent *Gnostic teachers, such as *Cerdo and *Valentinus, were in the city at the time; Hyginus' Greek name suggests the continuing influence of the foreign element among the Christians in the Latin capital.

HYPATIA (ca. 375–415)

A Neoplatonist philosopher in Alexandria, she followed her father, Theon, in writing works on philosophy and mathematics; *Synesius of Cyrene was one of her pupils; she was murdered by a Christian mob that held her responsible for some harsh actions by the local prefect, and many suspected that *Cyril of Alexandria was behind the attack, although that has never been proven.

HYPATIUS OF CONSTANTINOPLE (fl. 531–536)

Advisor to the emperor *Justinian (527–565) and champion of the *Theopaschite formula; he also represented the emperor in the fruitless negotiations with the *Monophysites.

HYPOSTASIS

Greek term meaning "substance" but, like many other Greek theological terms, susceptible of other meanings; the *Cappadocians brought theologians to use the term to mean an individual existing being in the sense of a person so that they could speak of three *hypostases* in the Trinity without meaning three gods; the oneness of God was emphasized in his *ousia*; the term "hypostatic union" defined the union of the divine and human natures in Christ at *Chalcedon.

I

IBAS OF EDESSA (d. 457)

Theologian and *bishop of Edessa in Syria from 435 to 449, when he was deposed by the Second Council of *Ephesus for supposed *Nestorian views, only to be reinstated by the Council of *Chalcedon in 451; he was condemned at *Constantinople II in 553 as one of the *Three Chapters because of his lack of complete support for the *Christology of *Cyril of Alexandria.

ICONOGRAPHY

Literally, "writing in images" (in Greek, *eikon*), the term refers to the study of Christian art for its content, for example, the portrayal of innocent suffering (Isaac, Job, Daniel) during the age of *persecution; symbols are prominent in iconography, for example, the peacock for eternal life, the vine for Christ's blood.

ICTHUS

Greek for "fish," it was an acrostic, that is, its letters are the initials of the words *Iesous Christos Theou Uios Soter* (Jesus Christ, God's Son, Savior). This symbol first appears in Christian art in the second century, but its origins are unknown.

IGNATIUS OF ANTIOCH
(d. ca. 115)

*Bishop of Antioch who was *martyred during the reign of the emperor Trajan (98–117); during his journey to Rome for execution he wrote seven letters, six to Churches and one to *Polycarp of Smyrna, which reveal that *Docetists and *Judaizers were both active in Antioch; they also reveal a *Monarchical concept of the episcopacy because Ignatius sees the bishop as a source of unity but also as a stand-in for Christ (at one point comparing the bishop and his *presbyters to Christ and his apostles). This represents an advanced concept of the episcopacy and one quite distinct from the collegial approach assumed to be common in the first century, but it could just as easily represent an emergency taken in Antioch to put an end to the confusion caused by sectional strife. Some scholars, however, believe that a monarchical episcopate existed in the Jerusalem Church from its beginning, and Ignatius' views represent an extension of that. Ignatius also expressed a passionate desire for martyrdom, likewise rather uncharacteristic of the age.

ILLTYD (ca. 440–ca. 535)

Welsh saint known primarily through medieval legend; he apparently migrated to Wales from Brittany and founded the monastery of Llantwit; *Gildas was probably one of his pupils.

INFANCY GOSPELS

Name given collectively to several apocryphal *gospels that describe the infancy of Christ; the best known are those of the *Protoevangelium of *James* and the *Infancy Gospel of *Thomas*; these works were very influential in medieval art, for example, the Giotto frescoes at Padua's Scrovegni Chapel.

INNOCENT I (d. 417)

Pope from 401; son of Pope *Anastasius I; he vigorously promoted Roman primacy in the West, insisting that Roman custom be the standard for all Western Churches; he con-

demned the *Pelagians but only after congratulating the African *bishops for deferring to the judgment of the Apostolic See on this matter—something the Africans simply did not do; he propagated the Roman canon of the Scripture; and he did all this not in his own name but that of Saint Peter. He was in Rome when the Visigoths began their siege in 410, but he left the city before its actual fall, returning only in 412. In the East he did not get involved in doctrinal matters, but he supported *John Chrysostom in his unsuccessful struggle to keep the see of Constantinople; indeed, he broke off communion with the bishops who had worked for John's deposition.

INSTANTIUS (fl. 380)

A Spanish *bishop who supported *Priscillian but who managed to escape his fate, although he was himself deposed from his now unknown see; many scholars think him the author of several unclaimed Priscillianist tracts.

IONA

Island off the southwest coast of Scotland on which *Columba founded a monastery in 565 and from which many of the pagan inhabitants of the area were converted; it was also the starting point for the Irish mission to the Angles and Saxons in the seventh century.

IRENAEUS OF LYONS
(ca. 130–ca. 200)

A native of Asia Minor, probably Smyrna, he migrated to Gaul and lived at Lyons, which had a sizeable Asian community; he visited Rome around 177 to discuss *Montanism with Pope *Eleutherius; this visit may have saved his life, since a fierce *persecution broke out in Lyons at the same time; the *bishop, *Photinus, died a *martyr and Irenaeus replaced him; Irenaeus, whose name means "peacemaker" (in Hebrew, "Solomon"), tried around 185 to end the *Quartodeciman controversy between Pope *Victor I and the bishops of Asia; after this nothing is known of his life. Irenaeus wrote several works, but only two survive, his *Demonstration of the Apostolic Preaching,* something of a fundamental theology, and his masterpiece, *On the Detection and Overthrow of the Pretended but False Gnosis,* usually and conveniently shortened to *Against *Heresies.* As the title suggests, Irenaeus attacked the *Gnostics, but in a new and effective way. Realizing that the Gnostics based much on their claims of secret traditions reaching back to the apostles, Irenaeus turned this approach on its head, insisting that he could trace what he taught back to the apostles and could prove it because his teachings had public verification, that is, they could be found in Scripture (here including the Old Testament and at least the four Gospels and probably some other New Testament books) and apostolic succession, that is, a succession of bishops who could be traced back to the apostolic age. He himself had been taught by *Polycarp, who, he claimed, had been taught by John (presumably he meant John of the Twelve), and thus Irenaeus understood apostolic succession as something organic, a living link to the first age of the Church. Thus, what had been the Gnostic strong point, the secret traditions, now became its weak point. This theological method, commonly called "Scripture and Tradition," became the standard approach for all other early Christian theologians, who insisted that what they taught was no more than what the apostles had taught. Irenaeus' book is also of great value because of the many varieties of Gnosticism it catalogues, and the modern discovery of Gnostic literature has in general upheld Irenaeus' descriptions of the beliefs of the Gnostic sectaries.

ISAAC OF ANTIOCH

Fifth-century anti-*heretical writer; he wrote in Syriac against the *Nestorians and the *Monophysites.

ISAAC THE GREAT

See Sahak.

ISAIAH, ASCENSION OF

Jewish *apocryphal work describing the *martyrdom of Isaiah and his ascension into heaven; very popular in the early Church (Heb 11:37), it was reedited by a second-century Christian. It describes the seven heavens and gives prophecies about Christianity, including one referring to Nero's *persecution.

ISIDORE (fl. ca. 150)

Disciple and possibly the son of the *Gnostic teacher *Basilides; he wrote a book on ethics and another one claiming that the Greek philosophers had taken some of their concepts from the biblical prophets.

ISIDORE OF PELUSIUM (d. ca. 435)

A well-educated Alexandrian who led a *monastic life, but scholars are uncertain whether he was a *hermit or *cenobite or, at different times, followed both lives; his writings include approximately two thousand letters, which throw much light on his personality and somewhat less light on the events of his day; a critic of *Cyril of Alexandria, he was theologically a moderate, defending the divinity of Christ against the *Arians and the humanity of Christ against the *Manichees.

ISIDORE OF SEVILLE (ca. 560–636)

Often called the last of the Western Church *Fathers, a title he would have appreciated, since his life's work was dedicated to preserving the *patristic heritage in Visigothic Spain; Isidore came from a noble family with a record of Church service; his older brother *Leander had reformed the Spanish Church. Leander headed the monastery in which Isidore studied; he later became *bishop of Seville, again to be followed by Isidore (ca. 600). Isidore was a man of great energy and encyclopedic learning, and although he wrote exegesis, pastoral works, and some dogmatic treatises, he is best known from his *Etymologiae,* an encyclopedia of the knowledge of his day divided into twenty categories of the arts and sciences with great emphasis upon the sciences. This work preserved much ancient knowledge—and some ancient nonsense—from now nonextant works. This handy compendium was widely used in the early Middle Ages, and almost one thousand *manuscripts of it survive.

ITALA

Term used by *Augustine to describe one branch of the Old Latin or *Vetus Latina* versions of the Bible; there is no way to tell exactly what text he meant, although scholars have not been unwilling to apply the name to particular versions.

J

JACOB BARADAI (ca. 500–578)

A Syrian *Monophysite, he was a desert monk until he went to Constantinople in 528 and stayed there in a monastery until 542, when an Arab king who was a client of the Romans requested from the emperor *Justinian (527–565) two *bishops for his people; the empress *Theodora arranged for Jacob's appointment as bishop of Edessa. A remarkably active man, he went about much of the East founding Monophysite Churches in spite of considerable danger and physical want; he ordained at least thirty other bishops. Most of his influence was in Syria; his attempts to work with the Egyptian Monophysites failed. Thanks to him the Eastern Monophysite Church was well founded and well organized and destined for a long life. Indeed, many Monophysite Churches were known as *Jacobite; his surname means "the ragged," no doubt applied to him because of his tireless schedule.

JACOBITES

Name given to those Churches founded by *Jacob Baradai; they were common in the East from the sixth century, through the period of Arab rule, until the thirteenth century.

JACOB OF NISIBIS (fl. 325–350)

Syriac *bishop, participant at the First Council of *Nicea, and lifelong opponent of the *Arians; little is known of his life.

JACOB OF SARUG (ca. 450–521)

Syriac *bishop, author of many letters, homilies, and *hagiographical works; he was educated at Edessa and was an itinerant *priest among Syriac communities from 503 to 519, when he became a bishop; many of his homilies were metrical and earned him the epithet "the Flute of the Holy Spirit."

JAMES, APOCALYPSES OF

Two short *Gnostic works found at *Nag Hammadi; their dates are uncertain; the format is a conversation between Jesus and James, the brother of the Lord.

JAMES, (APOCRYPHAL) EPISTLE OF

Second-century Jewish Christian work with *ascetical overtones; it claims to contain Jesus' final discourse to his disciples before the ascension.

JAMES, PROTOEVANGELIUM OF

Second-century *infancy gospel probably written by a Jewish Christian, it gives a vivid account of the life of Mary before the birth of Jesus, and it follows the Holy Family down to the Slaughter of the Innocents; it gives the names of Mary's parents as Joachim and Anna, a widely followed tradition in the Middle Ages; the book emphasizes Mary's perpetual virginity and explains the "brothers of the Lord" as children of Joseph by a previous marriage; this work enormously influenced Christian art.

JANUARIUS (d. ca. 305)

In Italian, Gennaro; bishop of Benevento, *martyred apparently under the emperor Diocletian (284–305); famous into the twentieth century for the supposed liquification of his blood, preserved in a special vial in the cathedral of Naples, on certain feast days.

JEROME (ca. 342–ca. 420)

His Latin name was Eusebius Hieronymus, but he is best known from the Anglicized form of his second name; he was born in Dalmatia, modern Croatia, and received a superb education in Rome; by 370 he was in Trier with a circle of friends intent on the *ascetical life, but he broke with this group and in 373 went to the East, where he began to learn Greek; from 375 to 377 he was a monk in the Syrian desert, where he quarreled with other monks, although, on the positive side, he learned Hebrew at this time. He left the desert and attached himself to Paulinus of Antioch, who ordained him; in 381 he accompanied Paulinus to the First Council of *Constantinople; in 382 he returned to Rome, where he became secretary to Pope *Damasus I. The pope was legitimately concerned about the deplorable state of the Latin versions of the New Testament, and he asked Jerome to prepare a revision; Jerome not only revised the Latin versions but also consulted the Greek, the beginning of his fruitful career as a translator. He also became a strong advocate of asceticism in Rome, associating himself with the wealthy and pious women *Paula and *Marcella; in the furtherance of ascetic ideals he criticized nonascetics, especially the Roman clergy, who took their revenge in 385 (after Damasus' death in 384) by driving Jerome from the city. He went with Paula to Bethlehem in 386 never to return to the capital, although he kept in constant contact with his friends there via his many letters. In Bethlehem Jerome undertook his *magnum opus,* the translation of the Old and New Testaments into Latin, a translation known as the *Vulgate (although not all of the extant Vulgate is from Jerome's hand). He also wrote many biblical commentaries, noted for their literal rather than *allegorical approach, and several polemical tracts, especially against the *Pelagians and those who disagreed with his ascetical stance. His book *On Famous Men* offers a catalogue of famous Christians, and his writings on the Old Testament canon, insisting that Christians follow the Hebrew canon, were rejected in his day but revived in the Renaissance and Reformation by both humanists and Reformers. Jerome was a great scholar and linguist but also a tortured personality, seeing enemies in even the slightest criticism, tart toward his friends and savage toward his supposed enemies; his groveling acceptance of ecclesiastical authority and his fear of being tainted with even the slightest suspicion of *heterodoxy led him to deny his own debt to *Origen and to engage in machinations against Bishop *John of Jerusalem and to break off an almost lifelong friendship with *Rufinus of Aquileia during the *Origenist controversies. He was and remains a controversial figure.

JEU, BOOKS OF

Two small *Gnostic treatises of the second century; they contain revelation from Jesus about a journey of the soul.

JOHN I (d. 526)

Pope from 523; he was a friend of *Boethius, and he worked to maintain the integrity of the Church under the *Arian Ostrogothic king Theodoric I; the king was suspicious that the Byzantine emperor Justin I (518–527) had designs on Italy and sent John on an embassy to Constantinople to negoti-

ate an end to the Arian persecution of Catholics and the reverse, including permitting forcibly converted Arians to return to their faith, something John said he could not recommend; although Justin received the pope with much honor, he did not agree to Theodoric's central demand, as the pope had suspected. John returned to Italy to find Theodoric angry and suspicious; fearful of an Eastern plot with Roman support, the king executed Boethius and was menacing John, who, already an elderly man, died before the king could act.

JOHN II (d. 535)

Pope from 533; a *priest named Mercurius, he adopted the name John II after the persecuted *John I, and he thus became the first pope to change his name upon election. He was a conciliatory man who worked well with the emperor *Justinian (527–565), even to the point of accepting the *Theopaschite formula, which he felt could be given an orthodox interpretation.

JOHN III (d. 574)

Pope from 561; he inherited the *Three Chapters controversy, which, ironically, was largely settled by the Lombard invasion of Italy in 568, which forced most Italian Churches into unity against the pagans; John had to get the assistance of Narses, the Byzantine governor of Italy and a very unpopular person there because of Byzantine autocracy and taxes; when Narses returned to Rome in 571, the popular reaction against this move forced John to leave Rome and to conduct papal business from a suburban church; he returned to the city just before his death.

JOHN, ACTS OF

*Apocryphal work of the second century and the earliest apocryphal *acts; Greek in origin and *Docetic in theology, it was enormously popular; it may have originated in Asia Minor. It gives an account of the Apostle John's missionary activities in various eastern Mediterranean cities.

JOHN, APOCRYPHON OF

*Gnostic text from *Nag Hammadi, probably of the third century, in which Jesus, after his resurrection, engages in a philosophical dialogue with John in which they speculate on the nature of God.

JOHN CASSIAN

See **Cassian, John.**

JOHN CHRYSOSTOM (ca. 350–407)

"John of the Golden Tongue" was born in Antioch from a noble Christian family; he studied with a famous pagan scholar, Libanius of Antioch, and with the theologian *Diodore of Tarsus; he became a monk for a short time (ca. 373–381), and his austerities at this time ruined his health for the rest of his life; in 381 *Meletius of Antioch, an early patron, ordained him a *deacon, and in 386 Flavian of Antioch ordained him a *priest with the special duty of preaching in the city's largest church, a post he held until 397. John was the finest preacher of his day; reliable traditions say that when he finished a sermon, the congregation would cry out for more. This ability combined with his personal sanctity made him famous, and when the *bishop of Constantinople died in 397, John was chosen, against his will, to succeed him, taking office in 398. John set about to do a good job, reforming the local Church and preaching mercilessly against moral abuses, only to find out that in the imperial capital intrigue took precedence over reform. Well-connected clergy joined forces with nobles unaccustomed to having their opulent way of life criticized by a bishop; by 399, joined by several bishops, John's enemies had turned against him the all-powerful empress *Eudoxia, whom John had also criticized. When John offered protection to some Egyptian monks being hounded by *Theophilus of Alexandria, he offended the most dangerous enemy of all. Theophilus, jealous of the rising power of the imperial see and the consequent eclipse of Alexandria, joined with the empress and, at the Synod of the Oak in 403, had John deposed. The deposition lasted only a day, due to popular support for the bishop and partly because of a minor earthquake, which was thought by many to be a sign of divine anger. But John did not change his policy, the intrigues continued, and when John compared Eudoxia to Herodias, "seeking again the head of John," no one could save him, and in 404 the emperor Arcadius (395–408) exiled him to the region of Antioch. When John inconveniently continued to live in spite of precarious health, he was forced into a harsh journey on foot to northern Asia Minor; he died along the way.

Even after his death he remained controversial. When Pope *Innocent I, a supporter of John, requested *Cyril of Alexandria, Theophilus' nephew and successor and a participant at the Synod of the Oak, to include John in the diptychs, that is, among the honored bishops of other sees, Cyril replied that he would rather put Judas back in the company of the apostles. His sermons *Against the Jews,* which were intended to keep his congregation from frequenting synagogues, were used in the Middle Ages to justify anti-Semitism. John was a good theologian as well as a great homilist, especially on the Scriptures, and many medieval exegetes, both Greek and Latin, used his works, which often rejected the *allegorical in favor of the historical and literal interpretation. His liturgical sermons also remained popular, as did some of his moral and *ascetical works. His epithet, "of the golden tongue," was first bestowed on him in the sixth century.

JOHN DIACRINOMENUS
(fl. 510–520)

Syrian *Monophysite who wrote about Christianity in the Eastern empire in the fifth century.

JOHN MALALAS (d. 577)

Also called John Scholasticus; a *Monophysite, he wrote a *Chronography,* or Church history, which stretches from the Creation to the sixth century but which deals largely with Antioch.

JOHN MANDAKUNI (d. ca. 485)

Armenian *patriarch and patron of the Armenian language; his genuine works include some prayers; some debated sermons are ascribed to him.

JOHN MAXENTIUS (fl. 519–533)

Leader of the Gothic monks at Constantinople and a strong supporter of the *Theopaschite formula.

JOHN MOSCHUS (ca. 550–619)

A widely traveled (Jerusalem, Egypt, Syria, Rome) monk and spiritual writer who left an account (*The Meadow*) of the famous *ascetics of his day; its edifying character made him an important spiritual writer for Eastern monks.

JOHN OF ANTIOCH (d. 441)

*Bishop of Antioch from 429; he led the Syrian bishops at the Council of *Ephesus in 431; he supported *Nestorius against *Cyril of Alexandria; when the latter rushed through a conciliar decision against the former before John arrived in Ephesus, John called a counter *council to condemn Cyril. In the aftermath of the council, John worked with *Theodoret of Cyrrhus to draw up a formula acceptable to Cyril and himself; this formed the basis of the *Union of 433. In the process of reconciliation, John had to abandon the cause of Nestorius.

JOHN OF APAMEA

Syriac spiritual writer of the early sixth century.

JOHN OF CAESAREA (fl. 510–520)

Anti-*Monophysite writer who worked to reconcile the differences between the *Christologies of *Cyril of Alexandria and the Council of *Chalcedon.

JOHN OF EPHESUS (ca. 507–586)

*Monophysite *bishop of Ephesus and later of Constantinople under *Justinian, he was imprisoned in 572 by the *Chalcedonian emperor Justin II (565–572) and ended his life as a wandering exile; he wrote in Syriac a Church history and the *History of the Eastern Saints,* a collection of biographical sketches of fifty-eight Mesopotamian monks.

JOHN OF GAZA (d. ca. 530)

Palestinian monk whose many (446) letters concern *ascetical topics; a teacher of *Dorotheus of Gaza.

JOHN OF JERUSALEM (d. 417)

*Bishop of Jerusalem from 386, he sided with *Rufinus of Aquileia during the *Origenist controversy and was subsequently attacked by *Jerome and *Epiphanius of Salamis.

JOHN OF SCYTHOPOLIS (fl. 500–530)

A highly educated and cultivated man, he wrote a defense of the Council of *Chalcedon as well as the earliest commentary on *Dionysius the Pseudo-Areopagite; few of his extensive writings survive.

JOHN PHILOPONUS (ca. 500–ca. 565)

An Alexandrian who worked to reconcile Christianity with the philosophy of Aristotle, although he was never loathe to criticize the great philosopher; for example, he argued for creation against the Aristotelian theory of the eternity of the world. John had *Tritheistic and *Monophysite leanings in his *Trinitarian theology.

JOHN THE FASTER (d. 595)

*Bishop of Constantinople from 582, his *asceticism earned him his nickname; he tried to reassert the authority of his see vis-à-vis that of Rome; his assumption of the title "ecumenical patriarch" enraged both *Pelagius II and his successor, *Gregory I, but John did not back down, and later Constantinopolitan *patriarchs used the title as well.

JORDANES (fl. 550)

Gothic historian in Italy who in 551 published a *History of the Goths,* an abbreviation of a similar work of *Cassiodorus; this book is important as the earliest account of Gothic history.

JOSEPH THE CARPENTER, HISTORY OF

Probably composed in Egypt in the fifth century, it tells the story of Joseph from the period just before the birth of Jesus to Joseph's own death; it is the first example of veneration of Joseph as a saint.

JOVINIAN (d. ca. 405)

Milanese monk who denied both that virginity was a higher state of life than marriage and that *asceticism was spiritually superior to a moderate use of food and material goods; Pope *Siricius condemned his view in 390 and again in 391, as did *Ambrose in 393, but *Jerome wrote a long and bitter attack against him, *Against Jovinian,* which in effect finished his career, but the book's unrestrained attack on marriage and women provoked a reaction against Jerome.

JUDAIZERS

Those Christians who felt that all Christians, Gentile converts included, must follow the Jewish Law; Paul combated them in his letters to the Galatians and the Philippians as did *Ignatius of Antioch, but elements of their thinking survived for some centuries.

JUDAS, GOSPEL OF

*Gnostic gospel mentioned by *Irenaeus of Lyons, and therefore at least from the second century; its contents are unknown. Irenaeus associates it with the *Carpocratians and *Nicolaitans among others, so it may be conjectured that it contained or at least reflected their views.

JULIAN OF ECLANUM (ca. 386–454)

Southern Italian *bishop from a noble episcopal family, he supported *Pelagius against the attacks of *Augustine; Julian, son of a bishop, married the daughter of a bishop; by 408 he was a *deacon and a bishop by 416; he was deposed in 418 for his *Pelagian views. He saw the danger in Augustine's views on sex and on *predestination, and from 421 he conducted a long and intense controversy with Augustine, which ended only with Augustine's death in 430. He traveled to the East in search of a home, staying for a while with *Theodore of Mopsuestia and *Nestorius, but was always forced to move on by the local civil or ecclesiastical authorities. In 431 the First Council of *Ephesus condemned him; he finally settled in Sicily and taught rhetoric, although in 439 he made one last futile attempt to return to the Church. Two of his works survive in Augustine's extensive citations from them; Julian may also have been the author of a Psalter commentary.

JULIAN OF HALICARNASSUS (d. ca. 530)

*Monophysite *bishop who was driven from his see around 518, he fled to Alexandria where he headed a group called the Aphthartodocetae (those teaching the incorruptibility of the flesh [of Christ]); he strongly opposed his fellow Monophysite theologian *Severus of Antioch.

JULIAN POMERIUS (late fifth–early sixth centuries)

African who migrated to Gaul, tutor of *Caesarius of Arles; Julian wrote a popular book on the contemplative life intended for both clergy and laity.

JULIAN THE APOSTATE (332–363)

Emperor from 361; son of *Constantine I's half brother who was murdered in 337 by the emperor's sons to ensure their succession, Julian was brought up as a Christian, but he resented the religion of the imperial family and, thanks to his tutors, came to believe in the old gods. *Constantius II had no heir and from 355 had to rely on Julian to rule in the West; he soon proved to be a good general, well liked by his troops. In 360 the wary and jealous Constantius ordered Julian to send some of his best troops to the East; the troops refused, proclaiming Julian emperor. A civil war was averted by Constantius' death. Upon becoming emperor, Julian proclaimed his allegiance to the old gods and tried to restore paganism by declaring religious freedom while subsidizing pagan clergy and temples. He allowed the *Donatist leaders to return home as well as *bishops of various *Arian and *Nicene factions who had been exiled; this guaranteed severe confusion among the Christians, who loathed this emperor. In 363 Julian invaded Persia and enjoyed some initial successes but was killed in a minor skirmish. After his death, many Christian writers wrote vituperative books about him, indicating an underlying fear of a return to pagan worship sponsored by a future emperor, but, in fact, he reigned for too short a time to make any real dent in Christianity's rise. His epithet, "the Apostate," was, of course, given to him by his Christian opponents.

JULIUS I (d. 352)

Pope from 337; strong supporter of *Nicea, he risked imperial wrath by providing refuge for *Athanasius and *Marcellus of Ancyra after they were driven from their sees; at a Roman synod in 340 Julius cleared them of all charges of doctrinal deviation. When the emperors Constans (337–350) and *Constantius II (337–361), at Julius' request, convened the *Council of Serdica in 343 to unite East and West, Julius insisted that Athanasius and Marcellus be invited, thus causing the (mostly *Arianizing) Eastern *bishops to withdraw; the largely Western group continued to meet—Julius himself was not present—and found in favor of Athanasius and Marcellus. The council also said that a deposed bishop could appeal to Rome, not a common practice but one designed to spread Roman primacy. Little is known of Julius' pontificate after Serdica. He built the Julian Basilica and the Church of St. Mary in Trastevere in Rome; he also pronounced the date of Christmas to be December 25, the first unambiguous citation of the now traditional date.

JULIUS AFRICANUS, SEXTUS (ca. 160–ca. 240)

Born in Jerusalem, he served with the emperor Septimius Severus (193–211) in the East and got to know the dynasty of Edessa, with whom he maintained good relations; a genuine polymath, he established a public library in Rome for the emperor Alexander Severus (222–235); he spent some time in Alexandria and made friends of *Origen and *Heraclas; he lived in Emmaus in Palestine until his death. His writings include a world history, the *Chronography*, the first Christian attempt at such a book, but only fragments survive; he also wrote an encyclopedia for the emperor Alexander Severus, which he entitled *Embroideries* because it drew from everything from magic to medicine. He also wrote two letters about the Scriptures, one to Origen on the authenticity of the story of Susanna, which Origen defended and which Africanus (correctly) maintained was a later addition, the second letter to an Aristides tries to harmonize the Gospel genealogies of Jesus; too much should not be made of brief letters, but they do demonstrate a good critical approach to the Scriptures, something not found often in his day.

JULIUS OF BRITAIN

See **Aaron and Julius.**

JULIUS THE VETERAN

Roman soldier who became a Christian and was *martyred; dates for his death range from 202 to 303, the dates of particularly large *persecutions.

JUNG CODEX

A *manuscript from *Nag Hammadi containing several *Gnostic writings and now in the possession of the Jung Institute in Zurich.

JUNILIUS (fl. ca. 542)

An African who wrote an introduction to the study of the Bible in the *Antiochene spirit of *Theodore of Mopsuestia; it was rather popular in the early Middle Ages.

JUSTINIAN (484–565)

Roman emperor from 527, when he succeeded his childless uncle, Justin I; the Western empire had passed into the hands of various barbarian tribes a half century before, and Justinian, urged on and strongly supported by his wife, *Theodora, purposed to reestablish the old imperial frontiers; his magnificent campaigns in the 530s brought Africa, part of coastal Spain, and much of Italy back into the fold. But, as emperor, he saw himself as the head of the Church, something the Eastern *bishops accepted but which caused many problems, especially for the papacy. He forced his will upon Rome, deposing Pope *Silverius in 537 (his general, Belisarius, actually did the deed), installing *Vigilius, and then brutalizing him into accepting the decrees of the Second Council of *Constantinople. In the East, Justinian asserted his orthodoxy by *persecuting the remnants of the *Montanists and by closing the old Athenian school of philosophy in 529. But the empress was a *Monophysite, and she averted his wrath from them. She convinced him to find some way to end the *Chalcedonian-Monophysite *schism; his solution was to condemn the *Three Chapters, for which he called Constantinople II in 553. By the time the council met, Theodora was dead, and, although the council obligingly condemned the Three Chapters, the Monophysites were not reconciled. Justinian fancied himself a theologian and wrote several anti-*heretical tracts. He also was a great builder of churches, the most famous being Santa Sophia in Constantinople; although not personally involved, he was generally responsible for the building of several churches in Ravenna, which was the seat of the Byzantine governor in Italy.

JUSTIN MARTYR (d. ca. 165)

The most prominent Christian *apologist; born a pagan in Palestine, he tried several philosophical schools in search of wisdom, turning finally to Christianity; sometime during the reign of the emperor Antoninus Pius (138–161) he removed to Rome, where he established a school; he angered a pagan philosopher named Crescens whose enmity proved implacable; about 165, according to evidence based upon a court report, he was decapitated along with six companions. Only three of his many writings survive, two addresses, or apologies, to the emperor and a debate with a Jew named Trypho. Justin's most important contribution to Christianity was his theory of the *Logos, or Word of God, who he said was present with God at the Creation and was only recently incarnated in Jesus Christ. Justin saw the Logos behind all true statements, including those of pagan sages and philosophers, and the concept of "Christians before Christ" appears in his writings; the ancients received only the "generative Word" (*Logos spermatikos*), whereas the Christians knew the incarnate Word. Much of Justin's theology is not sophisticated, but he is chronologically the first real theologian after the author of John's Gospel, and one should not expect too much. Justin also provides valuable early accounts of *baptism and the *Eucharist. Although thoroughly Christian, Justin knew and appreciated Greek philosophy and did not hesitate to incorporate it into his thinking, being the first important Christian to do so.

JUSTUS OF URGEL (fl. ca. 540–550)

Spanish *bishop and author of a commentary on the Song of Songs.

JUVENAL OF JERUSALEM (d. 458)

*Bishop of Jerusalem from 422; a consummate politician out to advance the cause of his see, he sided with *Cyril of Alexandria against *Nestorius at *Ephesus in 431, then with *Dioscorus of Alexandria at the Second Council of Ephesus in 449, only to turn against him at *Chalcedon in 451; the *Monophysite monks of his see made trouble for him and he required imperial assistance to maintain himself as bishop.

JUVENCUS, CAIUS VETTIUS AQUILINUS (fl. 325–350)

Spanish *priest from a noble family who wrote the first Latin Christian epic, a verse harmony of the four Gospels, although 80 percent comes from Matthew; Juvencus tried throughout to imitate the great Latin poet Virgil.

K

KENTIGERN (d. 603)

Also known as Mungo; according to tradition, he was the illegitimate son of a British prince; a monk who was consecrated *bishop for Strathclyde but had to flee a persecution there; he went to either Cumbria or Wales but eventually returned to Strathclyde and then worked in the Glasgow area, where he died.

KEVIN (d. ca. 618)

In Irish, Coemgen; according to tradition, he came from the royal family of Leinster; he decided to become a monk and settled at Glandalough, the Vale of the Two Lakes, which became a famous monastery.

L

LACTANTIUS (ca. 240–ca. 320)

A pagan African by birth and a rhetorician by training, he studied with the elder *Arnobius and later went to Nicomedia in Asia Minor to teach Latin rhetoric at the court of the emperor, Diocletian (284–305); while there he became a Christian and so lost his position in the Great *Persecution of 303, apparently returning to Africa around 305; in 317 the new emperor, *Constantine I (306–337), appointed him tutor to his son Crispus. Renaissance humanists called Lactantius the Christian Cicero because of his rhetorical elegance, but his theology did not match his eloquence. His most important work is *The Divine Institutes,* an attack on the shortcomings of paganism and the first Latin attempt at systematic theology in the manner of *Origen's *On First Principles,* but Lactantius was simply not up to the work, drawing largely from classical authors and Latin theologians and showing little knowledge of Greek theology.

Another of his books, *On the Deaths of Persecutors,* gives a vivid, even lurid account of the terrible fates suffered by those emperors who persecuted the Christians.

LAODICEANS, EPISTLE TO

At the end of the canonical Epistle to the Colossians (4:16) is a reference to "the epistle from Laodicea," not found in the canon; a fourth-century writer attempted to fill the gap with a Latin epistle, actually a pastiche of Pauline phrases, which, amazingly enough, was widely accepted as authentic and appears in many medieval Bibles as part of the New Testament.

LAPSED

In Latin, *lapsi;* those who apostasized during *persecution but who, after the persecution ended, wished to be readmitted to the Church; apostasy was originally considered to be unforgiveable, but when very large numbers lapsed in the Decian persecution (250–251), the *bishop of Carthage, *Cyprian, worked out a formula of *penance for their readmittance.

LATROCINIUM

Latin for "robber council," name given by Pope *Leo I to the Second Council of *Ephesus of 449.

LAURA

See **Lavra.**

LAURENCE; LAURENTIAN SCHISM

Laurence was a Roman *priest who was elected pope on the same day (November 22, 498) as *Symmachus; Laurence was the choice of the pro-Byzantine aristocracy, who wished an end to the *Acacian schism; both sides appealed to the real ruler of Italy, the Gothic king Theodoric, who acknowledged Symmachus in 499. Laurence accepted the decision and took a southern Italian *bishopric, but his followers did not abandon the cause, agitating with the king and making false accusations against the pope. In 501 Laurence returned to Rome, and from 502 to 506 he was the de facto pope; but Theodoric turned against him and deposed him in 506. Laurence retired to a life of *asceticism, dying around 507.

LAVRA

Sometimes spelled *laura,* literally, "a street" but in ecclesiastical parlance a colony of *hermits in cells branching off a central area and living together under the supervision of an abbot; these were very popular in Palestine from the fourth century onward.

LAWRENCE (d. 258)

In Latin, Laurentius; he was a Roman *deacon and *martyr in the *persecution of Valerian; an early tradition spoke of his having been grilled to death on a gridiron, an unlikely historical event; he was widely popular in Rome and Italy, referred to by *Ambrose and *Prudentius. The Church of San Lorenzo in Rome is built over his tomb.

LEANDER OF SEVILLE (ca. 549–600 or 601)

Son of a noble Romano-Hispanic family and older brother of *Isidore of Seville; around 580 he was an ambassador to Constantinople, where he made the acquaintance of *Gregory the Great and a lifelong friendship began; around 584 he returned to Spain to occupy the see of Seville; he was a great reformer who battled the *Arianism of the Visigoths; in 589 he saw his life's work rewarded at the Synod of Toledo, at which the Visigothic king *Recared abandoned Arianism; few writings of Leander survive, one being a rule for nuns.

LEONTIUS OF BYZANTIUM (d. 543)

A philosophically educated anti-*Monophysite writer whose life is virtually unknown; he was in Palestine as a monk before 520; by 531 he had gone to Constantinople on an embassy from a Palestinian monastery; he returned to Palestine but was again in Constantinople by 540. A strict adherent of *Chalcedon, he attacked *Nestorius and *Eutyches, demonstrating that a true Chalcedonian does not accept Nestorius, and he also attacked *Theodore of Mopsuestia; all these theologians were, of course, deceased, but Leontius also attacked the contemporary Monophysite leader, *Severus of Antioch. He concentrated on the Monophysite misunderstanding of *hypostasis.

LEO I THE GREAT (d. 461)

Pope from 440; apparently born in Rome, he was an influential *deacon both to *Celestine I, whom he advised in the *Nestorian controversy, and to *Sixtus III, whom he advised in the *Pelagian controversy. Leo, convinced that the Apostle Peter spoke through the popes, confidently asserted his authority on every possible occasion and succeeded in getting the emperor Valentinian III (425–455) to recognize his jurisdiction over all the Churches of the Western Roman provinces. The disorganization of Vandal-occupied Africa allowed Leo to influence that usually contrary Church, and in 450 he divided the *bishoprics of Gaul between the *metropolitans of Arles and Vienne, thus preventing any one Gallic see from gaining too much power. Leo's dealings with the East were initially less successful but improved with time. The monk *Eutyches appealed to him against *Flavian of Constantinople, but Leo rejected Eutyches' teachings and wrote his *Tome, which contained his own *Christological

teaching. When the Second Council of *Ephesus met in 449, Leo sent three legates and a copy of the Tome, but *Dioscorus of Alexandria ignored Leo and vindicated Eutyches. Leo condemned the council as a *latrocinium (robber council), but he could do nothing about it until a new emperor (Marcian, 450–457) called a new council at *Chalcedon in 451. At this council Leo's legates were treated honorably, and the council praised the teaching of the Tome, even acknowledging that Leo spoke with the voice of Peter; that did not, however, stop the council in its twenty-eighth canon from elevating the status of Constantinople to equality with Rome, because both were imperial capitals. Leo accepted the council's Christology but refused to acknowledge the twenty-eighth canon. After Chalcedon, Leo had to turn his attention to the sad state of Italy. In 452 he personally persuaded Attila the Hun not to attack Rome; in 455 he again tried personal diplomacy with Gaiseric the Vandal, but Gaiseric still attacked and looted the city, although few people were killed. The last years of his pontificate were uneventful.

LEPORIUS (fl. fifth century)

Gallic monk who taught that the divine Word was one person and the man Christ was another, but that Christ's virtues brought him ever closer to divinity until he eventually became divine; he was rejected in Gaul and so went to Africa, where *Augustine convinced him that the unity of human and divine did not compromise Christ's humanity; he abandoned his views and prepared a confession of faith acceptable to the Gauls.

LÉRINS

Island monastery off the southern coast of Gaul, founded around 410 by *Honoratus; it was famous as a cradle for fifth- and sixth-century Gallic *bishops.

LEUCIUS CHARINUS

Supposed author of the apocryphal *Acts of *John;* he would have lived in the late second century.

LIBELLATICI

Latin term for those who purchased a *libellus pacis* (a little book of peace) but actually a certificate from the Roman authorities acknowledging that the possessor had sacrificed to the gods; this mild form of bribery was widely used by Christians in Africa during the Decian *persecution (250–251) to avoid having to sacrifice; in a *martyr-oriented Christianity like that of Africa this was considered a serious sin, although not as serious as that of the *lapsed; *Cyprian and other leaders condemned the practice but treated the *libellatici* more leniently than the lapsed.

LIBERATUS (fl. 560–566)

Arch*deacon of Carthage, opponent of the *Three Chapters and author of a history of the *Nestorians and Eutychians (followers of *Eutyches) down to the sixth century.

LIBERIAN CATALOGUE

See **Chronographer of 354.**

LIBERIUS (d. 366)

Pope from 352; a Roman by birth and successor to the stong-minded *Julius I, Liberius had to deal with the *Arianizing emperor *Constantius II (337–361), who was determined to bring the Western *bishops to the Arian cause. Failing to stop the emperor's first moves, Liberius demanded a new *ecumenical council to settle matters; the emperor called a council in Milan in 355 and browbeat the bishops into condemning *Athanasius—only three bishops refused, and they were exiled. Liberius, who was not personally at the council, held out, was brought to Milan by force, and still held his ground. Constantius then exiled him to Thrace, where he eventually gave in to threats and cajolery, agreed to the excommunication of Athanasius, and signed a vague *creed capable of an Arian interpretation. In 358 the emperor permitted him to return to Rome, where he was wildly welcomed by the people, who promptly drove out *Felix II, an *antipope who had replaced Liberius during his exile. As long as Constantius was alive, Liberius maintained a discreet silence; after the emperor's death in 361 the pope again publicly spoke in favor of the Council of *Nicea, although he favored moderation in dealing with those bishops who had compromised themselves with the Arians. His pontificate weakened Roman prestige in both West and East.

LIBER PONTIFICALIS

Literally, "the papal book," this is a collection of popes' lives, beginning with Peter and continuing, in various recensions, to Hadrian II (d. 872) and even to the fifteenth century; its earliest section goes to *Felix II (d. 530) and was probably composed just after his death, probably by a Roman cleric; the work is formulaic but includes many dates and is of great value historically, especially from the fourth century onward.

LICINIAN OF CARTAGENA
(fl. 590–600)

Spanish *bishop, famous as a letter writer, but only three epistles survive, including one defending the incorporeal nature of the angels and of human souls.

LINUS (d. ca. 78)

Pope from about 66; according to the earliest papal lists of *Hegesippus and *Irenaeus, the first successor of Peter in Rome; the sources say he held the office of *bishop for twelve years, but the actual years are uncertain, as is the nature of the office of bishop in the first-century Roman Church; the sources also identify him with the Linus mentioned in 2 Timothy 4:21; this is historically possible although unprovable.

LOGIA

Literally, "sayings," the plural of the Greek word *logos; the term is used of an early *apocryphon, the *Sayings of Jesus, from Oxyrhynchus in Egypt.

LOGOS

Greek for "word," but in the sense of "expression of one's mind"; for the early Church the Logos, the term used of Jesus in the prologue of John's Gospel (1:1-18), was the term for Christ, not only because of its biblical foundation in both the Old and New Testaments but especially because of its long history in Greek philosophy, which enabled the *Fathers to relate Christian doctrine to Hellenistic thought. *Ignatius of Antioch was the first to use it that way, but *Justin Martyr was the first to make extensive use of the concept, followed quickly by *Clement of Alexandria. Later Fathers used the word primarily for *Christology, especially in the late fourth and early fifth centuries. Indeed, one could make a case that the history of the Logos doctrine is a history of *patristic Christology.

LONGINUS

According to tradition, the soldier who pierced Christ's side with a lance (in Greek, *longche*) in John 19:34; the origin of the story is apparently the *Gospel According to *Nicodemus,* a fourth-century apocryphal *gospel that contains the *Acts of *Pilate,* an account of Jesus' execution and his sojourn in the land of the dead before his resurrection. His legend was extremely popular in the Middle Ages.

LUCIAN OF ANTIOCH (d. 312)

Teacher of theology at Antioch, he had *Arius and *Eusebius of Nicomedia among his pupils; he apparently taught a *subordinationist *Christology; few fragments of his writings survive, so he is known primarily through his students. It is certain that he was a competent textual critic whose edition of the Greek Bible was widely used in the East and called the Lucianic Text; it is likewise certain that he was a man of great piety who died a *martyr after prolonged tortures.

LUCIAN OF SAMOSATA
(fl. ca. 170)

Pagan satirist; his satire *On the Death of Peregrinus* depicts the philosopher Peregrinus as a wandering rogue who, for a while, becomes a Christian and beguiles his well-intentioned corcligionists, who rush to his aid when he is arrested; Lucian wishes to portray the Christians as simpleminded and credulous, but, perhaps inadvertently, he paints a fine picture of Christian charity.

LUCIFERIANS

Sect claiming to be disciples of *Lucifer of Cagliari, they were fiercely *Nicene, even to the point of *schism from the Roman Church; *Damasus I acted harshly to break up this group.

LUCIFER OF CAGLIARI (d. ca. 370)

Sardinian *bishop known largely from his activities during the *Arian controversies; in 355, as a representative of Pope *Liberius to the *Council of Milan, he defied the Arianism of the emperor *Constantius II (337–361), and was exiled to the East for seven years; released in 362 by the pagan emperor *Julian (361–363), he went first to Antioch, where he became involved in and actually made worse the *Meletian schism by consecrating a West-

erner and a strong *Nicene, Paulinus, as bishop in opposition to Meletius. Lucifer eventually returned to Italy, where he disappeared from history. A fierce, uncompromising anti-Arian, he left behind five violent pamphlets attacking Constantius.

LUCILLA

Wealthy Spaniard who lived in Carthage in the early fourth century; her public veneration—by kissing—of a supposed *martyr's bone earned her the criticism of *Caecilian, *bishop of Carthage, whose perceived irreverence for the martyrs was one of the factors in initiating the *Donatist *schism.

LUCIUS (d. 254)

Pope from 253; Lucius was a Roman *priest who was banished with Pope *Cornelius by the emperor Gallus (251–253); when Cornelius died, Lucius, still in banishment, was elected pope. On Gallus' death, he returned to Rome; little is known of his pontificate except that he continued Cornelius' firm stance against *Novatian. *Cyprian wrote to him expressing sorrow that Lucius had not been able to die a *martyr and expressing hope that this might yet occur; Lucius, however, disregarded Cyprian's advice and died a natural death.

LUCIUS OF BRITAIN

According to legend, the first Christian king of Britain, who wrote to Pope *Eleutherius (ca. 174–189) to ask to be converted; based upon an entry in the *Liber Pontificalis, the legend was widespread in the Middle Ages, for example, in *The Ecclesiastical History of the English People* by the Venerable Bede.

LUCY (d. 304)

Sicilian virgin and *martyr who died in the *persecution of Diocletian (303-305); all accounts of her life are legendary.

LUPUS OF TROYES
(ca. 395-478)

A Gaul who married the sister of *Hilary of Arles, he separated from his wife by mutual agreement and entered the monastery of *Lérins around 426 but was called away the following year to be *bishop of Troyes; he traveled to Britain in 429 with *Germanus of Auxerre to combat *Pelagianism (an account some scholars doubt); later legend portrayed him as saving his province from Attila the Hun.

M

MACARII

Term given collectively to *Macarius of Alexandria and *Macarius of Egypt.

MACARIUS MAGNES
(fl. ca. 390–410)

*Apologist who wrote a dialogue against Neoplatonic criticisms of the Faith; this work preserves some pagan objections to Christianity, perhaps derived from Porphyry, a third-century Neoplatonist and strong critic of the Faith. Some scholars identify Marcarius with a *bishop of Magnesia in Asia Minor who attended the Synod of the Oak, at which *John Chrysostom was deposed.

MACARIUS OF ALEXANDRIA
(d. ca. 394)

Sometimes called Macarius the Younger; Egyptian *hermit who went to the desert around 335, possible disciple of *Antony; he was famous as a thaumaturge; no authentic writings of his survive.

MACARIUS OF EGYPT
(ca. 300–ca. 390)

Sometimes called Macarius the Elder; at the age of thirty he went to the desert, where he lived for sixty years, first as a *hermit, then as the head of a community in the district of Scete; he visited *Antony several times and supported *Athanasius in his struggles against the *Arians; Lucius, Arian *bishop of Alexandria, exiled him briefly. Macarius is famous because of the *Sayings of the Fathers (*Apophthegmata Patrum),* in which he figures prominently; many writings are attributed to him, but scholars are uncertain as to the authenticity of them.

MACARIUS OF JERUSALEM
(d. ca. 335)

*Bishop of Jerusalem, member of the First Council of *Nicea, and builder of

101

the famous Church of the Holy Sepulchre in Jerusalem, commissioned by *Constantine I.

MACEDONIANS; MACEDONIANISM

Name given to the sect of the *Pneumatomachi because of its supposed association with Macedonius, *bishop of Constantinople (d. ca. 362).

MACRINA (ca. 325–379)

Sometimes known as Macrina the Younger because her grandmother was known as Macrina the Elder; she was the elder sister of *Basil of Caesarea and *Gregory of Nyssa, who wrote her *vita; she was a strong personality who influenced Basil to take up an ecclesiastical career; after her fiance's death, she became a consecrated virgin; she later founded a convent on her own property; and Gregory, who was himself a great theologian, praised her theological abilities.

MALCHION OF ANTIOCH (fl. ca. 270)

*Priest of Antioch who interrogated *Paul of Samosata about his *Christology; he was probably also the person who wrote the synodal letter condemning Paul.

MAMERTUS OF VIENNE (d. ca. 470)

Gallic *bishop, brother of *Claudianus Mamertus; he advanced the claims of his see in Gaul, only to be reproached by Pope *Hilarus; he introduced the Rogation Days before the feast of the Ascension.

MANDAEISM

Small sect of approximately fifteen thousand currently living in Iraq and parts of Iran and descended from a probably *Gnostic sect of the second or third century but claiming descent from John the Baptist (whose movement did indeed survive his death; see Acts 19:2-3); their most important book is the *Ginza* (Treasure), an eighth-century document but containing older material; Mandaean teaching is similar to much in *Manicheism, stressing the opposition of flesh and spirit; because of the late date of the *Ginza,* scholars cannot determine in which direction the influence went; the value of Mandaeism for the understanding of early Christianity is a debated point.

MANES; MANICHEISM; MANICHEES

Manes (ca. 216–276) was a Persian *priest who, although he was brought up in a Jewish-Christian milieu, around 240 underwent a conversion experience that caused him to abandon the prevailing orthodoxy of Zoroastrianism and attempt to found a universal religion. Driven into exile, he returned around 242, won over the Persian king Sapor I, who later turned against him; the next king, Bahram, had him executed for *heresy. Manes taught a fundamental and cosmic dualism, a conflict between light and dark, between good and evil, with opposing forces struggling for the souls of humans. This may have been derived from a *Gnosticism current in his day. He claimed that all the great religious teachers, Jesus included, had come to teach people about the world of light and how they might struggle toward it, largely by *ascetical practices such as celibacy and vegetarianism—these practices being taught by the Elect to the Hearers, that is, the initiates. By the year 300 Manichean missionaries had arrived in the Roman Empire, in Syria and Egypt. The religion's most famous convert was *Augustine, who belonged to the sect for a dozen years and who wrote against it after converting to Catholic Christianity. Manichean sectarianism, astrology, excessive asceticism, and simplistic approach to the question of evil made it an easy target for intellectuals, but, in spite of *persecutions by both Persians and (pagan) Roman emperors, there is no reason to consider the movement either subversive or immoral.

MANUSCRIPT

From the Latin manuscriptum (written by hand), the term for a hand-written book, the normal way in which books were produced before the invention of the printing press.

MARCELLA (325–410)

Roman noblewoman who was widowed at a young age; she devoted herself to a life of charity and *asceticism; she was an enormously learned woman who studied the Bible in the original languages and corresponded with *Jerome about the linguistic difficulties of particular passages; she died as a result of injuries sustained during the Gothic capture of the city of Rome in 410. Sixteen letters of Jerome to her survive; unfortunately, none of her own survive.

MARCELLINA (d. ca. 398)

Sister of *Ambrose of Milan; she was a famous *ascetic—indeed, too ascetical for her brother.

MARCELLINUS (d. 304)

Pope from 296; according to the *Liber Pontificalis he apostasized during the Great *Persecution in 304, handing over Christian books to the pagans and even offering sacrifice to the gods. It goes on to say that he was inspired by *penance and became a *martyr, but *Eusebius of Caesarea, who said the pope "was overtaken by the persecution," does not mention this nor do Marcellinus' later defenders, such as *Augustine. It is likely that he was deposed from office for this offense.

MARCELLUS I (d. 308)

Pope from 306; after a two-year delay due to *persecution, the *priest Marcellus succeeded Pope *Marcellinus; he took a strong stance against the *lapsed, probably because his precedessor's apostasy had weakened the prestige of the Roman see; his policy, however, brought a strong reaction by those favoring reconciliation of the lapsed; the dispute became increasingly bitter and eventually violent, so that the emperor Maxentius (306–312) sent him into exile, although where is unknown. He died in exile.

MARCELLUS OF ANCYRA
(d. ca. 374)

Along with *Athanasius, the leading defender of the First Council of *Nicea against the machinations of *Eusebius of Nicomedia; Marcellus fell victim to the politics of the age when, in his defense of Nicea, he so emphasized the oneness of Son and Father in the Trinity as to suggest *Sabellianism, which his enemies used against him to get him deposed from his see in 336. He was restored in 337 but deposed again in 339; he was repeatedly condemned by Eastern *councils. He fled to Rome and was with Athanasius and Pope *Julius I during the many conflicts with the *Arians in the 340s. Marcellus submitted to Julius a profession of faith, which the pope found orthodox. But his later teaching, saying that the kingdom of Christ is not eternal, continued to get him into trouble, and he was posthumously condemned at the First Council of *Constantinople in 381, which appears to have added the phrase "and his kingdom will have no end" to the *creed to refute his teaching.

MARCELLUS THE MARTYR
(d. 298)

Roman centurion stationed in the African province of Mauretania; as a Christian, he symbolically rejected his calling by throwing down his soldier's belt; he was tried for treason and executed.

MARCIA (d. 193)

According to *Hippolytus, the mistress of the emperor Commodus (180–192) and, if not a Christian herself, a supporter of the Church; she is best known for using her influence to get Christian prisoners (one of whom was the future Pope *Callistus) released from the mines on Sardinia; an accomplice in Commodus' assassination, she was executed in 193 by his successor.

MARCIONITE PROLOGUES

A set of brief prologues to the Pauline epistles, which are found in many medieval *Vulgate *manuscripts; they are of second-century Marcionite origin, but no one is certain how they won acceptance in orthodox circles; they describe the place, date, and circumstances of each letter.

MARCION OF PONTUS
(fl. ca. 140–160)

Wealthy shipowner and son of the *bishop of Pontus, who excommunicated him for his immorality, according to *Epiphanius, but more likely for his teaching; he came to Rome around 140, gave a huge financial gift to the community, and became part of the congregation; soon his teaching caused misgivings, and by 144 the community had returned his gift and excommunicated him. Marcion went to the East and used his fortune to establish churches of his own, which lasted in the Orient into the Middle Ages. Marcion's own writings do not survive, except for fragments, but his importance is unquestioned, because several important writers, such as *Irenaeus and *Tertullian, wrote against him. Marcion taught that there is an unknown God, from whom Jesus came, and this God is distinct from the God of the

Old Testament, the *Demiurge, the creator of the material world and the stern judge of people. Jesus' gospel of love differed from Jewish legalistic teaching, and after Jesus' death his Jewish disciples did not maintain his teaching. Fortunately, Paul restored the balance, and Marcion understood Christianity through his understanding of Paul. To promote his cause, Marcion produced the first real New Testament canon, in two parts, *Apostle* and *Gospel,* the former being an edition of ten supposed Pauline epistles (including the Pastorals) and the latter being an expurgated version of Luke, Marcion's having deleted the Jewish elements, which he thought had crept in. Ancient writers placed Marcion among the *Gnostics, and his doctrine of an unknown God beyond the God of the Old Testament has a Gnostic flavor, but he founded his teaching upon Paul, not upon secret teachings or cosmological speculations. To later readers, his approach appears untenable and anti-Semitic (was there ever a Paul who rejected the Old Testament?), but his clear and abrupt solution to the tension between Old and New Testaments by means of eliminating the authority of the former had a clear appeal to his contemporaries, and his New Testament canon forced his opponents to speed up their own consideration of the question.

MARCION OF SMYRNA (fl. ca. 150)

Author of the *Martyrdom of *Polycarp,* an account of the famous *bishop's death.

MARCUS; MARCOSIANS

Marcus was a disciple of the *Gnostic teacher *Valentinus, but little is known of his teaching; *Irenaeus accuses him of magic and womanizing; his followers, the Marcosians, were prominent in Gaul in the second century, where they made wide use of *apocryphal scriptures.

MARINUS (d. ca. 260)

Roman soldier *martyred in Palestine in the mid-third century; patron saint of San Marino.

MARIUS MERCATOR (d. ca. 435)

An Italian by birth, he was a monk who lived in the Eastern portion of the Roman Empire; he wrote treatises against the *Pelagians, one that survives and two that are known because *Augustine mentions that Mercator had sent them to him.

MARIUS VICTORINUS

See **Victorinus.**

MARK (d. 336)

Pope for nine months in 336; in 313 *Constantine I wrote a letter to "*Miltiades, *bishop of Rome, and Mark," indicating Mark to be of great importance, recipient of an imperial letter and named after the pope; many scholars consider this Mark to be the later pope. He built two basilicas, one named San Marco, and is credited with instituting the practice whereby the bishop of Ostia heads the group of three bishops who consecrate the bishop of Rome.

MARK THE HERMIT (fl. 430–440)

Possibly a pupil of *John Chrysostom, he was first an abbot but in his old age became a *hermit; little is known of his life; he wrote several spiritual treatises, a treatise against an unknown group who considered Melchizedek an incarnation of the divine *Logos and another treatise against *Nestorius.

MARTIN OF BRAGA (ca. 520–580)

From the Balkans he went to Palestine as a monk and then migrated to northwest Spain, where he was *bishop of Dumio and then of Braga, the capital of the barbarian kingdom of the Sueves, who were *Arians; Martin worked throughout his episcopate to convert the Sueves, and he achieved considerable success. He wrote on a variety of subjects, from *asceticism to canon law to liturgy, including a translation of the *Apophthegmata Patrum, and his writings show a solid knowledge of classical literature.

MARTIN OF TOURS (ca. 320–397)

Born in the Balkan Roman provinces, he was an army medic until a vision of Christ impelled him to convert; after leaving the army he went to Milan, only to be driven out by the *Arian *bishop *Auxentius; by 360 he was with *Hilary of Poitiers, the Western anti-Arian hero, and he founded a monastery at Ligugé, the first monastery in Gaul. His personal saintliness and his reputed miracles—possibly some of the cures derived from his experiences as a medic—made him the people's choice for the bishopric of Tours around 372. The other Gallic

bishops resented the foreign *ascetic, but Martin appears to have been an able bishop, especially in the conversion of rural pagans. He opposed the execution of *Priscillian and risked his position in so doing. His *vita, one of the most influential books ever written in the Western Church, was composed by his disciple, *Sulpicius Severus, before his death; *Gregory of Tours included some other details. These works helped to make him one of the most popular saints of the Middle Ages; the account (by Sulpicius) of his dividing his military cloak and giving half to a beggar became a staple of medieval Christian art.

MARTYR

In Greek, martyros means "one who gives witness"; into the third century, the word could mean those who had suffered for the Faith as well as those who had died for it, but by the fourth century "martyr" meant only those who had died for the cause, the word "*confessor" being used for those who had suffered but had not died.

MARTYROLOGY

A list or registry of those regarded by a particular Church as having died for the Faith; normally these are also calendars that record the date of the martyrdom; they were widely used after the fourth century.

MARY, GOSPEL OF

*Apocryphal work of *Gnostic origin probably dating to the third century; Mary Magdalene describes the gnostic's progress through the planetary spheres, information given to her by Jesus, who often spoke privately to her.

MARY OF EGYPT

According to saintly legends, she was a prostitute for seventeen years when, on a trip to Jerusalem, an invisible power prevented her from entering a church, and she was convinced to convert; she became an *eremite; her return to nature was so complete that when her clothes wore out, she covered herself with her long hair; a *priest named Zosimus comforted her before her death and buried her. The legend may have a factual basis; it was enormously popular in the Middle Ages.

MARY, QUESTIONS OF

*Gnostic gospel in which Mary Magdalene asks questions of Jesus; the gospel was written to promote libertine values; it probably dates to the third century.

MASHTOTS

See Mesrob.

MASTER, RULE OF

See Regula Magistri.

MATTHIAS, GOSPEL OF

Mentioned by *Origen, this was a second-century *Gnostic gospel of the sect of *Basilides; it is no longer extant.

MAXIMIANUS (d. 434)

Successor of *Nestorius as *bishop of Constantinople (elected in 431); during his short episcopate he worked to bring together the *Alexandrian and *Antiochene factions estranged by the bitter tone of the Council of *Ephesus (431); he also tried to root out Nestorian sympathizers in his see.

MAXIMILIAN (d. 295)

Roman soldier stationed in Numidia, North Africa, who, as a Christian, refused to serve in the army; he was executed and eventually buried in Carthage next to *Cyprian.

MAXIMILLA (fl. ca. 156)

*Montanist prophet and one of the three leaders of the movement; according to one account preserved by *Eusebius of Caesarea she hanged herself along with Montanus at the collapse of the movement; a few of her oracles survive.

MAXIMINUS (ca. 365–ca. 430)

Latin *Arian best known for his debate with *Augustine in 427; several of his works survive, showing him to be a good scholar and Latin sylist.

MAXIMUS OF TURIN
(d. ca. 408–423)

*Bishop of Turin; nothing is known of his life except that he died between the dates just given; 240 sermons are attributed to him; although scholars consider most of these spurious, they give a picture of popular preaching in his day.

MAXIMUS THE CYNIC

The tool of Peter II of Alexandria to force *Gregory of Nazianzus out of the see of Constantinople; Peter had Maximus consecrated *bishop in 380, but the First Council of *Constantinople declared Gregory the authentic bishop; Maximus convinced some Westerners, including *Ambrose of Milan, to support him, but in 382 a synod at Rome withdrew any recognition; his nickname comes from his support of Cynic philosophy.

MELANIA THE ELDER
(ca. 341–ca. 410)

Wealthy Roman noblewoman who became an *ascetic after her husband's death (ca. 365); in 372 she moved to Palestine, where she established a double monastery (one for men and one for women) on the Mount of Olives with *Rufinus of Aquileia as her spiritual advisor; she returned to Italy around 400, where she stayed until 408, when, fleeing the advancing Goths, she returned to Jerusalem, where she died.

MELANIA THE YOUNGER
(ca. 383–438)

Granddaughter of *Melania the Elder; she and her husband Pinian jointly practiced the *ascetic life; they fled the Gothic invasion of Italy in 410 and went to Africa, where they founded two monasteries in 417; they later moved to Palestine, where they joined *Jerome's circle at Bethlehem; after her husband's death in 431 Melania founded another monastery on the Mount of Olives; she visited Constanti-nople in 436 and met the empress *Eudoxia; she died shortly therafter.

MELCHIADES
See Miltiades.

MELCHIZEDEKIANS

Name given to two Christian groups who took their name from the Old Testament priest Melchizedek (Gen 14:18-20), claimed in the Epistle to the Hebrews as a type of Christ (Heb 5:1-10); *Epiphanius said that one of these groups was led by the *Monarchian theologian *Theodotus the Banker; another was apparently active in Asia Minor, but little is known of them.

MELETIAN SCHISM; MELETIUS
(d. 381)

Meletius of Antioch, *bishop from 360, was driven from his see by the *Arians but returned in 362; he lacked the support of *Athanasius of Alexandria, and a party opposed to him at Antioch consecrated the *priest Paulinus, who was recognized by Rome as bishop of Antioch. Meletius stayed in his see under difficult circumstances and was exiled twice by the Arianizing emperor Valens (364–378), from 365 to 366 and from 371 to 378. *Basil of Caesarea strongly supported Meletius in the *schism and fruitlessly tried to get Rome to give up its support for Paulinus. The Eastern bishops showed their support for him and their defiance of Rome by electing Meletius president of the First Council of *Constantinople in 381; he died during the council.

MELITIAN SCHISM

Named for Melitius, *bishop of Lycopolis in Egypt, who opposed the lenient treatment of the *lapsed by *Peter I of Alexandria around 306. Peter excommunicated him, but after Peter's *martyrdom and Melitius' own exile by the pagans, he returned to found his own Church. The First Council of *Nicea worked out an agreement to restore peace, but, after the council, *Eusebius of Nicomedia, working to discredit *Athanasius, persuaded Melitius to renew the *schism, which lasted, albeit in decreasing size, until the coming of the Muslims.

MELITO OF SARDIS (d. ca. 190)

Christian *apologist from Asia Minor, he was the first to suggest that the Roman Empire and the Christian faith could be joined peacefully to the benefit of both; he was also the first known Christian to visit the Holy Land as a pilgrim. His sermon *On the Pasch* deals with Jesus' passion in strongly Old Testament terms, although Melito attacks the Jews rather strongly; in spite of this, he opted for the Jewish Christian method of dating Easter during the *Quartodeciman controversy. He emphasized the humanity of Christ, probably against the *Docetists; the context of this work is probably a Christian paschal service. He also wrote many sermons that do not survive.

MENANDER

Second-century *Gnostic theologian who, his opponents said, came from Samaria and was a disciple of *Simon Magus; to protect the divine majesty from contact with the material, Menander claimed that angels, not God, created the world; amazingly, he taught that his disciples would neither grow old nor die, which obviously forced him and his followers to explain his teachings in a symbolic or at least a nonliteral way.

MENAS (d. ca. 305)

Egyptian *martyr, reputedly a Roman soldier; most of the information about him is either legend or of dubious historical value, but his cult was enormously popular in his native land.

MENAS OF CONSTANTINOPLE (d. 552)

*Patriarch of Constantinople, consecrated by Pope *Agapetus in 536 to succeed the patriarch Anthimus, deposed for his *Monophysite convictions; Menas was a weak man, bullied by *Justinian into condemning *Origen and then into condemning the *Three Chapters, a condemnation that got him excommunicated by Pope *Vigilius in 547 and again in 551.

MESROB (ca. 350–440)

Also called Mesrop and Mashtots; Armenian civil servant, soldier, and then monk who worked with the *patriarch *Sahak to create an Armenian ecclesiastical literature; borrowing from the Greek and Syriac alphabets, he created an Armenian alphabet in 406; he headed a group of translators who by 410 had translated the New Testament into Armenian; the

Old Testament translation appeared around 414. He was also a famous preacher, and he tried to keep abreast of theological developments outside his province. Mesrob succeeded Sahak as *patriarch but died after only six months in office.

MESSALIANS

Fourth-century Mesopotamian sect devoted to excessive prayer on the grounds that that was the only way to drive out the demon in each one's soul; sometimes called *Euchites* (those who pray). Supporters of *asceticism, they believed that constant prayer would eliminate all bodily passions and make the believer eligible for a Trinitarian vision; their prayer book, the *Asketikon,* written around 400, was condemned at the First Council of *Ephesus in 431. The Messalians seem to have been rather simple believers; sources indicate many were illiterate. Although repeatedly condemned by Greek authorities, their doctrines were popular among many spiritually minded Christians.

METHODIUS OF OLYMPUS
(d. ca. 310)

Because he opposed *Origen, *Eusebius of Caesarea ignored him in his *Ecclesiastical History,* and little is known of Methodius' life; he was apparently a Macedonian by birth, became a *bishop in Asia Minor, and was *martyred. He admired Plato and tried to write in his style; his best-known book, *The Banquet,* an exaltation of virginity, imitates a Platonic dialogue; this text refers to Christ as the bridegroom of the Church, an image widely used by later writers. He wrote some exegesis, attacked Origen's notion of the preexistence of the soul, and defended free will against some *Gnostic writers. Many of his works are nonextant, although fragments suggest he favored the *allegorical exegesis of the Bible.

METROPOLITAN

*Bishop of a province; the early Church often used Roman geographical divisions, and by the fourth century the bishop of the largest or most influential diocese came to speak for the whole province, for example, the bishop of Carthage in Africa. At the First Council of *Nicea, this arrangement was formalized. The system worked well in the East, especially when metropolitans called provincial synods, but there were many difficulties in the West when the popes insisted that they had power over all the West, even over the metropolitans of Gaul, who waged a losing battle to preserve their autonomy vis-à-vis Rome. Metropolitans were often called by other titles such as archbishop and *primate, and the metropolitans of Alexandria, Antioch, Constantinople, Jerusalem, and Rome were called *patriarchs.

MILAN, EDICT OF

According to *Eusebius of Caesarea, in February of 313 *Constantine I and his ally in the Roman civil wars, Licinius, met at Milan and decided to grant the Christians freedom of worship and to restore their ecclesiastical property; the document announcing this, which was not issued at Milan nor was it technically a Roman edict, has not been preserved in pristine state, since *Lactantius and Eusebius both give different forms of it.

MILLENARIANISM

See **Chiliasm.**

MILTIADES (fl. ca. 180–190)

Name is sometimes given as Melchiades; from Asia Minor and possibly a pupil of *Justin Martyr, he was an *apologist whose writings are now lost; he wrote against the pagans and also against dissident Christians such as the *Montanists and *Valentinians.

MILTIADES (d. 314)

Pope from 311; the emperor Maxentius (306–312), not originally a *persecutor, was goaded into that role by his ally Galerius, a fierce anti-Christian, and the Roman Church was without a leader for twenty-two months after the death of *Eusebius of Rome; Miltiades was a Roman *priest whose first act was to receive back from Maxentius all the Church property he had confiscated—this in anticipation of *Constantine I's descent upon Rome and the need for peace in the city. Constantine defeated Maxentius, who died in battle, and then he and his ally Licinius issued the Edict of *Milan, which gave the Christians freedom of worship and restored their property. Miltiades was thus the first pope to enjoy this new freedom. In 313 Constantine, still a pagan, gave the pope the Lateran Palace as a residence, but the new emperor soon made it clear the gift had a string attached—he expected order in the Church. When *Donatus

and his followers accused *Caecilian of Carthage of having succeeded to a *traditor,* Constantine asked Miltiades to intervene as a judge, which he did at a *council in the Lateran in 313, siding with Caecilian against Donatus, who soon led his followers into *schism—just what Constantine did not want—but Miltiades died before having to face the emperor's wrath.

MINUCIUS FELIX (fl. ca. 200)

Probably an African and a lawyer, he wrote a dialogue called *Octavius,* in which Octavius, an African lawyer visiting Rome, discusses Christianity with Caecilius, a pagan, with Minucius as judge; Octavius attacks pagan belief and defends the Christians against calumnies; Caecilius is convinced and decides to become a Christian. The tone is civilized, stressing philosophical ideas such as immortality and ethics, and the dialogue takes passages from a wide variety of pagan authors.

MODALISM

A type of *Monarchian *Trinitarianism that held that there were really no persons in the Trinity but rather modes of operation temporarily adopted by God for specific purposes, such as creation; this was popular in the West in the third century.

MONARCHIANISM

A *Trinitarian theology that attempted to preserve the unity of God by denying the independence of the persons of the Trinity; Dynamic Monarchianism took an *Adoptionist position, that is, that Jesus was a man upon whom God poured out his grace and power; *Modalist Monarchianism stressed that the persons of the Trinity were names for modes of divine operation. The movement was prominent at Rome and associated with *Noetus and *Sabellius.

MONARCHIAN PROLOGUES

A set of four Latin Gospel prologues found in many medieval *Vulgate *manuscripts; once thought to be *Monarchian, they are now known to be *Priscillianist; they purport to give the places, dates, and circumstances under which the Gospels were written.

MONASTICISM

Something of a catchall term; as the name implies, it originally referred to *eremites (in Greek, *monos,* "one"), but later it came to mean all those who withdrew from the world to practice a life of *asceticism. Soon, however, monasteries were built in urban environments, such as Constantinople, and it was quite common for *bishops to be chosen from the ranks of the monks, for example, many Gallic bishops of the fifth century. Monastic writings such as the *Apophthegmata Patrum* made accounts of great monks and their teachings familiar to the Church at large. No one knows who the first Christian monks were, but the founder of Christian monasticism was *Antony of Egypt, a famous hermit and reluctant abbot; he was soon followed by *Pachomius, the founder of *cenobitic monasticism. By the mid-fourth century monasticism had spread from Egypt to Syria and Asia Minor;

by the end of the century it was known in the West, largely through the career of *Martin of Tours and the writings of John *Cassian and *Sulpicius Severus. *Basil of Caesarea wrote a Rule for monks that has largely governed Eastern houses; in the West *Benedict of Nursia's *Rule* came to dominate. In both East and West, however, the eremitic tradition continued. Monasticism offered to Christians the chance for the rigorous self-sacrifice of the *martyrs; as the martyrs died once, the monks died every day (mortification). Not surprisingly, this withdrawal from the world presented problems for bishops; if the ideal Christians lived without the *sacraments and the daily life of the Church, why should others bother with them? There were some early conflicts; Cassian tells of an Egyptian ascetic who warned his disciples to flee from women and bishops. But a *modus vivendi* was soon worked out, and the monks were often among the most loyal followers of the bishops, for example, the tremendous support given to *Athanasius by the Egyptian monks during the *Arian controversies. The monastic literature played up the mythic themes of the return to the natural world (Eden) and the combat with Satan in the desert, but the real success of monasticism lay not in its imagery but in its holy men and women, whose lives inspired others to endure and triumph.

MONICA (ca. 331–387)

Mother of *Augustine and ethnically a Berber, she was a devout Christian married to Patricius, a pagan until shortly before his death; she had three children but recognized early the talents of Augustine and strove for his conversion and social success; when he surreptitiously abandoned her in Carthage and went to Italy, she followed him, first to Rome and then to Milan, where she aligned herself with *Ambrose in his struggles against the *Arians; she lived to see Augustine converted, and she died shortly thereafter.

MONOPHYSITISM; MONOPHYSITES

The term comes from two Greek words, *monos* (one) and *physis* (nature); *Cyril of Alexandria had spoken of the one nature of Christ, but he did so when Greek *Christological terminology was still somewhat confused; when his successor, *Dioscorus, advanced this teaching at the Second Council of *Ephesus in 449, many *bishops and theologians thought he was denying the reality of Christ's humanity; at the Council of *Chalcedon in 451, the assembled bishops declared that Christ has one person and two natures, human and divine. The council also deposed Dioscorus. In Egypt the humiliation of the *patriarch and the apparent rejection of Cyril's theology brought about an immense popular reaction, and soon a Monophysite Church came into being in Egypt. Imperial attempts to settle the situation with force backfired; later attempts to reconcile the Monophysites, for example, with the *Henoticon, were rejected by other Christians as a betrayal of Chalcedon. Monophysitism spread into Syria and soon acquired important leaders such as *Severus of Antioch. *Theodora, wife of the emperor *Justinian (527–565), was a Monophysite and pushed her cause with her husband, but by the mid-sixth century it was clear that the break could not be healed. The main Monophysite areas were overrun by Islam, and Monophysitism is the faith of comparatively few Christians today, but in the sixth century it held the allegiance of probably more then half the Christians of the East, dominating Armenia, Syria, Egypt, Ethiopia, and part of Mesopotamia.

MONTANUS; MONTANISM

Called in its day the New Prophecy, Montanism was a conservative reaction in the second century to the growing authority of *bishops and the growth of the New Testament canon; Montanus, possibly a pagan priest but definitely a recent convert, was a resident of the Phrygia, a province of Asia Minor; he claimed that the Spirit still spoke to the Church and indeed was speaking through him and two women associates, *Maximilla and and *Priscilla. Clearly they had hit a nerve, because many Christians flocked to hear their ecstatic and apocalyptic utterances; the movement's *asceticism also appealed to many, for example, its most famous convert, *Tertullian. But the prophecies of an imminent end proved untrue, and soon many non-Montanists began severely to criticize it. *Eusebius of Caesarea reports that the movement also attracted frauds, further that, according to one account, Montanus and Maximilla hanged themselves in despair at the movement's collapse. Although its actual duration was short, possibly just a few years (either 156 or 172; the sources do not permit final dating), its impact was enormous. Isolated groups of Montanists survived into the sixth century; although there are literary references from many areas, Montanist inscriptions survive largely from Phrygia.

MURATORIAN FRAGMENT

Portion of an eighth-century *manuscript containing a New Testament canon list; discovered by the Italian scholar L. A. Muratori (d. 1750). Although some scholars date the list to the fourth century, the majority consider it of the second century and thus the oldest Latin canon list. It does not include all the twenty-seven books of the eventual canon, excluding Hebrews, James, 1 and 2 Peter, and 3 John, but it does include two books (the *Apocalypse of *Peter* and the *Wisdom of Solomon*) that did not make it into the New Testament canon, although the latter appears in the Old Testament canon of several denominations. This text testifies to the early and widespread acceptance of the (now) four canonical Gospels, the Acts of the Apostles, and the epistles of Paul. It rejects several *Gnostic works but stresses the acceptability of John's Gospel, hitherto a Gnostic favorite.

MUSANUS

Second-century *apologist who wrote against the *Encratites.

N

NAASENES

A second-century *Gnostic sect, most scholars think that its adherents are to be identified with the *Ophites, the serpent worshipers. *Hippolytus claimed that their name came from *nass,* Hebrew for "serpent"; they considered humans to be enslaved to a creator God, from whom Christ liberated them.

NAG HAMMADI

The site on the Nile River in Egypt where a large collection (forty-nine) of *Gnostic treatises in thirteen fourth-century *codices was discovered in 1945; the treatises are largely in Coptic, the dialect of the native Egyptians outside Alexandria (where Greek was spoken), and this library represents the largest surviving body of Gnostic texts, including the *Gospel of *Thomas* and the *Apocryphon of *John.* These are a particular boon to scholars because many Gnostic teachers and teachings were previously known only through their opponent's citations or characterizations.

NARSES (ca. 400–ca. 503)

Also spelled Narsai; a *Nestorian theologian; he was an orphan who was brought up in a monastery; he studied at the school of Edessa and became its head in 437; expelled from there by an anti-Nestorian *bishop, he founded the school of Nisibis, which was in Persian, not Roman, territory and which offered him haven from his theological and imperial opponents. He wrote many exegetical works, which do not survive, and poems, which do survive; he was an important figure in the establishment of the Nestorian Church.

NAZARENES

A group of apparently Jewish Christians in Syria who observed some parts of the Jewish Law not followed by most other Christian groups; they flourished in the fourth century.

NAZARENES, GOSPEL OF

Another name for the *Gospel According to *Hebrews.*

NECTARIUS OF CONSTANTINOPLE (d. 397)

A layman and an imperial official, he was chosen, although not yet even *baptized, by the emperor *Theodosius I (379–395) to be *bishop of Constantinople after the resignation of *Gregory of Nazianzus in 381; he had an uneventful tenure.

NEMESIUS OF EMESA (fl. ca. 390–400)

Disciple of *Eusebius of Caesarea and *bishop of Emesa in Syria, he was trained in Platonic philosophy, and his one extant work, *On Human Nature,* attempts to reconcile Platonic and Christian teachings on the soul.

NEREUS AND ACHILLEUS

Roman *martyrs of the second (or even possibly the first) century; according to an inscription of Pope *Damasus I on their tomb, they were Roman soldiers who converted to Christianity, abandoned their military careers, and were decapitated; they are buried in the *catacomb of *Domitilla.

NESTORIANISM; NESTORIANS

Nestorianism is a theological position deriving from the teaching of *Nestorius of Constantinople that separates the divine from the human in Christ, largely from a concern that a too-close union of the two would lead to *Sabellianism. After the condemnation of Nestorius at the First Council of *Ephesus in 431, many *bishops from Syria who supported his position slowly but surely formed a separate Church, first at Edessa and later at Nisibis, because the former was in Roman territory and thus subject to harassment and the latter was in Persian territory; soon the center of the Church moved farther in Persia to Seleucia-Ctesiphon on the Tigris River. Although occasionally suspected of being Roman sympathizers by the Persians, the Nestorians generally lived in peace; even the Islamic conquest of Persia did not change their state. In the thirteenth century some Nestorian missionaries made important converts among the Mongols, but when the Mongols adopted Islam, they began to persecute the Nestorians. A small group of Nestorians known as Assyrian Christians today survives in the Middle East and in the United States.

NESTORIUS (ca. 382–ca. 451)

Of Persian descent, he was a monk and a *priest at Antioch, where he became a famous preacher; in 428 the emperor *Theodosius II (408–450) chose him to be *bishop of Constantinople. Like *John Chrysostom before him, this Antiochene monk did not know his way around the intrigues of the court and the church of the capital, and he soon became embroiled in controversy. He promised to root out *heresy, but his methods against peaceful people with whom the Constantinopolitans had learned to live antagonized many. The real difficulty lay with his theology. He was concerned that Christians did not really distinguish the human and divine in Christ, and he opposed the title *Theotokos (God-bearer) for the Virgin Mary, saying instead that she was Christotokos. This offended not only many theologians but also the piety of the populace, which was devoted to Mary; furthermore, the term had been used since the early third century and was widely accepted. At this point the theologically brilliant but politically unscrupulous *Cyril of Alexandria entered the picture, attacking Nestorius' theology as dividing Christ into two (which is not what Nestorius intended). When both men appealed to *Celestine I of Rome, the pope backed Cyril. At the request of Nestorius, who expected to be vindicated, the emperor called the First Council of *Ephesus in 431, where Cyril brilliantly engineered Nestorius' downfall, that is, his deposition from the see of Constantinople, his return to his monastery in Antioch, and in 436 his exile to a monastery in Egypt. He lived long enough to hear about the Council of *Chalcedon, whose teaching he considered a justification of his own. Nestorius was not the *heretic of tradition, but he obviously had not worked out the implications of his own theology; he did not clearly determine what was the unitive element in Christ. It is regrettable that an important theological question was buried under the ecclesiastical politics of the age. His own view of the situation can be found in his strangely titled book, *The Bazaar of Heracleides.*

NEW PROPHECY

See **Montanus; Montanism.**

NICEA, FIRST COUNCIL OF

When the controversy over the teaching of *Arius of Alexandria could not be settled either within his diocese or by local councils, Emperor *Constantine I (306–337) decided to call a council of the *bishops of the inhabited world, the *oikumene,* and thus Nicea in 325 became the first *ecumenical council; its main achievement was the formulation of a *Trinitarian statement, *homoousios,* which affirmed the divinity of the Son and his equality with the Father and which could not be accepted by Arius. Most scholars believe that *Hosius of Cordova, the emperor's theological advisor and a Westerner, suggested the term, which had had a rather checkered history in the East. The disputes after the council made it clear that Nicea was not considered authoritative in the fourth century, but the First Council of *Constantinople made its teachings a criterion for orthodoxy, a method used by subsequent ecumenical councils; all parties at the councils of *Ephesus in 431 and *Chalcedon in 451 claimed to be consonant with this first council. Nicea also passed some disciplinary decrees, for example, on the *Melitian schism and on the date of Easter, a topic of great importance to Constantine. The so-called Nicene *Creed is not from this council but, more likely, from the First Council of Constantinople. (Although the present volume speaks of this simply as the Council of Nicea, there was a second one in 787 to discuss the question of the use of images in Christianity.) The adjectival form of its name is Nicene.

NICETAS OF REMESIANA
(d. after 414)

As *bishop of a city in the Balkans, he had both Eastern and Western contacts, for example, he visited *Paulinus of Nola in Italy; since his area was one frequently invaded by barbarian tribes, he also did some missionary work. He left behind a mixed bag of writings, including some anti*heretical writings, liturgical works, and, the most important, a book of *catechetical instructions in six parts, the fifth of which discusses the *Apostles' Creed, a valuable witness to that document. Nicetas is the first person to use the phrase "the communion of saints."

NICHOLAS OF MYRA
(fl. ca. 290–300)

Although he is the most popular Christian saint in the world, virtually nothing is known about his life except that he was apparently a *bishop in southwestern Asia Minor who suffered but was not *martyred during the *persecution of Diocletian (303–305); he may have attended the First Council of *Nicea in 325. Legends about him and his miracle-working powers grew almost immediately; by the sixth century he had a major cult in the East, which soon spread to the West. In 1087 some enterprising adventurers from Bari, Italy, stole his body from its burial place in Myra, which was by then in Muslim hands, and brought it to their city. Nicholas is the patron saint of children, to whom he brought gifts on his feast day, December 6. Through a series of complicated metamorphoses, he became the British Father Christmas and the American Santa Claus.

NICODEMUS, GOSPEL ACCORDING TO

*Apocryphon attributed to Nicodemus, the Jewish teacher who came to Jesus at night (John 3:1-15) and who aided in his burial (John 19:39); this work includes the Acts of *Pilate.

NICOLAITANS

Sect mentioned in the second chapter of the Book of Revelation (2:1-7) and again by several Christian writers around 170–200, for example, *Irenaeus, *Clement of Alexandria, and *Tertullian, although they are referring to a *Gnostic sect. For some inexplicable reason, the *Fathers identified Nicholas, the founder of this sect, with one of the seven chosen by the apostles in Acts 6. Little is known of this sect except what can be deduced from Revelation, although some Fathers accused the Nicolaitans of sexual immorality.

NILUS OF ANCYRA (d. ca. 430)

Abbot of a monastery in Asia Minor, he was a disciple of *John Chrysostom to the extent that in 407 he refused to offer a prayer for the well being of the city of Constantinople because the emperor Arcadius (395–408) had deposed and exiled John; his extant writings include letters and *ascetical treatises.

NIMBUS

In artistic representations, the circle of light emanating from the head of a sacred or divine figure; it appears first in pagan art of the Hellenistic and Roman periods; by the third-century Christian artists were using it of Christ and by the fifth century of the saints. The *halo, or circle of light floating above the head, is from a later period.

NINIAN (ca. 360–ca. 420)

A Briton who evangelized in southern Scotland (then Pictland), he is known only from a brief passage in the *Historia Ecclesiastica* of the Anglo-Saxon Bede (d. 735); from his foundation at Whithorn, Candida Casa (White House) he carried out his work not only among the Picts but also among the Britons, but the extent of this work is much debated.

NINO (ca. 325–335)

Slave in Asia Minor who was famous as a healer; her fame reached the kingdom of Georgia, whose queen asked for her; according to the account of *Rufinus of Aquileia, she cured the queen and saved the king from an accident by invoking Christ's name; the royal family converted, and Nino evangelized much of the kingdom, although *priests had to be sent from Constantinople to regularize worship in Georgia.

NITRIA

Region of Egyptian desert west of the Nile and close to Libya, where, from the fourth century, many *ascetics founded monasteries.

NOETUS OF SMYRNA (fl. ca. 200)

He is known only through the writings of *Hippolytus, who says he was a *modalist and the first to teach *Patripassianism; he also opposed the *Logos doctrine of Christ, already at the time a popular form of *Christology. A synod in the city of Smyrna in Asia Minor condemned his teaching.

NONNUS OF PANOPOLIS (ca. 400–ca. 435)

An Egyptian, he wrote in Alexandria an epic poem, *Dionysiaca,* about the journey of the god Dionysos to India; he then apparently converted to Christianity, because around 431 he wrote a metrical *Paraphrase of Saint John's Gospel;* virtually nothing is known of his life.

NOVATIAN (d. 258)

*Antipope from 251; the date of his birth is unknown, but by 250 he was the leading figure in the Church at Rome, a *presbyter who governed the Church there after the martyrdom of Pope *Fabian. In 251 the Romans overwhelmingly chose as *bishop the priest *Cornelius to the chagrin of Novatian, who got himself consecrated bishop by three southern Italian bishops. Novatian took a rigorist stance on the readmission of the *lapsed, although since his earlier stance was more moderate, this may have been a device to separate himself from Cornelius. Novatian made a vigorous attempt to establish communion with other bishops, but *Cyprian of Carthage and *Dionysius of Alexandria rejected his claim, although the latter attempted to make peace between Cornelius and him. Cornelius acted decisively, however, calling a synod of sixty bishops, which excommunicated Novatian. But Novatian's group spread anyway, as far as Spain and Syria. The founder himself died in 258, probably as a *martyr, a death befitting a rigorist; Novatianist Churches survived for centuries. Novatian's chagrin at not being chosen bishop resulted not only from his feeling that his service to the community had been overlooked but also because he was far more learned than Cornelius or his successors. Novatian was the first great Roman theologian to write in Latin, and his theological terminology considerably affected later Roman theology. Several of his writings survive, most dealing with moral questions, but his reputation rests on his treatise *On the Trinity,* in which he united the *Logos doctrine of Christ while maintaining a *Monarchian approach to the Trinity.

O

OECUMENIUS (fl. 550)

Greek writer of unknown provenance; he was a philosopher and rhetorician and wrote the earliest Greek commentary on the Apocalypse; a *Monophysite, he was a follower of *Severus of Antioch.

OLD LATIN VERSION OF THE BIBLE

See Vetus Latina.

OLYMPIAS (ca. 365–ca. 415)

Member of an influential family in Constantinople, she married Nebridius around 385, an imperial official who soon died (386); the young widow stymied an attempt of the emperor *Theodosius I (379–395) to marry her to one of his relatives, and she decided to live an *ascetic life and one devoted to charity; her social position was significant, and she became a friend of *Nectarius, *bishop of Constantinople, who ordained her a *deaconess; Olympias used her wealth to aid Nectarius and his successor *John Chrysostom, and she stood by the latter in his trials with the imperial family; when he was exiled in 407, so was she; she died some time before 419.

OLYMPIODORUS (fl. ca. 510–520)

*Deacon in Alexandria; anti-*Monophysite writer who opposed *Severus of Antioch; he wrote commentaries on several Old Testament books not commonly treated by the *Fathers, such as Ecclesiastes, Job, Jeremiah, and Baruch.

OPHITES

A *Gnostic sect that praised the Genesis serpent for bringing knowledge to humanity when the Old Testament God wished to keep people in ignorance; the pagan critic *Celsus accused them of being magicians and sorcerers. The Ophites are usually identified with the *Naasenes.

OPTATUS OF MILEVIS
(fl. ca. 370–380)

Catholic *bishop in the African province of Numidia, he wrote against the *Donatists in a work usually called *Against Parmenian the Donatist,* Parmenian being the successor of Donatus in Carthage; the book attacks the Donatist ecclesiology, especially its exclusiveness and the claim that the Donatist sect (*pars Donati*), as Optatus called it, alone was holy; his book also includes information on *baptism and some other ritual practices of the African Church. He also includes some documentary material much used by historians, especially for information about the *Circumcellions.

ORANGE, COUNCILS OF

*Council held in Arausio in Gaul; the first was held in 441 under *Hilary of Arles and dealt largely with practical matters such as marriage and church ownership; the second, more important one, was held in 529 with *Caesarius of Arles presiding—this council condemned *Semi-Pelagianism and basically supported the teaching of *Augustine on grace and original sin, an important gesture in the country where Semi-Pelagianism had flourished; indeed, after this council Gaul followed the Augustinian position.

ORIENTIUS (fl. ca. 430–450)

A poem entitled the *Commonitorium* identifies its author as Orientius, identified in other sources as a Gallic *bishop who tried to mediate between the Romans and the Visigoths around 439; the poem deals heavily with the demands of Christian life, and it also gives a vivid picture of the destruction of Gaul caused by the Germanic invasion in 407.

ORIGEN (ca. 185–ca. 253)

The first great Christian writer known to have been born of Christian parents, Origen lost his father, Leonidas, in the *persecution by the emperor Septimius Severus in 202; *Eusebius of Caesarea says that Origen wished to follow his father, but his mother hid his clothing, thus preventing his martyrdom. A child prodigy, Origen was asked by Bishop *Demetrius to take over the Alexandrian *catechetical school when *Clement of Alexandria decided to leave the city during the persecution; Origen was a genius with immense energy who turned his hand to all that was around him. He practiced a life of *asceticism, and Eusebius preserves a rather unreliable account that he castrated himself in response to Matthew 19:12. Origen devoted his energies to biblical exegesis, but since, to him, virtually all Christian teaching revolved around the Bible, his exegesis led him into many other areas. Origen's fame spread, and Eusebius says that this made Demetrius jealous. In 215 during a visit to Palestine, Origen accepted an offer from the local bishops to preach; Demetrius claimed that since he was a layperson, he had no right to do so, and the bishop recalled him to Alexandria. When, on another visit to Palestine in 230, Origen had himself ordained by the local bishops, Demetrius made him unwelcome at Alexandria, depriving him of his position at the catechetical school.

Origen settled in Palestine at Caesarea and opened a school there; when his pupil *Heraclas became bishop of Alexandria, he returned there, but the former pupil supported the former bishop, and Origen had to return to Palestine. He taught in Caesarea for twenty years; during this time *Gregory Thaumaturgus (the Wonder-Worker) studied with him and wrote his famous encomium to this great teacher. Origen traveled widely, going to Rome in 212, where he met the most important local theologian, *Hippolytus; by 215 he was in Arabia (the Roman province) to instruct the local governor at his request; he spoke before the emperor Severus Alexander (222–235) and his mother, Julia Mammaea, at the latter's invitation, although the date is uncertain; in 244 at the invitation of the local bishops, he traveled again to Arabia, this time to correct the theology of a local bishop. In 250 the emperor Decius decided to persecute the Christians; this most famous of Christian teachers was arrested and tortured for a year in hopes of getting him to apostasize. The desire for martyrdom Origen had manifested a half century before had not weakened, and he did not give in. He was released upon the emperor's death in 251, but he died soon afterward as a result of the tortures. Origen was a remarkably prolific writer who, supposedly, could simultaneously keep dozens of secretaries busy. He was remarkable not only for the number of books but also their range. For example, in his debates with the Jews of Alexandria he found that the different parties read different texts of Scripture, so he engaged in textual criticism, that is, in determining what the Old Testament actually said by comparing and evaluating *manuscripts; the result was the magnificent *Hexapla, a monument of scholarship. Origen considered himself a man of the Church, and much of his energy went into homilies and moral works. He wrote many biblical scholia, short treatises on biblical topics, as well as a considerable number of long works on the Bible, clearly his greatest achievement. Indeed, after him, every great theologian down to the Scholastic age was an exegete. Furthermore, Origen's use of the allegorical method, that is, to look beyond the literal meaning of the biblical text for a spiritual or moral or dogmatic meaning, enabled him to tackle the most unpromising topics, for example, his homilies on the Book of Leviticus. Between 220 and 230 he wrote his famous work, *On First Principles,* the first treatise to deal systematically with several aspects of Christian theology; in this text he advanced some of his controversial theories, such as the preexistence of souls. His *Against Celsus,* a reply to the criticisms of Christianity by the pagan *Celsus, is the most thorough *apology from the early Church. He was also a mystic, although his mysticism does not appear in any one treatise but is found in several. Origen was and considered himself to be primarily an exegete, and thus the bulk of his work was exegetical, but he is best known for some of his speculative work. He defended the unity of God by asserting the eternal generation of the Son; he had no use for *apocalyptic or *millenarian notions and attacked them ruthlessly; he could not believe that God was inactive before the creation of the world and speculated that this world was one of many; his theory for the preexistence of souls, including the soul by which the divine *Logos was joined to a human body, carried *Christology into a new realm; his suggestion that even the devil could be saved challenged notions of *soteriology. While Origen was alive, some, such as Sextus *Julius Africanus, criticized him, but no one really challenged his theology. After his death and especially in the fourth century when the *Arian controversies had produced a new orthodoxy, some theologians attacked the more adventurous parts of his teachings (*See* **Origenist Controversies**). These attacks reached their highest point around 400 and again at the Second Council of *Constantinople in 553, at which several of Origen's teachings were condemned. This resulted in the destruction of many of his books, today known only by their names; yet even with this Origen's extant literary output is exceeded only by that of *Augustine. He paid the price of being a pioneer during and after his life, but his impact on the development of Christian theology was enormous.

ORIGENIST CONTROVERSIES

In the latter part of the fourth century, as *Nicene orthodoxy was triumphing, some people with little sense of historical development applied current standards to theologians of the past, particularly *Origen. *Epiphanius of Salamis, a poor intellect but a self-appointed *heresy hunter, decided Origen was a threat to doctrine; in 393 he sent a *priest named Atarbius to Palestine to demand a condemnation of Origen for heresy by local monks; to the surprise of all, *Jerome, an avowed admirer of Origen, agreed to the condemnation, although *Rufinus of Aquileia and Bishop *John of Jerusalem refused. Epiphanius came to Jerusalem and denounced John; Jerome soon joined the cause. In 397 Rufinus went to Rome to protect Origen's reputation, but some of Jerome's friends stirred up trouble between Rufinus and Jerome by telling Jerome that Rufinus had claimed that the two of them agreed on their views of Origen. While the two Latins were being driven apart, the unscrupulous *Theophilus, *patriarch of Alexandria, entered the fray. Formerly a supporter of Origen, he had turned against him and proceeded to attack John of Jerusalem in 400. In that same year Theophilus condemned Origen at Alexandria, and when he wrote to Pope *Anastasius I (who personally knew nothing about Origen), the combination of Alexandria and Jerome's Roman friends convinced the pope to condemn Origen and to urge other Italian *bishops to do likewise. In 402 Theophilus condemned some monks in *Nitria who favored Origen, and when four of them, the so-called *Tall Brothers, fled to their fellow monk *John Chrysostom, bishop of Constantinople, they gave Theophilus the opportunity to attack his real target. Jerome joined in the attack on Chrysostom with a Latin translation of a sleazy pamphlet written by Theophilus, who was by now masterminding the entire affair. Indeed, when Epiphanius saw how the events were being orchestrated to destroy Chrysostom, he took ship for home, only to die during the trip. Theophilus was successful, John was deposed, and Origen's teaching was discredited. The whole sordid affair was caused largely by Epiphanius' ignorance and Jerome's fear of being in any way associated with heresy; when personalities and ecclesiastical politics became involved, there was no way for reason to win out. This was not, however, the end of the affair. When, around 542, some Palestinian monks again began to read Origen, their local opponents used a letter of the emperor *Justinian (527–565) to his patriarch in Constantinople, *Menas, condemning Origen as a heretic in order to discredit them. In 543 Justinian had Origen's teachings condemned at a synod in Constantinople, a condemnation signed not just by Eastern bishops but also by Pope *Vigilius; the condemnation was repeated at the emperor's Second Council of *Constantinople in 553. As a consequence of this, many of Origen's books were destroyed, and unless they had been translated into some other language, many were irretrievably lost.

OROSIUS (ca. 375–d. after 420)

Spanish *priest and admirer of *Augustine, he went to Africa partly to escape the effects of the invasion of Spain by Visigothic barbarians and partly to give Augustine a copy of his book against the *Priscillianists and *Origenists; Augustine sent him to *Jerome in Jerusalem, where the *Pelagian controversy was heating up; in 415 Orosius testified against *Pelagius before *John of Jerusalem only to find out that his views had become badly misrepresented via translation from Latin to Greek, and he ended up writing a book defending himself against *heresy. Because of a barbarian invasion in Spain, he returned to Africa in 416, where Augustine asked him to write a world history to point out the evils of the past (Augustine was at the time writing *The City of God* to refute pagan claims that things were better before the empire became Christian). No more is known of Orosius after about 417. He did write the history, called *The Seven Books of History Against the Pagans,* which basically repeats material from older writers but which is of great value for the period from 378 down to the author's own day. His books against the heretics and in his own defense also survive.

ORSISIUS (d. ca. 380)

Sometimes spelled Horsiesi; when the great *monastic founder *Pachomius died, he was succeeded by one Petronius, who died after two months, and Orsisius became superior of the monastery of Tabennisi; although a saintly man, he was not an organizer and had to appoint a coadjutor named *Theodore to assist him, and eventually he had to resign in favor of Theodore; upon the latter's death in 368, he again became superior; he prepared a monastic Rule, not just a continuation of the Rule of Pachomius but a new document with many insights into Pachomian life; it survives in a Latin translation. Orsisius continued the monks' traditional support of *Nicene orthodoxy, and he himself received two letters from *Athanasius.

OUSIA

Greek term for "being," often rendered as *substantia* in Latin and thus "substance" in English; unfortunately many Greek terms, especially in the early Christian period, were subject to more than one interpretation when used theologically, and this term could also mean "an individually subsisting being." Thus, when the First Council of *Nicea in 325 proclaimed that the Father and the *Logos were *homo-ousios*, that is, of the same *ousia*, many Greek *bishops thought (albeit after the council) that the term meant that Father and Logos were the same being and that the council had canonized *Sabellianism. During the long debates and controversies of the fourth century the *Cappadocians were able to clarify the language, so that *ousia* was understood as "being" or "substance" while *hypostasis* came to mean "an individually subsisting being"; thus the Trinity was understood to be three *hypostases* sharing one *ousia*.

P

PACHOMIUS (ca. 290–346)

Born a pagan in Egypt, he converted to Christianity when, while an army conscript during the Roman civil wars (ca. 310), he saw Christians doing charitable work; he studied briefly with an Egyptian *hermit named Palemon; around 320 he founded a *cenobitic community near Tabennisi on the Nile, the first cenobitic community, not in the sense that monks had not lived together before but rather that Pachomius promoted a sense of community and common goals. He also drew up the first *monastic rule, emphasizing order but also charity, *asceticism, poverty, and obedience to the abbot. He established other foundations, which numbered nine for men and two for women by the time of his death. His monastic rule also influenced other founders and legislators, such as *Basil of Caesarea and John *Cassian. The name "Pachomian Koinonia" (community) is given to a variety of literature from the Pachomian monasteries, including several biographies of the saint.

PACIANUS OF BARCELONA (ca. 310–ca. 390)

Spanish *bishop who worked to eradicate pagan practices among his congregation; he wrote treatises on *penance that are valuable for understanding early Christian penitential practice; he also wrote three letters to a *Novatianist named Sympronianus that attacked the Novatianist ecclesiology.

PALIMPSEST

*Manuscript on which the original text has been scrubbed away, usually with pumice, and then written on again; this was done for several reasons, such as a simple shortage of writing materials or a rejection of the original contents; several manuscripts of the works of *Ephraem the Syrian survive as palimpsests.

PALLADIUS OF HELENOPOLIS
(ca. 363–425)

Born in Asia Minor, he followed his brothers into the *monastic life, first at the Mount of Olives in Palestine; around 388 he went to Egypt, staying at several locations and becoming a disciple of *Macarius the Egyptian and then *Evagrius Ponticus; around 399 he had to leave the desert because of ill health. He became *bishop of Helenopolis in northern Asia Minor in 405 and soon became involved in the *Origenist controversy on the side of *John Chrysostom, whose cause he pleaded at Rome; his support of John earned him an exile in Egypt; around 411 he was freed and became bishop of Aspuna, also in Asia Minor. He left behind three valuable writings. The shortest is an account of India and the Brahmins who lived there, although it is likely that only part of this is from Palladius. The second is a dialogue on the life of John Chrysostom, a valuable biographical account. His most important work is the *Lausiac History,* an account of the Egyptian monks based on his personal experiences and also upon some written sources; it is a basic work for understanding the character of early Christian monasticism.

PALLADIUS OF IRELAND
(fl. 431–440)

The Gallic chronicler *Prosper of Aquitaine says that in 431 Pope *Celestine I sent a *deacon named Palladius to be the *primus episcopus* (first *bishop) of the Christian Irish; this Palladius is apparently the same man Prosper mentions elsewhere as having urged the pope to send *Germanus of Auxerre to Britain to combat *Pelagianism, so it is likely that he was sent to Ireland to prevent the spread of Pelagianism from the neighboring island; Palladius' work in Ireland is virtually unknown, especially since it was swallowed in the legends about his contemporary *Patrick.

PAMMACHIUS (ca. 340–410)

Roman noble who became a monk after the death of his wife; he was a friend and confidant of *Jerome, who dedicated several treatises to him; Pammachius was famous for his works of charity for the Roman poor.

PAMPHILUS (ca. 240–309)

An adherent of *Origen, he established a *catechetical school in Caesarea in Palestine, where he got to know the Church historian *Eusebius of Caesarea, who wrote a now nonextant life of him; during a *persecution Pamphilus, who was eventually *martyred, spent some time in prison, where he wrote a defense, or *apologia, for Origen; Eusebius used this in his own account of Origen in the *Ecclesiastical History.*

PANCRAS (d. 304)

Roman *martyr who was supposedly martyred at the age of fourteen; he was widely venerated, but virtually nothing historical is known of him.

PANTAENUS (fl. ca. 170–190)

A Sicilian, he traveled considerably, even as far as India; around 180 he came to Alexandria, where he was converted from Stoic philosophy to Christianity; he soon became head of the *catechetical school of Alexandria, where he taught *Clement of Alexandria, who referred to his teacher as the "Sicilian bee" because he went from source to source drawing out the best, as the bee does in seeking out various flowers. Although only single-sentence quotations of his works have survived, there can be little doubt that this educated, cosmopolitan man gave the Alexandrian school its liberal character.

PANTALEON (d. ca. 305)

According to tradition, he was the son of a pagan father and a Christian mother, initially a Christian, then a pagan, then a Christian again; he was a physician who numbered the emperor Galerius (305–311) among his patients, but even that could not save him during a *persecution; he died a *martyr and was widely venerated in the Christian East.

PAPIAS OF HIERAPOLIS
(ca. 60–ca. 110)

*Bishop of Hierapolis in Asia Minor and one of the *Apostolic Fathers, he left behind no writings but only fragments preserved by *Irenaeus and *Eusebius of Caesarea; he held *millenarianist views, and Eusebius says he was a man of little intelligence, a view that the extant fragments of his works do not contradict. He is an early witness to the authorship of Matthew's and Mark's Gospels.

PAPYRUS

Writing material made from reeds grown along the banks of the Nile; this was the most widely used material in the Roman Empire, although *parchment largely replaced it in the West toward the end of antiquity; the English word "paper" ultimately derives from it.

PARCHMENT

Writing material made from treated animal skins; this was not as popular as *papyrus in the ancient world but was used more and more toward the end of the Roman period and widely used in the Middle Ages; many *patristic *manuscripts survive on parchment.

PAROUSIA

The imminent second coming of Christ; belief in this was widespread in the earliest Church (1 Thess 4:13-18) and continued to be popular into the second century, but Alexandrian attacks on the literal interpretation of *apocalyptic prophecies plus the gradual passage of time without the return of Christ caused this belief to fade (see, for example, 2 Pet 3:8-9).

PASCHASINUS OF LILYBAEUM
(d. ca. 440)

Sicilian *bishop who was one of *Leo the Great's legates to the Council of *Chalcedon in 451.

PATRIARCH

Biblical title for the earliest major male figures (Noah, Abraham); it came to mean the *bishops of large sees, although often limited to Alexandria, Antioch, Constantinople, Jerusalem, and Rome; the widespread use of the title dates to the fifth century.

PATRICK (ca. 385–ca. 461)

Born in Roman Britain and kidnapped by Irish pirates around 400, Patrick (or Patricius, as he would have been called in his day) spent six years in Ireland and then escaped, later returning as a missionary *bishop somewhere between 432 and 435. Unlike *Palladius, who worked among Christians, Patrick worked primarily among pagans in the northern half of the island; despite the avalanche of later legends, his two extant writings make no mention of snakes, shamrocks, or druids; on the contrary, they emphasize his struggles and difficulties and his solid faith in God, which enabled him to persevere through the hardships of the mission. Although not the traditional wonder-worker of legends and parades, Patrick was a great missionary who earned the title "Apostle of Ireland."

PATRIPASSIANISM

Literally, "the suffering of the Father"; a form of *Monarchianism that so linked the Father and Son that what happened to the Son could be said to have happened to the Father, thus the term "Patripassianism"; this is also a form of *Sabellianism. Patripassianism was most prominent in the early third century and *Noetus was its best known proponent.

PATRISTICS

The study of the *Fathers (in Latin, *Patres*) of the Church; originally limited to the orthodox Fathers, it now means the study of virtually any aspect of early Christianity.

PATROLOGY

Originally equivalent with *patristics, it now means handbooks or manuals of early Christianity.

PAUL, ACTS OF

*Apocryphon of the second century, written, *Tertullian said, by a *presbyter who wished to glorify Paul; it tells of Paul's adventures as a missionary, including his famous dealings with *Thecla. This also contains the famous story of Paul's baptizing a lion (which later refuses to attack him in the arena) and the *Third Epistle to the Corinthians,* a melange of citations from genuine Pauline letters. This text offers an entertaining narrative, and it was very popular in the early and medieval Church, frequently circulating in parts as the *Acts of Paul and Thecla,* the *Martyrdom of Paul,* and the *Third Epistle to the Corinthians.*

PAUL, APOCALYPSE OF

Also called the *Vision of Paul;* a fourth-century *apocryphon based upon 2 Corinthians 12:1-10, that is, Paul's having been taken up into the third heaven, where he "heard things that cannot be told" (v. 4); this book tells of them with vivid descriptions of heaven and hell; it was very popular in the Middle Ages and was used by

Dante for his description of hell in the *Divine Comedy*.

PAUL, ASCENSION OF

Nonextant *Gnostic work mentioned by *Epiphanius of Salamis.

PAULA (347–404)

Roman noblewoman, widowed at thirty-two with five children, she decided in 380 to lead a life of *asceticism and to aid the destitute of the city. She soon came under the tutelage of *Jerome and proved to be an excellent student, especially of Scripture; she learned both Hebrew and Greek, demonstrating the possibilities for the Christian education of women, but other tutors did not follow Jerome's lead. When he had to leave Rome in 385, she and her daughter *Eustochium accompanied him to the Holy Land, where she used her considerable wealth to found a monastery for men and a convent for women, over which she presided until her death.

PAULINUS OF MILAN (d. ca. 425)

Possibly a native of the area around Florence, he met *Ambrose about 394 and went back to Milan with him, where he served as the *bishop's secretary until Ambrose's death in 397. Some years later Paulinus went to Africa, where he aided *Augustine in his campaign against the *Pelagians; while there he wrote the *vita of Ambrose, which follows the vita of *Martin of Tours by *Sulpicius Severus and which contains some personal biographical details, although disappointingly little on Ambrose's

public career, especially in Church-state matters.

PAULINUS OF NOLA (ca. 353–431)

Born Meropius Pontius Anicius Paulinus in Bordeaux, he came from a noble Gallic family and was enormously wealthy; he studied with *Ausonius, a famous rhetorician; around 373 he went to Rome to succeed his father in the senate; by 379 he was a governor in southern Italy, where he first heard of Saint *Felix of Nola, a reputed martyr during the persecution of the emperor Decius (250). Paulinus was soon back in Gaul, where he met *Martin of Tours and *Sulpicius Severus. He married a Spanish noblewoman named Therasia, was *baptized in 389, and ordained a *priest in 394 in Barcelona (on condition that he not have to stay in Spain). What caused this change in his life is uncertain, although the violent death of his brother and an uncertain subsequent danger to him as well as the influence of his wife contributed to it. He soon gave away much of his money and retired with Theresia to Nola, where he established a monastery and a pilgrimage hostel for those visiting the tomb of Felix. He lived in Nola for the rest of his life and was elected *bishop there in 409; however, his many letters kept him in contact with many of the great Christians of his day (*Augustine, *Ambrose, Martin of Tours, Sulpicius Severus). His letters also describe his *ascetic views. He is best known for his poetry, much of it in honor of Felix.

PAULINUS OF PELLA (376–ca. 460)

A Gaul by descent and grandson of *Ausonius, he was born and lived in Macedonia; his family returned to Gaul where he lived for years with his wife; the barbarian invasions and the resultant disorders deprived him of much of his property; he retired to Marseilles for some years after 422; he returned to Macedonia to die. He wrote a poetic autobiography in which he considers all that happened to him in the light of divine Providence; the book gives a valuable account of life in the Western provinces during the barbarian invasions.

PAULINUS OF PERIGUEUX (fl. ca. 470)

Author of a verse *vita and some poems on *Martin of Tours; the contents are borrowed from the works of *Sulpicius Severus.

PAUL OF SAMOSATA (fl. ca. 265–275)

Procurator of either the Syrian or the Roman province of Commagene (scholars debate this point), treasurer for Zenobia, queen of Palmyra, a small state in southern Syria, and *bishop of Antioch from 260; between 264 and 268 he was deposed by three local church *councils for teaching a *Monarchian *Christology, although Zenobia was able to prevent his deposition. When she fell from power in 272, the Christians in Antioch appealed to the Roman emperor Aurelian (270–275) to get the local Church property, which Paul had managed to keep. Paul's career after 272 is unknown, although a group called Paulicians kept his name and theology alive; they were condemned at the Council of *Nicea in 325. Ironically, the term *homoousios, the Nicene touchstone of orthodoxy, was also used by Paul of Samosata in his Christology, albeit in a different sense; this does, however, indicate how vulnerable Greek theological terms were to misunderstanding.

PAUL OF THEBES (d. ca. 340)

According to *Jerome, Paul was the first great Egyptian monk, antedating *Antony; the existence of Paul is known only from Jerome's *vita of him, and both ancient and modern scholars have doubted Paul's existence.

PELAGIANISM; PELAGIAN CONTROVERSY

The teaching of *Pelagius and his followers, particularly *Celestius and *Julian of Eclanum. Pelagius initially reacted against current fatalist teachings such as those of the *Manichees, and he argued that people could be saved by their own free will if they had the necessary self-discipline. He did not deny the salvific influence of divine grace, but he believed that humans could move toward the good and accept the grace on their own, although he seems to have allowed for human perfectibility via the discipline of the will alone. Celestius, however, pushed this to its logical conclusion, suggesting that if one could be saved by disciplining the will, then divine grace, especially that given by *baptism, was not absolutely necessary. He also rejected the common teaching that original sin was passed along to all and that it corrupted human nature. *Augustine, who at first admired Pelagius personally, realized that this meant a denial of the universal human responsibility resulting from the sin of Adam and Eve and thus a denial of the need for divine grace. By 412 Augustine was preaching against the teaching of Pelagius and was heading rapidly into a rigid *predestinationism. Pelagius realized that Augustine's theology meant a denial of human freedom and a frightful picture of a God who saved whom he would and damned the rest. The gap was too wide to be breached, and Pelagius generally refrained from the fray. Celestius, however, tried to prove his orthodoxy but was not successful, and both he and Pelagius were condemned by African and Roman *councils as well as by the Christian Roman emperor Honorius in 416. Celestius continued to strive for recognition and convinced Pope *Zosimus to reopen his case in 418, but African pressure soon put an end to that. Celestius tried in 429 to get a sympathethic hearing from *Nestorius of Constantinople, but the First Council of *Ephesus in 431 condemned them both. The Italian bishop Julian of Eclanum continued the struggle, less for Pelagian teachings than against Augustinian predestinationism, but the Africans were too strong and Julian soon had to flee his see. The battle never really ended; in Gaul in the fifth century arose what scholars have rather misleadingly labeled *Semi-Pelagianism. Medieval admirers of Augustine tried to soften the rigidity of his teaching, but the early Protestant Reformers enthusiastically supported his predestinationism; in general, modern Christian denominations have abandoned it, although they have equally avoided the Pelagian emphasis on the possibility of human perfectability without divine grace.

PELAGIUS (ca. 354–ca. 420)

A Briton by birth, he migrated to Rome, where he became a spiritual advisor to wealthy families; in 410, when the Goths took Rome, he fled with his friends to Africa, where his disciple *Celestius soon got into trouble with his teaching; Pelagius escaped censure and went to Palestine; in 415 he found himself accused of *heresy by *Jerome and his friends and also by the Spanish *priest *Orosius, whom *Augustine had sent to Palestine. Pelagius, who may have known Greek, ably defended himself at a diocesan synod in Jerusalem and at a provincial synod in Diospolis; he even succeeded in putting Orosius on the defensive. But the African *bishops were firmly against him, and they got Pope *Innocent I to go along with them in condemning Pelagius and Celestius in 416. Pope *Zosimus (417–418) was willing to reopen the case, but the Africans bullied him into repeating Innocent's condemnation; the Africans also succeeded in getting the emperor Honorius (395–423) to condemn them as well. Pelagius disappears from history after 418; later sources suggest he returned to Britain. His writings consist of a very important and learned commentary on the Pauline epistles, some moral treatises, and several letters. Augustine and some of his other opponents have quoted him in their own works, but there is no way to check the accuracy of their citations. For his teaching, *see* **Pelagianism.**

PELAGIUS I (d. 561)

Pope from 556; a wealthy Roman and a *deacon, he accompanied Pope *Agapetus to Constantinople, where he got to know the emperor *Justinian I (527–565); Pelagius worked with Pope *Vigilius and was in charge of Rome during the pope's absence when the Gothic king Totila besieged the city in 546. Pelagius energetically cared for the slowly starving population and, knowing the city would fall, convinced Totila to spare most of the population. Totila sent him to Constantinople to negotiate with Justinian in 547. While there he took the side of Vigilius on the question of the *Three Chapters, even to the point of sharing the pope's privations; but when Vigilius abandoned the cause, Pelagius abandoned him and even wrote a defense of the Three Chapters. When the Second Council of *Constantinople condemned the Three Chapters in 553, Pelagius abruptly joined in the condemnation, possibly because he accepted the teaching of an *ecumenical council and possibly because he knew his old friend Justinian would make him the next pope. His confidence was vindicated; the emperor secured his election, although Pelagius could not find three *bishops to consecrate him—he had to settle for two bishops and a *priest representing the bishop of Ostia. The Roman clergy and people shunned him, and he was forced into the humiliating and un-heard of situation of proving his orthodoxy, a complete reversal of the papal attitude of declaring that what was taught by Rome was orthodoxy and other Christians had to prove their orthodoxy to the pope. His efforts failed; the northern Italian bishops went into *schism, and the Gauls ignored him. A man with an outstanding career behind him did little as pope.

PELAGIUS II (d. 590)

Pope from 579; a Goth by race but a Roman in his upbringing; he was elected pope during a Lombard siege of Rome, and this event set the tone for his pontificate. He sent the *deacon *Gregory (later Pope Gregory the Great) to Constantinople to ask for imperial aid against the Lombards, but all Gregory's efforts came to naught. Pelagius also appealed to the Franks, but likewise to no avail. Not until 585 was a truce effected with the Lombards. Freed from the immediacy of the threat, Pelagius attempted to get the northern Italian *bishops back into communion and thus end the *schism caused by the affair of the *Three Chapters and by the questionable roles of popes *Vigilius and *Pelagius I in the affair, but the northern Italians would not budge. Pelagius could take some pleasure in the conversion of the Spanish Visigoths under their king, *Recared, but he also became embroiled in a dispute with the bishop of Constantinople over that bishop's use of the title "ecumenical patriarch," which the pope felt was reserved for the bishop of Rome, proof that Roman concerns about primacy, which soured relations with the Byzantines, transcended any concern about the Lombard threat, which only the Byzantines could counter. Pelagius was an energetic man who tried to restore the city of Rome, so damaged by the barbarian invasions of the sixth century, but he succumbed to the plague that infested Rome in 590.

PENANCE

One of the four *sacraments of the early Church; penance was the rite of reconciliation and forgiveness; in the earliest communities, *baptism was the penitential sacrament; the *Shepherd of *Hermas* in the mid-second century is the first real reference to a postbaptismal rite of forgiveness; rigorists like *Tertullian and *Novatian thought that some sins committed after baptism, such as apostasy, could not be forgiven, but Pope *Callistus (217–222) was willing to extend forgiveness to acts previously thought beyond it. The Council of *Nicea took a middle course, affirming deathbed penance for recidivists. By the fourth century, penance's sacramental character was widely held, for example, by *Athanasius, who compared its efficacy to that of baptism; this view was universally held in the fifth century. The act of penance was called *exomologesis,* and it was public and liturgical; strangely, it was more rigorous in the usually more tolerant East than in the usually more juridical West; both involved exclusion from the liturgy or at least from the complete liturgy, but the Western rite usually took about a year while the Eastern one could go on for several years. Private and repeatable confession awaited the coming of the Irish monks, who brought the *monastic practice of a novice's confessing faults to a senior (for spiritual correction, not for sacramental penance) into the rite of penance.

PENITENTIAL

A book containing a list of sins and penances appropriate to those sins; these arose in Celtic circles, mostly Irish, and they spread to the continent with the Irish monks; they fit in well with the practice of private confession and soon became enormously popular, eclipsing the older penitential system.

PERPETUA, VIBIA (d. 203)

An African noblewoman and convert to Christianity, she and her slave *Felicity are the heroines of the *Passion of Saints Perpetua and Felicity,* an important Latin document of the early third century; Perpetua was the mother of a young son, and some of the most moving scenes in the *Passion* are between her and other members of her family as she tries to convince her father why she must die and arranges for the care of her son. She had several visions while in prison, and they reflect the typical African emphasis on the importance of *martyrdom and of the presence of the Holy Spirit over institutional affiliations. The *Passion* shows strong *Montanist influences, indicating the strength of this movement among Carthaginian Christians around 200, although there is no reason to believe that Perpetua herself was a Montanist.

PERSECUTION

An attack on the Christian religion by representatives of the Roman state; the term can cover a variety of topics, including plain mob violence, although it usually is reserved for conscious, legalized action. Nero (54–68) was the first Roman emperor to persecute the Christians, blaming them (as the pagan historian Tacitus says) for the fire of 64, which burned much of Rome; other emperors either did not persecute or did so sporadically until the time of Decius, who in 250 launched the first empire-wide persecution, which ended with his death in 251. There was one more persecution in the third century, that of Valerian in 257–259, which took the life of *Cyprian of Carthage. In 303 Diocletian began what historians have called the Great Persecution because of its extent, time (two years), and number of victims. This ended in 305, and although there were several persecutions in the early fourth century, none threatened the survival of Christianity. Ironically, after the empire became Christian, some emperors persecuted *heretics and *schismatics; also, some Christians were persecuted in Persia in the fourth century, apparently because they were thought to be sympathetic to Persia's ancient enemy, the (now Christian) Roman Empire.

PESHITTA

The Syriac translation of the Bible, completed in the fifth century, although begun most likely in the second century; possibly the Old Testament sections were begun by Jews, since those books were translated from the Hebrew; noncanonical books, often accepted by Christians, were translated from the Greek. The New Testament translation, at least in its final form, was the work of *Rabbula of Edessa, while the Old Testament may derive from older Jewish translations. The New Testament did not include 2 Peter, 2–3 John, Jude, or Revelation, although in later centuries they gradually came to be accepted.

PETER, ACTS OF

Second-century *apocryphon of Eastern origin, it recounts Peter's adventures in Rome, including a contest with *Simon Magus, his vision of the Lord (the *Quo Vadis* vision), and his crucifixion upside down. The work has a strong narrative quality and no apparent theological ax to grind, which probably explains its considerable popularity.

PETER, APOCALYPSE OF

Second-century work purporting to give Peter's vivid vision of heaven and hell; it was thought by both *Clement of Alexandria and the author of the *Muratorian Fragment to be a candidate for the canon, and *Methodius of Olympus in the fourth century considered it inspired; its teaching was basically moral with an emphasis on sternness; it does not reflect the theology of a particular sect. The complete text survives in Ethiopic, with fragments from other languages.

PETER, GOSPEL OF

Second-century *Docetic work of Syrian origin, which *Serapion of Antioch (ca. 190) says was used liturgically in Asia Minor; it tends to exculpate the Romans and to blame the Jews for Jesus' death.

PETER, PREACHING OF

Second-century treatise that proclaims the superiority of Christianity to paganism and Judaism but which also strongly criticizes Pauline theology; it is probably a *Gnostic work.

PETER CHRYSOLOGUS
(ca. 390–454)

*Bishop of Ravenna from around 428; little is known of his life; *Eutyches appealed for help from him in his conflict with *Flavian of Constantinople, but Peter referred the matter to *Leo the Great and made a very deferential comment about Roman primacy in the process; Peter was a famous homilist, whose 176 homiles (not all of which may be authentic) paint a picture of the see of Ravenna at the end of the Western Roman Empire, especially of Peter's efforts to root out paganism.

PETER MONGOS (d. 490)

*Monophysite *bishop of Alexandria from 477; he was elected to succeed another Monophysite, but the emperor *Zeno (474–491) forced him to give up his see; Peter, however, agreed to help compose the emperor's *Henoticon, a formula for reuniting the Monophysites and *Chalcedonians; this diplomatic act enabled him to keep his see despite the suspicions of both groups in Alexandria; his nickname means "the Hoarse."

PETER OF ALEXANDRIA (d. 311)

*Bishop of Alexandria from 300; he survived the *persecution of Diocletian in 303; in another persecution in 306 he went into hiding; in his absence and taking advantage of his lenient treatment of the *lapsed, Melitius of Lycopolis occupied his see, thus initiating the *Melitian schism; Peter returned to his see to deal with this but was captured and decapitated during the persecution of the emperor Maximinus Daia in 311.

PETER THE FULLER (d. 488)

Monk of the *Acetemae in Constantinople and a fuller in the monastery, he had to leave because of his *Monophysite views. He became a confidant of the emperor *Zeno (474–491), who enabled him to become *bishop of Antioch in 470, although within months the *Chalcedonians drove him from his see; he returned in 475, was driven out and even imprisoned in 477, coming back for good in 482 when he agreed to support the *Henoticon, Zeno's formula for reunion between the Monophysites and Chalcedonians.

PETER THE IBERIAN (411–491)

Member of the Iberian royal house who emigrated to Palestine, where he became a *Monophysite *bishop; he significantly influenced *Severus of Antioch; his *vita by *Zacharias of Mytilene is a good picture of the rise of that movement in the sixth century.

PETROC (sixth century)

Also spelled Pedrog; the most famous of the saints of Cornwall; very little is known of him historically; tradition says that he was a *hermit who lived in harmony with nature and who had some contacts with prominent Welsh and Irish saints; his cult was extensive in Cornwall and, to an extent, in Devon and even Brittany.

PETRONILLA

Since the sixth century identified in tradition as the daughter of Saint Peter the Apostle; she was a historical personage who died as a *martyr in Rome; she is buried in the *catacomb of *Domitilla.

PHILEAS (d. ca. 307)

Egyptian *bishop *martyred at Alexandria; he wrote a letter to his Church while in prison, and *Eusebius of Caesarea has preserved the letter.

PHILIP, ACTS OF

Fifth-century *apocryphon that survives only in fragments; it depends upon older apocrypha such as the Acts of *Peter.

PHILIP, GOSPEL OF

*Gnostic treatise discovered at *Nag Hammadi; it may date to the second century; it is a wandering, speculative work with only occasional references to Christ and possibly a collection made from other writings.

PHILIP SIDETES (fl. 430–440)

Sometimes called Philip of Side; he was from Asia Minor but moved to Constantinople and became a friend and partisan of *John Chrysostom; he tried three times to become *patriarch of the city (426, 428, 431); fortunately for historians he failed and thus turned his energies to writing what he called *Christian History,* which chronicled the world from the Creation down to 426. Philip could not, however, concentrate on his theme and brought into the work astronomy, music theory, geography, and whatever else struck his fancy; much of Philip's history does not survive, but what does is of some value.

PHILIP THE ARAB (d. 249)

Roman emperor from 244, he is reported by *Eusebius of Caesarea to have been a Christian, which, if it were so, would make him the first Christian emperor. This does, however, appear unlikely, since in 247 Philip presided over the celebration of Rome's millennium with a pagan ceremony. Yet Philip was at least sympathetic to Christianity. He died fighting the emperor Decius (249–251), who was a vicious *persecutor of the Church.

PHILOCALIA

Literally, "the love of what is beautiful"; name given to a collection of excerpts from *Origen's writings made by *Basil of Caesarea and *Gregory of Nazianzus in 358; because later generations condemned and destroyed much of Origen's works (*see* **Origenist Controversy**), this collection preserves many passages from Origen not found elsewhere.

PHILOMENA

Formerly a saint of the Roman Catholic Church because of an inscription found in the *catacomb of Saint *Priscilla in Rome mentioning a Filumena; inside the tomb were the bones of a teenage girl; research, however, demonstrated that the bones were not those of the original burial; in 1960 the cult of Saint Philomena was quietly dropped.

PHILO OF ALEXANDRIA
(d. ca. 50)

Jewish scholar who favored *allegory as a means of interpreting the Bible; although a pious Jew and a spokesperson for his community on important civic matters (he once led an embassy to the emperor Gaius Caligula on behalf of the Alexandrian Jews), Philo was also much influenced by Hellenistic culture. With the Greeks, he thought that an anthropomorphic presentation of God was inaccurate, and he tried to interpret some biblical accounts, such as Genesis, in a way that preserved a sound Jewish interpretation but avoided the anthropomorphisms. In this he was influenced by the Greek scholars who had allegorized the Homeric epics, and he in turn influenced Alexandrian Christian scholars such as *Clement, *Origen, and *Cyril.

PHILOSTORGIUS (ca. 368–ca. 439)

From Asia Minor, went to Constantinople around 410; he was a layman and an *Arian, a follower of *Eunomius, and his *Church History,* which survives only in fragments, defends Arianism and gives accounts of some Arian figures otherwise ignored by *Nicene Church historians.

PHILOXENUS OF MABBUG
(ca. 440–523)

Syriac *Monophysite and *bishop of Mabbug from 485; he urged another Monophysite named Polycarp to produce a Syriac version of the New Testament, often called the Philoxenian version, which contained the New Testament books omitted by the *Peshitta; Philoxenus was also a theologian and an *ascetical writer; he suffered for his theological views, having been exiled in 519.

PHOCAS OF SINOPE

*Bishop from Asia Minor who was *martyred under the emperor Trajan (98–117). He soon became confused with Phocas the Gardener, who died in 303 and who was also confused with Phocas of Antioch; in any event, very little is known historically about any of them.

PHOEBADIUS (d. ca. 395)

Gallic *bishop and friend of *Hilary of Poitiers; he signed the formula of the Arianizing *Council of Rimini in 359 under pressure from the delegates of *Constantius II, but only with qualifications that, he felt, vitiated its *Arian content; he was a strong opponent of Arianism and wrote a book against it, a book that reworked the *Trinitarian theology of *Tertullian to support the *Nicene tradition; little is known of his life.

PHOTINUS OF LYONS (d. 177)

Sometimes spelled Pothinus; *bishop of Lyons, *martyred in a severe local *persecution, and succeeded by *Irenaeus.

PHOTINUS OF SIRMIUM (fl. ca. 340–360)

Pupil and disciple of *Marcellus of Ancyra and a *Sabellian in his theology; he was a *bishop in the Balkans but lost his see; at the First Council of *Constantinople he and a group known as Photinians were condemned.

PIERIUS OF ALEXANDRIA (d. ca. 310)

Head of the *catechetical school of Alexandria from about 281; well educated and dedicated to poverty, he was so highly thought of that the Alexandrians called him *Origen Junior; he suffered during the *persecution of the emperor Diocletian (303–305) and went to Rome after the persecution, where he died; he was a famous exegete and also a homilist; fragments of his work survive.

PILATE, ACTS OF

*Apocryphon of the fourth century, it purports to give an account of Christ's trial, execution, and resurrection; some *manuscripts of the work also include an account of Christ's liberation of the souls of the good people who died before his coming—this section of the work was often printed separately and is known in English as the *Harrowing of Hell;* when the two sections are found in one work, it is usually called the *Gospel According to* *Nicodemus; this was an enormously popular work and one that exercised great influence on Christian art and legend.

PIONIUS (d. 250)

*Martyr from Smyrna in Asia Minor during the *persecution of the emperor Decius (250–251); around 300 someone wrote an account of his martyrdom replete with lengthy speeches by him to his fellow prisoners; in spite of this, many scholars think this vivid account may preserve a contemporary account of a Decian martyrdom. Pionius himself is credited with preserving, although not writing, the account of another martyrdom, that of *Polycarp of Smyrna.

PISTIS SOPHIA

Literally, "faith wisdom"; a *Gnostic work of the third century, it contains the instructions Jesus gave to his disciples, especially John and Mary Magdalene, at the end of his stay on earth after the resurrection—a stay that now lasts twelve years!—and an account of the fall of Pistis Sophia, a heavenly being hounded by a demon; it emphasizes *ascetic values.

PIUS I (d. ca. 155)

Pope from around 142; he has a Latin name, but the *Muratorian Fragment says that he was the brother of *Hermas, author of the visionary *Shepherd,* and that name is Greek; Hermas, however, says that he was a slave, and owners were allowed to give their slaves any names they chose; more importantly, scholars consider the *Shepherd of Hermas* to be a Jewish Christian work, which means that if the tradition of the Muratorian Fragment is correct, Pius was Jewish, continuing proof of Jewish influence in the Roman community. Little is known of his episcopate, although he presumably presided over the synod that expelled *Marcion of Pontus around 144; various sources say that during Pius' episcopate the *Gnostic teachers *Cerdo and *Valentinus were in Rome, as was *Justin Martyr and, of course, Marcion, so clearly Rome was a major center of Christian intellectual ferment, although there is no way to determine Pius' contribution to that.

PNEUMATOMACHI

Literally, "the fighters against the spirit"; a name given to those Greek theologians who denied the divinity of the Holy Spirit; they appeared—and were condemned—at the First Council of *Constantinople in 381 for denying that the Spirit was *homoousios with the Father and Son; several fifth-century writers claimed their founder was Macedonius of Constantinople (d. 362), so they are also called *Macedonians.

POLYCARP OF SMYRNA
(d. ca. 156)

*Bishop of Smyrna in Asia Minor; *Irenaeus says that he sat at the feet of the Apostle John; Polycarp received a letter from *Ignatius of Antioch; he visited Rome, where he met with Pope *Anicetus about the *Quartodeciman controversy; he wrote a letter to the Philippians; and he died a *martyr at age eighty-six by being burned at the stake. He was a vigorous opponent of the *Gnostics. The account of his martyrdom, written by *Marcion of Smyrna, is the first account of a Christian martyrdom outside the New Testament, although it is in the form of a letter to the Church of Philomelium in Phrygia. Polycarp's letter and the account of his martyrdom are two of the writings classified under the title "*Apostolic Fathers."

POLYCHRONIUS OF APAMEA
(d. ca. 430)

Brother of *Theodore of Mopsuestia and *bishop of Apamea in Syria; he wrote several commentaries on the Old Testament in which he avoided *allegorical exegesis in favor of a rationalizing approach.

POLYCRATES OF EPHESUS
(fl. ca. 190)

He is known from only one event, preserved by *Eusebius of Caesarea; as the *Quartodeciman controversy worsened, *Victor of Rome insisted that all Churches follow Rome and observe Easter always on a Sunday, so Polycrates called a synod of Asian *bishops, who defended their method of reckoning the date on the grounds of a tradition deriving from the apostles Philip and John; this caused Victor to break off communion with them.

POMERIUS, JULIUS (d. ca. 500)

African *priest who migrated to Gaul and wrote a book for clerics entitled *On the Contemplative Life,* an indication that the Gallic tradition of introducing *monastic values into clerical life continued into the sixth century, although the third part of the book was ostensibly for all Christians.

PONTIAN (d. 236)

Pope from 230; a Roman about whom little is known; he presided over a Roman synod that confirmed *Demetrius of Alexandria's condemnation of *Origen, and he had to deal with the continuing *schism of *Hippolytus. The *persecuting emperor Maximinus (235–238) exiled Pontian and the *antipope to the mines in Sardinia, where the two became reconciled before their death; realizing that he would not return from what the Romans called "the island of death," Pontian resigned, the first pope to do so, and he very probably outlived his immediate successor, *Anterus. Pope *Fabian arranged for the bodies of both Pontian and Hippolytus to be returned to Rome for a decent burial in 236 or 237.

PONTIUS (fl. ca. 260)

According to tradition, a *deacon of the Church of Carthage and author of a *vita of *Cyprian.

POSSIDIUS OF CALAMA (ca. 365–ca. 440)

Converted pagan who joined *Augustine's community in Hippo around 391; at Augstine's recommendation he became *bishop of Calama, where he followed his great friend's lead in attacking the *Donatists; when the barbarian Vandals invaded Africa in 428, he fled to Hippo, where in 430 he witnessed Augustine's death; he returned to his see in 431, but in 437 the *Arian Vandals, who now ruled the area, drove him out; nothing of his life is known after that; his one literary work is a biography of Augustine, and it is a very valuable one, having been written by someone who knew him intimately for forty years and had spent several years in the same community. Presuming that his readers know Augustine's *Confessions,* that is, the account of his early life, Possidius deals largely with Augustine the bishop.

POTAMIUS OF LISBON (d. ca. 360)

Originally a friend of *Hosius of Cordova, by 357 he had become a leading Western *Arian, even to the point of helping to compose Arian *creeds such as the one at *Sirmium in 357, although he later abandoned Arianism; his four surviving brief works are divided into two doctrinal ones and two homiletic ones; he is the first known *bishop of Lisbon.

PRAEDESTINATUS

A book written during the pontificate of *Sixtus III (432–440); it reproduces sections of *Augustine's book on *heresies and then criticizes his *predestinationism.

PRAXEAS

*Patripassian theologian known only from *Tertullian's attack upon him; apparently from Asia Minor, he had moved to Rome.

PRAXEDES

Second- or even first-century Roman woman who is buried in the *catacomb of *Priscilla; the written material about her makes her a virgin and *martyr and a relative of *Pudentiana.

PREDESTINATION; PREDESTINATIONISM

The belief that God, in his unfathomable wisdom, has chosen a certain number of people for eternal salvation. This was a centerpiece of the theology of *Augustine, who argued that although God willed to save all people, sinners chose to sin and thus needed grace for salvation. God gave saving grace to some but not to all; this is not unjust, since God cannot be unjust. Christians must accept that they cannot understand God's ways in this. This view was opposed by *Pelagius, *Julian of Eclanum, and their followers, who felt it corrupted the freedom of the will.

PRESBYTEROS; PRESBYTEROI

Greek for "elder," from which the English word "priest" comes; there is no scholarly consensus on the exact functions of presbyteroi in the early Church, although by the mid-second century they had emerged as a distinct group from the *episkopoi and *diakonoi. They were subject to the episkopos (bishop) and performed liturgical functions, although as Christianity grew in both population and geographical range, the presbyteroi took on many of the functions of the bishops, such as heading local Churches.

PRIEST

See Presbyteros.

PRIMASIUS OF HADRUMENTUM (d. ca. 555)

African *bishop who, unlike most of his colleagues, accepted the condemnation of the *Three Chapters. He wrote a commentary on the Apocalypse, which borrowed from the important work on that book by *Tyconius the *Donatist but which included much of his own theology. The commentary was influential in the Middle Ages.

PRIMATE

Literally, "the first bishop"; title given to the chief *bishop of a province, similar to a *metropolitan or a *patriarch.

PRISCILLA

A *Montanist prophet, one of the two women who shared the leadership of the movement with Montanus; Priscilla is reported to have claimed that in a vision Christ appeared to her in the form of a woman; little is known about her.

PRISCILLIAN OF AVILA (d. 386)

Spanish layman who, according to *Sulpicius Severus (the only source), taught a rigorous *asceticism and possibly practiced sorcery; he preached and won over two *bishops to his cause, but most of the Spanish hierarchy opposed him and condemned his teaching at a synod in 380; the two bishops who supported him promptly consecrated Priscillian as bishop of Avila. His enemies next got the emperor Gratian (375–383) to condemn his teaching, and Priscillian and his followers had to leave Spain, migrating first to Gaul, where he won over a wealthy woman named Euchrozia. Next, all journeyed to Italy, where *Damasus I and *Ambrose refused to meet with them, although they were able to get the imperial court to annul Gratian's decree. But in 384, when the usurping emperor, Maximus, who had murdered Gratian in 383, wanted to look like a supporter of orthodoxy, he had Priscillian put on trial for sorcery, a capital crime. *Martin of Tours intervened to stop the trial, but Maximus pushed on. Priscillian, Euchrozia, and some others were decapitated, while others of his followers were sent into exile. This was the first time a Christian had been executed for *heresy, and it produced a belated protest from many Church leaders, including Ambrose. The two Spanish bishops who had led the attack on Priscillian both lost their sees, one by deposition and the other by resignation to avoid deposition. Priscillian was widely regarded as a holy man, and his cult grew immediately in Spain. *Leo the Great had to condemn it in 447, and the Spanish *council of Braga repeated the condemnation in 563 but with mixed success. Scholars have debated how much of later Latin literature is of Priscillianist origin.

PROBA, FALCONIA
(fl. ca. 350–360)

Roman noblewoman who wrote a biblical cento, that is, a new poetic work made by taking complete or half lines from another, a widely recognized literary device of the day; its 694 lines dealt with the Creation story down to the Flood and then with Jesus' redemptive activity; it was a popular text in Christian schools.

PROCLUS OF CONSTANTINOPLE
(d. 446)

Appointed *bishop of the Asian city of Cyzicus, across the water from Constantinople, he could not occupy his see because of ecclesiastical factionalism; he stayed in Constantinople and became, in 429, one of the earliest opponents of the bishop *Nestorius. He was appointed bishop of Constantinople in 434; in 437, with the assistance of the empress *Pulcheria, he brought the bones of *John Chrysostom back to the city. In that same year, he sent his *Tome,* a statement of doctrine relying upon *Cyril of Alexandria's teachings, to the Christians of Armenia, and he introduced the *Trisagion into the liturgy of Constantinople. His extant writings include a few homilies and a *Christological treatise against *Theodore of Mopsuestia, the second of his seven letters.

PROCOPIUS OF CAESAREA
(fl. 520–560)

Palestinian layman, he accompanied *Justinian's general, Belisarius, on his conquest of Italy; from 542 he lived in Constantinople, where he wrote a history of the Byzantine reconquest of the West, an account of Justinian's building projects, including the great churches of the capital, and an account of the private lives of Justinian and *Theodora.

PROCOPIUS OF GAZA
(ca. 470–ca. 538)

A rhetorician and an exegete who compiled his work from the writings of earlier Eastern exegetes; his writings were largely on the Old Testament, especially its first eight books; more than 150 of his letters survive.

PROSPER OF AQUITAINE
(ca. 390–455)

Gallic layman who went to Marseilles and became acquainted with the *Lérins circle; in 426 he entered the *Semi-Pelagian controversy on the side of *Augustine, with whom he was in contact; he attacked *Vincent of Lérins and John *Cassian, and after Augustine's death, he went to Rome to get Semi-Pelagianism condemned but found that Pope *Celestine I was not anxious to make the controversy worse. Prosper returned to Marseilles and kept up the attack until the death of Cassian around 435, when Prosper abandoned the fight and moved to Rome, where he served *Leo the Great and may have aided him in writing the *Tome; he was a productive writer of theology, poems, letters, and a brief history of the world, which repeats much from earlier works, such as those of *Eusebius of Caesarea and *Jerome, but which gives valuable information for the Gallic Church in the fifth century.

PROTASIUS

See Gervasius and Protasius.

PROTOEVANGELIUM OF JAMES

See James.

PRUDENTIUS (348–d. after 405)

Aurelius Prudentius Clemens was a Spanish layman who began his career as a lawyer but soon turned to government, a field in which he enjoyed conspicuous success until, moved by his conscience, he abandoned public life and dedicated himself to writing Christian poetry. His poems included theological topics, hymns, *allegories, antipagan polemic, and spiritual themes. His most important work was the Psychomachia (literally, the battle for the soul [between vices and virtues]); it was widely used in the Middle Ages not just by poets but also by spiritual writers. Another poem, Peristephanon, contains fourteen hymns in honor of Christian *martyrs, mostly Spanish; many hymns and several lesser poems survive.

PSEUDO

Greek for "false," it is often attached to writings of unknown authors who were at one time thought to be Church *Fathers, for example, Pseudo-Justin; at times this can be almost as confusing as the original mistake, for example, at least seven authors are known as Pseudo-Jerome. Some great authors fall into this category, such as *Dionysius the Pseudo-Areopagite; the name is also applied to some literary works, such as the Pseudo-*Clementine Recognitions.

PTOLEMY

Italian *Gnostic teacher of the second century; pupil of *Valentinus; his *Letter to Flora* is a good example of Gnostic biblical exegesis; its use of literary analysis in regard to the Mosaic Law, concluding that more than one person composed it, was well in advance of its time.

PUDENTIANA

According to tradition, she was a first- or second-century Roman *martyr, although she is not mentioned in any ancient source but rather in medieval ones. Scholars believe that the Church of Saint Pudentiana takes its name from the house of a Christian senator named Pudens, the adjectival form of whose name would have produced Ecclesia (church) Pudentiana. The latter word, if it were a proper name, would be female, and this gave rise to the legend of Saint Pudentiana.

PULCHERIA (399–453)

Daughter of the emperor Arcadius (395–408) and elder sister of *Theodosius II (408–450), she was a devout woman who was responsible for overseeing her younger brother's activities, at least until his marriage to *Eudoxia in 421; she was less of an influence upon him after that, although she did convince him to condemn *Nestorius in 428. In 437 she arranged to have the bones of *John Chrysostom returned to Constantinople, thus bringing some religious peace to the capital. She was an early opponent of the teaching of *Eutyches, but her brother favored it; when it triumphed at the First Council of *Ephesus in 449, she looked to Rome for support, but in 450 her brother was thrown from a horse and died, and she became empress. Fearful that Roman society and politics would not permit a woman to govern alone, she married Marcian, an elderly senator, and together they called the Council of *Chalcedon in 451, at which Eutyches' theology was rejected. She is venerated as a saint in the East.

Q

QUADRATUS (fl. ca. 120–125)

The earliest Christian *apologist, he is known only from a passage from *Eusebius of Caesarea, who says that he composed an apology to the emperor Hadrian (117–138) early in his reign; this was the first defense of Christian teachings, which some scholars think to be identical with the *Letter to *Diognetus. Nothing is known of Quadratus' life.

QUARTODECIMAN CONTROVERSY

Literally, the "fourteenth-day" controversy; this refers to a conflict in the second-century Church as to whether Christians should follow the Jewish Christian reckoning for Easter, that is, on the fourteenth day of the month of Nisan; or whether it should be kept on the first Sunday after that day. Rome and many other Churches favored Sunday as a recognition of the newness of Christianity, but in Asia Minor many favored the Jewish Christian method. *Polycarp of Smyrna, during a visit to Rome around 155, met with Pope *Anicetus, and they agreed to disagree, but around 189 Pope *Victor I insisted that the Asians, represented in the dispute by *Polycrates of Ephesus, follow his practice, and he excommunicated them when they did not. The Asian Churches continued their practice for some time; those that did not conform eventually went into *schism. Although Victor's action brought in an unfortunate note of legalism, the controversy was a major one, since the date of Easter determined the entire liturgical year, and it was not settled until the Council of *Nicea in 325.

QUODVULTDEUS (d. ca. 454)

*Deacon in Carthage who in 428 asked *Augustine for a catalogue of *heresies in order to keep his own teaching inviolate; Augustine's reply was the treatise *On Heresies*. Quodvultdeus became *bishop of Carthage around 437 but had to flee from the Vandal king Gaiseric; Quodvultdeus went to Naples where he spent the rest of his life; his extant writings are homiletic in nature except for the treatise *The Book of God's Promises,* which deals with Old Testament passages that he thought pointed to Christ and the Church; two letters also survive.

R

RABBULA (d. 435)

Born a pagan, he became a Christian around 400, then an *ascetic, and finally *bishop of Edessa in Syria in 412. He supported the theology of *Cyril of Alexandria and was very anti-*Nestorian, a rarity for a Syrian bishop, and he attacked *Theodore of Mopsuestia, a leading *Antiochene theologian; he also attacked paganism and Judaism, destroying temples and at least one synagogue. According to a tradition, he translated the New Testament into Syriac, a translation called the *Peshitta, in order to weaken the popularity of the *Diatesseron of *Tatian, which was widely used in Syriac Churches.

RADEGUNDE (518–587)

A princess of the barbarian Thuringians, she was captured by the Franks and eventually consented to marry their king, Clotaire, in 536; when her violent and adulterous husband murdered her brother (ca. 550), she left him, became a *deaconess at Noyon, and eventually founded a monastery near Poitiers, where she spent the rest of her life.

RECARED (d. 601)

King of the Visigoths in Spain who converted from *Arianism to Catholic orthodoxy in 587, largely through the work of *Leander of Seville.

REGULA MAGISTRI

Latin for "Rule of the Master"; this is an Italian *monastic rule of the late fifth or early sixth century, and it is an important source for the *Rule* of Saint *Benedict of Nursia. The *Regula Magistri* is much longer and more detailed than Benedict's, and it is more theoretical in character, in contrast to the very practical Benedictine *Rule*.

RELIC

A physical object associated with some holy person; it can be an actual part of the person's body or some object such as clothing; relics became popular in Christianity in the fourth century, although the practice of preserving remains is known at least from the time of the *martyrdom of *Polycarp of Smyrna in the mid-second century; relics were believed to pass on spiritual power and were enormously popular, although easily subject to abuse, for example, fraudulent relics were routinely sold to the unsuspecting pious, or emphasis on the power of a relic diverted attention away from Scripture or the *sacraments. About 400 a Gallic writer named Vigilantius attacked the cult of relics in his Church, and this provoked *Jerome's defense of relics in his *Contra Vigiliantium*.

REMIGIUS (d. 533)

Also known as Remi; Gallic by birth, he evangelized the pagan Franks who had occupied his country; his crowning achievement came when, as *bishop of Rheims, he baptized the Frankish king *Clovis I in 496, largely because of the king's belief that Remigius' prayers had saved the king's son and aided his victory over his enemies, the Alemanni.

RETICIUS OF AUTUN (fl. ca. 330)

*Bishop and Latin biblical commentator whose works do not survive.

RHODON (fl. ca. 150–160)

Also spelled Rhodo; native of Asia Minor and disciple of *Tatian, he wrote against the *Gnostics and particularly against *Marcion of Pontus and his disciple *Apelles, whom he debated in person.

ROMANUS MELODUS (ca. 490–ca. 560)

Although a Syrian by birth, he became *deacon at the Church of the Resurrection in Constantinople, where he was said to have composed one thousand hymns; several dozen do survive, and they indicate clearly not only his great gifts but also his liturgical concerns, since their poetic meter was clearly aimed for a general congregation; Romanus was for centuries a major force in the Byzantine hymnody.

RUFINUS OF AQUILEIA (ca. 345–410)

Born in northern Italy, he became friends with *Jerome when both studied in Rome (359–368); from 368 to 373 he lived as a monk near Aquileia before going to Egypt (373–380) to live with the monks there and to study with *Didymus the Blind; in 381 he went with *Melania the Elder to Jerusalem, where he lived in a monastery on the Mount of Olives until 397, when he returned to Italy; he had to flee the Gothic invasion of the mainland in 407, and he eventually went to Sicily, where he died. While in Palestine, he sided with *Bishop *John of Jerusalem during the *Origenist controversy, which caused Jerome and him to break up their friendship. They renewed it just before Rufinus returned to Italy, but when he got to Italy he translated *Origen's great work, *On First Principles,* with a preface implying Jerome still admired the great Alexandrian; he also deleted some of Origen's statements, which he considered heretical and thus dangerous to Origen's reputation. This caused the conflict to heat up again, fanned by the unsavory tactics of Jerome's Roman contacts; Jerome wrote vicious attacks against Rufinus (who attempted to reply), and in 407 Pope *Innocent I almost condemned Rufinus for *heresy. *Augustine was one of many Christians who lamented to Jerome on the breakup of such a friendship, but the gap was too great to be bridged. Rufinus wrote some original works, including two *apologies during his controversy with Jerome and a commentary on the *Apostles' Creed, but his real contributions to early Christian theology and literature were his translations of many Greek writers, including Origen and *Eusebius of Caesarea, including the latter's *Ecclesiastical History,* a signficant boost to Latin learning.

RUFINUS THE SYRIAN

Disciple of *Jerome at Bethlehem, virtually nothing is known of him; he may be called ''the Syrian'' not because of the place of his birth but because of his time in the Holy Land. He carried letters of Jerome to Rome during the *Origenist controversy. He is the apparent author of a *Liber de fide* (a book of the faith), written about 411 and rather sympathetic to *Pelagian teachings, although this was before *Augustine, Jerome, and others began their denunciations of *Pelagius.

RUSTICUS (fl. 540–555)

Roman *deacon, nephew of Pope *Vigilius, and a strong opponent of *Justinian's attempt to condemn the *Three Chapters. When Uncle Vigilius followed Justinian's lead at the Second Council of *Constantinople in 553, Rusticus was deposed and excommunicated, but he found refuge in the monastery of the *Acemetae in Constantinople, where he maintained his opposition to the council. He also edited the acts of the councils of *Ephesus (of 431) and of *Chalcedon.

RUSTICUS HELPIDIUS (d. ca. 501)

Native of Gaul and correspondent of *Sidonius Apollinaris, he wrote some poems and epigrams, although he may also be identified with a Rusticus who was a correspondent of *Eucherius of Lyons, who died around 450—the chronological link, though awkward, is not impossible.

S

SABAS (439–532)

From Asia Minor, he was originally a hermit but in 478 founded a *lavra in Palestine; by 492 he was archimandrite of all Palestinian *eremites; he was a strong anti-Origenist and took part in the *Origenist controversies; his stand on behalf of the Council of *Chalcedon had considerable influence among the monks of Palestine.

SABELLIUS; SABELLIANISM

Little is known about Sabellius, who was a theologian active in Rome around 220; he taught a *Modalist *Monarchian theology, apparently with such success that this theology often bore his name; he may have been a Libyan.

SABINA

According to Roman tradition, an early second-century Roman noblewoman who was *martyred; the fifth-century Church of Santa Sabina in the city is named for her.

SACRAMENTS

Traditionally, seven outward signs instituted by Christ himself for the giving of grace; this is, in fact, a much later development; the earliest Church knew only two sacraments, *baptism and the *Eucharist, although *penance appeared rather early, possibly in the second century; *confirmation, as a separate sacrament, dates from the fourth century. There is no early Christian evidence for matrimony, holy orders, or extreme unction being considered sacraments.

SAHAK (ca. 350–439)

Name sometimes given as Isaac the Great; Armenian *bishop who was appointed *metropolitan or *catholicos* in 390; he won from the patriarch of Constantinople the independence of the Armenian Church from the bishop of Caesarea in Cappadocia; along with the scholar *Mesrob he translated the Old Testament into Armenian; he also furthered a nationalist literature.

SALONIUS OF GENEVA (fl. 439–455)

Son of *Eucherius of Lyons and correspondent of *Salvian, he was an active Gallic *bishop, but his only extant writing is a letter he wrote to Pope *Leo I with his brother Veranus and another bishop named Ceretius.

SALVIAN (ca. 400–ca. 475)

Son of a Christian family from either Trier or Cologne, he married a pagan, Palladia, who converted; they had a daughter, but shortly after both agreed to lead celibate lives; around 424 Salvian left his wife and went to the island monastery of *Lérins; by 429 he was a *priest at Marseilles. He was in the city during the barbarian invasions, a terror he had also experienced earlier in his life. In *De gubernatione Dei* (On the Governance of God), he writes movingly of the destruction the invasions caused, but he interprets these as God's judgment on a sinful Christian people, even to the point of favorably contrasting barbarian to Christian moral behavior, especially in the treatment of the poor. This work also provides important contemporary evidence of the administrative confusion and fiscal oppression that prevailed in Gaul at the time. *Gennadius of Marseilles says that Salvian was a prolific writer, but little else survives; a treatise *Ad Ecclesiam* warns about cupidity and recommends alsmgiving.

SAMSON OF DOL (d. 565)

Welsh monk famous for his piety, which attracted so many disciples that he constantly moved in order to live the *eremitic life; he lived first on the Severn River, then moved to Cornwall and finally to Brittany.

SARABITES

Name given by *Benedict of Nursia in his *Rule* to monks who wandered about with no fixed home.

SATORNIL

See **Saturninus.**

SATURNINUS (fl. ca. 150)

Name sometimes given as Satornil; *Gnostic teacher, probably a Syrian, a pupil of *Menander; he taught that the God of the Jews was the creator of the physical world but the supreme Deity sent a Savior to rescue the world from him; Saturninus' repugnance of the physical world extended to forbidding marriage and requiring vegetarianism of his followers.

SAYINGS OF JESUS

Term used by scholars to describe several fragmented *papyri from Oxyrhynchus in Egypt, which include short sayings attributed to Jesus; these sayings parallel some material in the canonical gospels but scholars now think that they are derived from the *Gnostic Gospel of *Thomas.

SCHISM

A break within the Church, usually over disciplinary matters, whereas *heresy usually involves doctrinal matters; the word appears as early as the second century; there were many schisms in early Christianity, such as those of *Novatian and the *Donatists.

SCHOLASTICA (fl. ca. 540–550)

According to *Gregory the Great's *vita of Saint *Benedict of Nursia, she was the saint's sister; she was mistress of a convent not far from her brother's monastery at Monte Cassino.

SCHOLIA

Brief, often marginal commentaries on a text; the Alexandrian exegetes prepared many scholia on the Bible.

SCILLITAN MARTYRS

Around 180, twelve Christians from the African town of Scilli became the first African *martyrs; an anonymous account survives about their trial. It shows how early was the African attitude of defiance to the state and the exaltation of martyrdom. This account also includes the first unabiguous reference to New Testament books in Latin translation.

SCRIPTORIUM

A room for scribes, that is, a place where *manuscripts were prepared.

SEBASTIAN

Roman *martyr during the *persecution of Diocletian (303–305); his martyrdom is authentic and is mentioned by the *Chronographer of 354, but the story, so popular in Christian art, that

he was shot to death with arrows is a later legend.

SECUNDUS (fl. late second century)

*Gnostic teacher, disciple of *Valentinus; little is known of him.

SEDULIUS (fl. 425–450)

Gallic or possibly Italian *priest; he was a famous Latin poet in his own day and widely cited throughout the Middle Ages; his great work, *Paschale Carmen,* written before 431, is a five-book work describing the mighty works of God in both the Old and New Testaments, although, for purposes of rhyme, he quotes the biblical text rather freely, engages in *allegory, and even cites *apocryphal works; he also wrote hymns on Christ.

SEMI-ARIANS

Literally, the nonsensical "half an *Arian," but actually a term created by scholars to describe those fourth-century theologians and *bishops who could not accept the decrees of the First Council of *Nicea about the Trinity but who could also not accept the radical Arian position of the Son of God as a creature; the Semi-Arians preferred terms like *homoios or *homoiousios to describe the relation of the Father and the Son.

SEMI-PELAGIANISM

An inaccurate, catchall term for the anti-*Augustinian movement, mostly in Gaul, to protest the African's extreme *predestinationism; the Semi-Pelagians accepted that grace was necessary for salvation, thus denying a central tenet of classical *Pelagianism, but they insisted that human beings can cooperate with the effects of grace by taking the initial steps toward salvation; since the initial steps would thus be good and since this would mean that humans could do something good without the aid of grace, the Augustinians opposed this. Many leading Semi-Pelagians were Gauls, such as *Cassian and *Vincent of Lérins; so were their opponents, such as *Prosper of Aquitaine and the *bishops at the Second Council of *Orange in 529, which condemned Semi-Pelagianism.

SENAN (d. ca. 544)

Irish monk and abbot; tradition makes him the founder of several important monasteries in the southwest of Ireland, particularly Scattery Island.

SENECA (ca. 4 B.C.–A.D. 65)

Pagan philosopher, tutor of Nero (54–68) and victim of the emperor's suspicions—Nero forced him to commit suicide; he was a leading Stoic whose ideas were congenial to many Christians, so much so that an *apocryphal correspondence between him and Saint Paul (Letters of Paul and Seneca) appeared in the third century, in which Seneca is so sympathetic to Christianity that *Jerome, in his book On Famous Men, ranks Seneca as a Christian.

SEPTUAGINT

Literally, "the work of the seventy," often abbreviated as LXX; this was a Greek translation of the Old Testament, apparently begun in Alexandria in the third century B.C.; tradition says that the translation was done by seventy scholars, hence the name; Jews outside Palestine considered the version to be inspired, as did many Christians; it was routine for the *Fathers to cite the Old Testament in this version, and many important *manuscripts of the Septuagint were prepared by Christian scribes.

SERAPION OF ANTIOCH (d. 211)

*Bishop of Antioch from about 190; his writings survive only in fragments, but even these are important; there is an anti-*Montanist letter and one to the Church of Rhossus in Asia Minor rescinding his earlier approval of the *apocryphal Gospel of *Peter.

SERAPION OF THMUIS
(d. after 362)

*Monastic abbot until 339, when he became *bishop of the Egyptian town of Thmuis; although few of his writings survive, his importance is unquestioned—he was an associate of *Antony, who mentioned Serapion in his will, and a correspondent of *Athanasius, who sent him on a diplomatic mission to the emperor *Constantius II (337–361); some letters and a treatise against the *Manicheans survive.

SETHIANS

*Gnostic sect claiming to honor the teachings of Seth, the third son of Adam and Eve (Gen 4:25); the Sethians had a very complicated cosmology with a divine triad consisting of Father, Mother, and Son, with Adam as a Primal Human, a struggle with lesser beings, the conflict between spirit and matter; accounts of the sect are confused, so that scholars cannot posit certain dates or places for the group, although its writings are well represented in the *Nag Hammadi find.

SEVEN SLEEPERS OF EPHESUS

According to sixth-century legend, seven Christians from Ephesus fled from the *persecution of Decius (250) by hiding in a cave; they fell into a miraculous sleep from which they awakened two centuries later when their city was Christian; this was a very popular story in the West, especially in the version of *Gregory of Tours.

SEVERIAN OF GABBALA
(d. ca. 410)

Homilist and opponent of *John Chrysostom at the Synod of the Oak; he was a strong *Nicene and a fighter against *heresy; he wrote a commentary on the Pauline epistles and based many of his homilies on Genesis; he wrote in Greek, but his extant works appear in Greek, Ethiopic, Syriac, Armenian, Coptic, and Arabic, a tribute to their popularity.

SEVERINUS (d. 482)

An Easterner by birth, he worked in the area of modern Austria after the death of Attila the Hun in 453 and made it safe for Christians; he founded monasteries and did his best to ameliorate the sufferings of the victims of the barbarian invasions; what is known of him comes from his *vita by his friend *Eugippius, whose work tells not only of the saint but also of Roman provincial life during the barbarian invasions.

SEVERUS OF ANTIOCH
(ca. 466–538)

*Monophysite leader and molder of much of the Monophysite theology; after study in Alexandria and a career as a monk, in 508 he convinced the emperor Anastasius (491–518) to cease the persecution of *Monophysite monks; in 512 Severus became *bishop of Antioch, a post he lost in 518 at the accession of the emperor Justin I (518–527); he fled to Alexandria, where Monophysitism was so strong that he was safe from the emperor; he tried, however, to reconcile himself in 532 to *Justinian, whose wife, *Theodora, was a Monophysite, but the reconciliation fell through and a *council at Constantinople in 536 condemned him. Severus was a busy man, strengthening the Monophysite Churches and sharpening Monophysite *Christology, and his huge extant *opera* include dogmatic treatises, liturgical treatises, 125 homilies, and more than 4,000 letters. The lasting success of Monophysitism in the East owed much to his spiritual authority and organizational ability.

SEXTUS, SENTENCES OF

A collection of moral sayings attributed to a pagan Pythagorean philosopher named Sextus; it was revised at the end of the second century by a Christian, possibly an Alexandrian, since *Origen is the first to mention these sayings; *Rufinus of Aquileia translated them into Latin and identified the author as Pope *Sixtus II. There is a mild *asceticism in the sayings as well as more Platonic ideas.

SHENOUTE (ca. 332–ca. 450)

Egyptian monk and abbot of the monastery of Atripe from 385; although he was addicted to strenuous corporal punishment, especially whipping, he was quite popular, and the population of his monastery grew considerably, probably because of his organizational abilities; he demanded his monks sign a written profession of obedience, something unique in its day; like many Egyptian monks, he strongly supported the *patriarch of Alexandria, in this case *Cyril, whom he accompanied to the First Council of *Ephesus in 431. He was also a bitter adversary to the surviving remnants of Egyptian paganism. He was a great monastic organizer, and his many letters are among the most important Christian documents in the Coptic language.

SIBYLLINE ORACLES

Sometimes called the Christian Sibyllines; this is a collection of oracles prepared by Jews and Christians in imitation of the famous pagan oracles; scholars think Jewish elements may date to the second century B.C., with most of the Christian additions dating to the second century A.D., although some are as late as the fourth century; they were edited probably in the fifth century. There were originally fifteen books but three (9, 10, 15) are now missing. The exact composition of the books is uncertain, that is, scholars cannot determine with finality how much Christians edited the Jewish sections; in general the books indict Rome for its many crimes and promise retribution, although the sixth book has a hymn to Christ and the eighth has the famous formula of the *fish as a symbol of Christ.

SIDONIUS APOLLINARIS (ca. 430–ca. 480)

Gallic nobleman and son-in-law of the Roman emperor Avitus (455–457); he was a famous poet who wrote much secular verse, including panegyrics to imperial statesman; thanks to his father-in-law, he became known in Rome and in 469 was appointed prefect of the city; in that same year, however, he was elected *bishop of Clermont, although he was still a layman. He reluctantly accepted the election, gave up writing poetry, and devoted himself to the welfare of his diocese, which was occupied in 475 by the Visigoths, and Sidonius was taken prisoner; he was released in 476 and returned to his diocese, where he made a collection of his many (147) letters, which provide a good picture of contemporary life.

SILVERIUS (d. 537)

Pope from 536; son of Pope *Hormisdas; only a subdeacon at the time, he was propelled into the papacy by the Gothic king, Theodahad. Silverius was less pro-Gothic than pro-peace with the Byzantines, but events were against him. His predecessor, *Agapitus, had antagonized the Byzantine empress, *Theodora, who plotted with the

Roman *deacon *Vigilius by promising him the papacy if he would go along with her wishes. When Vigilius arrived in Rome too late to be chosen pope, the Byzantine general Belisarius had Silverius arrested and condemned him for pro-Gothic sympathies; the pope was deposed and exiled to Asia Minor, where the local *bishop convinced the emperor *Justinian (527–565) that the pope deserved a fair trial; surprisingly, the emperor agreed and Silverius was returned to Rome for trial, but Vigilius, now pope, had him arrested and sent to a prison island, where he was forced to abdicate on November 11; he died less than a month later.

SILVESTER I (d. 335)

Pope from 314; name sometimes spelled Sylvester; first pope to live under a Christian emperor. In 314 at the request of *Constantine I, the *Donatist question was reopened at a *council in Arles in Gaul, a rebuke to the 313 Synod of *Miltiades; the *bishops, however, deferred to Rome and again condemned Donatism; significantly, Silvester was not at this council, and yet the council referred its decisions to him. Constantine accepted Rome's will in this matter and condemned the Donatists; he then showed his good will toward the pope by founding seven churches in Rome, including the Lateran Basilica and Saint Peter's in the Vatican, but this generosity was never matched by a concern for Rome's advice; indeed, in the great religious crisis of his reign, *Arianism, the emperor acted largely without the pope. Silvester declined to attend the First Council of *Nicea, sending two *priests to represent him, thus beginning on the *ecumenical level a process previously used on a regional one, that is, the popes kept themselves from active involvement in disputes while maintaining a decisive voice; it also kept the participants slightly off balance, since they could never be sure just what Rome would do. The two Roman priests, Vincent and Vitus, approved the decision of Nicea, as did Silvester. Nothing is known of his last ten years, although he presumably enforced Nicea in the West. Later legends about him were abundant, including his *baptism of Constantine, his conversion of the emperor's mother, *Helena, from Judaism by defeating Jewish magicians in a thaumaturgical contest, and the immuring of the Vestal Virgins' anthropophagous pet dragon in the Tarpeian Rock. A more important tradition, much used by medieval popes, was the so-called *Donation of Constantine,* a document claiming that the emperor had given to Silvester and his successors secular authority in the Western empire. In 762 Pope Paul I reburied either Silvester's whole body or just his head—the sources disagree—in the Church of San Silvestro in Capite (which seems to answer the question).

SIMEON STYLITES (ca. 390–459)

The first and most famous of the *stylite saints, that is, *hermits who sat on top of pillars of stone, sometimes for years; he began his religious life as a monk in Syria, near Antioch, became a hermit, and then, around 423, built himself a pillar, which he mounted one day and never came down; he stayed there praying. This caught the popular imagination; throngs came to see him and others imitated him; he was enormously influential and not just with the general populace—the emperor *Theodosius II (408–450) asked his help in mediating the break between Antioch and Alexandria following the First Council of *Ephesus. Simeon was a strong *Chalcedonian in his (probably rudimentary) theology, and his support helped the Chalcedonian cause in Syria.

SIMON MAGUS (d. ca. 70)

This mysterious person, a native of Samaria, appears in Acts 8:9-24, where he is practicing magic, becomes a Christian, and then offers to buy the Apostle Peter's power (thus providing the basis for the word "simony") but is rebuked. He then disappears from the New Testament but reappears in second- and third-century Christian writings as the founder of a *Gnostic sect, although a pre-Christian one; he apparently claimed divine power and also that his traveling companion, Helen, whom he had taken from a brothel, was the incarnation of a fallen spirit, whom he redeemed. He figures prominently in Christian legends, especially the *Clementine literature.

SIMPLICIANUS OF MILAN (d. 400)

Successor to *Ambrose as *bishop of Milan in 397; he was already famous for converting the Neoplatonic philosopher Marius *Victorinus around 360; he then became the tutor of Ambrose and even played a small role in the conversion of *Augustine, who addressed some of his books to him; ironically, his tenure as bishop is the least-known and least-significant part of his life.

SIMPLICIUS (d. 483)

Pope from 468; he was pope when the Roman Empire in the West ceased to be—in 476 a barbarian chieftain named Odoacer deposed the child emperor Romulus Augustulus (475–476) and informed the Eastern emperor *Zeno (474–491) that he would rule Italy as king with no more resident emperor. Since this event simply finalized what had been fact for some time, that is, barbarian rule in Italy, it probably did not produce much change in Church life. Simplicius was a vigorous upholder of papal authority in the West, and he appointed the *bishop of Seville to be papal vicar in Spain. As usual, the East was a different story. The *patriarch of Constantinople, *Acacius, wanted papal acceptance of canon twenty-eight of the Council of *Chalcedon, which gave Constantinople an equivalent status with Rome but which Simplicius refused to recognize. Acacius also sought, with the aid of the emperor Zeno, to placate the *Monophysites in hopes of restoring them to communion. Relations between Rome and Constantinople worsened, and in 482 the two Churches went into *schism.

SIRICIUS (d. 399)

Pope from 384; he was a long-time member of the Roman Church, having been a lector and then *deacon under *Liberius. Siricius took a dignified and businesslike approach to his task; offended by the excesses of the *ascetics, he was cool to them—*Jerome had to leave Rome and *Paulinus of Nola found himself unwelcome in the city. Siricius was not personally opposed to asceticism but wished the ascetics to realize they were in the Church, not above it. The pope condemned *Jovinian and others who denied Mary's perpetual virginity, but he avoided the *Trinitarian and *Christological theological questions that divided the East. He also avoided offending the Easterners by claims for Roman primacy, a disastrous policy, which his predecessor, *Damasus I, had pursued. For example, when two claimants to the see of Bostra in Arabia asked for his intervention, he told them to consult the much closer *bishop of Alexandria. From his pontificate come the first complete and genuine papal *decretals dealing with *sacraments, episcopal consecrations, and the rule of life for clerics; these show the growing authority of Rome, based upon Petrine claims, since Siricius was the first pope to claim not that he was speaking about some matter but that the still-present Saint Peter was speaking through him. The pope was most successful in Italy, Gaul, and Spain, less so in Africa, in extending his authority.

SIRMIUM

A *council called in 357 by the *Arian emperor *Constantius II; it propagated an extreme Arian formula and moved many *Semi-Arians to realize that they had little in common with the radicals; this council's *Christological formula is often known as the Blasphemy of Sirmium, an epithet given to it by *Hilary of Poitiers.

SIXTUS I (ca. 125)

Pope from around 116; Sixtus is known only by his name and that from a list preserved by *Irenaeus; indeed, his real name was probably the Greek *Xystus, since the foreign element in the Roman community was strong at this time.

SIXTUS II (d. 258)

Pope from 257; first pope to have the same name as one of his predecessors, although his name was probably the Greek *Xystus. He followed the turbulent *Stephen I, and it is clear that the Roman community wanted a different course from that of Stephen; where Stephen preferred confrontation, Sixtus preferred conciliation; he maintained the Roman stance against rebaptism but made peace with *Cyprian of Carthage; he also maintained good relations with *Dionysius of Alexandria, who wrote twice to the pope about the need for the churches to accept each other's customs in the face of the spreading *heresy of *modalism. In 257 the emperor Valerian began to *persecute the Christians; in the following year he made the Christians liable to execution without trial. Defying the emperor, Sixtus held a liturgy; when Roman troops appeared the pope realized that if he tried to escape, there would be a general massacre as the troops went after him;

this true pastor identified himself and was decapitated on the spot along with four of his *deacons.

SIXTUS III (d. 440)

Pope from 432; successor to the activist *Celestine I, whose correspondence to the First Council of *Ephesus he had helped to prepare, Sixtus worked to end the split between Antioch and Alexandria, which resulted from that council. He also worked to keep the *Pelagians in their place, denying the exiled *Julian of Eclanum permission to return to Italy; the pope also struggled to keep the *bishops in the northern Balkans, hitherto subject to Rome, from accepting the authority of Constantinople. In Rome itself, he tried to rebuild parts of the city damaged by the barbarian invasions.

SOCRATES (ca. 380–450)

Native of Constantinople, he received a good education from pagan teachers and became a lawyer; at the insistance of one Theodore, possibly a *priest, he decided to write a continuation of *Eusebius of Caesarea's *Church History* in seven books, from the abdication of the *persecuting emperor Diocletian (305) to the year 439. Although Socrates concentrated on Church history, he also included many secular events and much about the city of Constantinople; he used the earlier historians Eusebius and *Rufinus of Aquileia, although when he later found that the latter's history had many errors, he produced a second, corrected edition of his own work.

SOLOMON, ODES OF

The earliest Christian hymn book, a collection of forty-two hymns possibly dating to the first century but more likely to the second; they are Syriac in language, having originated in eastern Syria or Edessa, and Jewish Christian or even *Gnostic in character; they testify to the virgin birth of Jesus, the *Logos, and to the harrowing of hell; they are liturgical in character and some were used for the *baptismal rite.

SOLOMON, TESTAMENT OF

Third-century Jewish Christian work on angelology and demonology.

SOPHRONIUS OF JERUSALEM (ca. 560–638)

Native of Damascus, he became a monk, first in Egypt, then Palestine, and finally in Syria; he was a strong supporter of *Chalcedon, and this won him appointment as *patriarch of Jerusalem where, the year before his death, he had to endure the fall of the city to the Muslims.

SOTER (d. ca. 174)

Pope from about 166; little is known about his pontificate; he introduced Easter as an annual festival in Rome, following a date different from that of the Asians, thus reviving the *Quartodeciman controversy, although nothing bitter appears to have happened during his tenure; *Dionysius of Corinth wrote Soter a letter thanking the Roman Church for its generosity and mentioning an earlier letter to the Corinthians written by *Clement of

Rome, the chief means of identifying Clement as the author.

SOTERIOLOGY

Literally, "the theology of salvation"; this became an important consideration in the debates about Christ's humanity, with *Gregory of Nazianzus insisting that Christ had to have a full humanity in order to redeem us because "what had not been assumed [by Christ] could not be saved"; this principle was also used by other *Fathers.

SOZOMEN (d. after 450)

A native of Palestine and a layman, he went to Constantinople to practice law; between 439 and 450 he decided to write his *Church History* with an intent similar to that of *Socrates, that is, to continue the narrative of *Eusebius of Caesarea. He wrote a now nonextant epitome of world history to the year 323, then started his own account, which went down to 425. His work parallels that of Socrates, who tells more about the Church at this time, but, inevitably, he includes material Socrates does not, such as the history of Christianity among the Armenians and the Persians as well as information about early *monasticism; he also includes some legendary material.

SPYRIDON OF TREMITHUS (d. ca. 350)

Cypriote *bishop who, according to his *vita, suffered during the *persecution of Diocletian and attended the Council of *Nicea; it is historically

verified that he attended the Council of Sardica in 343; his vita contains many miraculous accounts of no historical value.

STATUTA ECCLESIAE ANTIQUA

Latin for "the ancient statutes of the Church"; once thought to be an ancient text, this collection of rites for ordination and rules for clerical behavior dates to the fifth century and is from Gaul.

STEPHEN I (d. 257)

Pope from 254; a Roman *priest who, resentful of the influence of *Cyprian of Carthage on the Roman Church, set out to break it. In 254 the two men skirmished over the deposition of two Spanish *bishops, with Cyprian supporting the deposition by the Spanish hierarchy and Stephen moving to restore the two—the outcome of the affair is unknown. In 255 Cyprian supported the efforts of Gallic bishops to depose Marcian of Arles, a supporter of *Novatian, but Stephen refused to get involved—again the outcome is unknown. The real struggle began in 256 over the rebaptism of *heretics and *schismatics. The Africans considered *baptism by those outside the Church, that is, heretics and schismatics, to be of no value, and so when converts from those sects came to the African Church they were rebaptized—or, as the Africans would have viewed it— baptized for the first time; the Roman tradition called for saying some prayers and laying on hands but no baptism. Cyprian called a *council in

256, which confirmed the African position, and he wrote to the pope to explain that; Stephen, however, upheld Roman tradition and claimed that, as the *primatial see of the West, the see of Peter and Paul, Rome would decide what others would do; he told the Africans to follow the Roman way. Cyprian called another council, received unanimous support for his position, and prepared for a break with Rome. For his part, Stephen refused to meet the African delegates, excommunicated the African episcopacy, and wrote to the Eastern bishops not to communicate with "the false prophet" Cyprian. He cited Roman tradition deriving from Peter and Paul. Cyprian, however, also wrote to the Easterners, particularly the Asians, who supported him, citing their own customs; Stephen excommunicated them, too. One of them, *Firmilian of Caesarea, remarked that Stephen was ready to excommunicate the rest of the Church. *Dionysius of Alexandria tried to intervene as a peacemaker, urging Stephen to respect the traditions of other sees and pointing out that there was no crisis until Stephen provoked it. The pope did stop short of excommunicating the bishops of the great sees of Alexandria, Antioch, and Jerusalem, but he did not retreat from his position. The flames of controversy were burning vigorously when Stephen died on August 2, 257. Regrettably, Stephen's actions are known primarily from the letters of Cyprian; scholars would clearly like to know much more about this early attempt to assert Roman jurisdiction over other Churches on the basis of Petrine and Pauline authority, especially since fourth-century popes dropped the Pauline emphasis.

STEPHEN GOBARUS
(fl. ca. 565–575)

*Monophysite theologian who followed the *Tritheism of *John Philoponus; he lived in either Syria or Egypt; some few fragments of his work survive.

STYLITE

From the Greek for "pillar," it refers to those *ascetics who, from the fifth to the tenth century, lived on top of pillars, where they prayed for the Church and tried to reconcile disputes, including theological ones, a rather dubious practice for those with no formal contact with current theology. Their disciples would provide them with food and would meet their sanitary needs; the most famous of these was *Simeon Stylites.

SUBINTRODUCTAE

Women who lived a spiritual marriage with men, that is, they did not consummate the marriage physically; it is known from the second century and survived into the early fifth; whatever merits the practice might have had, its blatant dangers were so significant that most *Fathers, especially *John Chrysostom, opposed it.

SUBORDINATIONISM

The belief that within the Trinity the Son is subordinate to the Father; this was a widespread and theologically respectable notion in the second and third centuries, but it died out in the fourth because of its obvious relation to *Arianism.

SULPICIUS SEVERUS
(ca. 360–ca. 425)

A Gallic nobleman, he married and planned a public career, but his wife's early death caused him to forgo his career and be *baptized; influenced by his longtime friend *Paulinus of Nola, Sulpicius lived the *ascetic life on his estate. The turning point of his life was his meeting with *Martin of Tours, whom he admired and to whose cult he devoted his literary life. Before Martin had even died (397), Sulpicius had written his masterpiece, the *Vita Martini, a brilliant propaganda piece that advanced the cause of *monasticism by popularizing this Eastern monk who had come to the West; Gallic bishops who had opposed Martin became in this book obscurantists (at best) who tried to deter the work of God's chosen one; the best-known passage, Martin's cutting his military cloak in two and giving half to a beggar, became a standard feature of medieval art. Sulpicius also wrote two dialogues and three letters, also about Martin, as well as a Chronicle, an account of world history down to the fifth century; much of it repeats the work of earlier writers, but its treatment of the *Priscillianist affair is particularly valuable, *Gennadius of Marseilles says that late in his life Sulpicius was duped by the *Pelagians, and, realizing this, led a life largely of silence until his death. Although not a great thinker, Sulpicius was a true literary artist whose Vita Martini was, after the Bible, the most popular Latin Christian book of the early Church.

SUSANNA

Roman *martyr who apparently died during the *persecution of Diocletian (303–305); traditionally, she was a noblewoman who refused to marry a pagan.

SYLVESTER

See Silvester.

SYMMACHUS (d. 514)

Pope from 498; a Sardinian pagan, he converted and became a Roman *deacon. The clergy who disagreed with the conciliatory policy of Pope *Anastasius II toward the Byzantines chose him, but there was a disputed election with the archpriest *Laurence, the candidate of the pro-Byzantine aristocracy. The effective ruler of Rome, Theodoric the Ostrogothic king, intervened and installed Symmachus; Laurence withdrew but his followers kept putting him forward; this problem occupied much of Symmachus' pontificate, especially from 502 to 506, when Laurence was able to rule in the Lateran as pope until Theodoric drove him from office. Symmachus combated *heresy vigorously, driving out the *Manicheans and opposing the *Arians, although without offending Theodoric too deeply; he also tried to improve the physical condition of Rome, especially that of Saint Peter's, so that he could work more effectively. Since Laurence was the candidate of the pro-Byzantine faction, Symmachus remained a staunch opponent of reconciliation with the Byzantines, a policy that finally induced the Byzantine emperor Anastasius (491–518) to give in and suggest a reconciliation *council, but Symmachus died before the offer reached him.

SYNESIUS OF CYRENE
(ca. 370–ca. 414)

Born a nobleman and possibly a pagan in Libya, he studied in Alexandria with the famous woman philosopher *Hypatia (who was murdered by a Christian mob in 415); in 399 he successfully represented Pentapolis in Libya before the emperor Arcadius (395–408) in Constantinople on a tax matter. He moved to Alexandria in 402, where he married a Christian woman, an indication of his own conversion; his civic sense had not diminished, and he labored on behalf of the citizens of Ptolemais, which had suffered from barbarian incursions, and in 410 the citizens chose him as their *bishop, although he had not yet been baptized. He agreed as long as he could keep his wife and continue to write philosophic works, conditions accepted by both the citizens and the *patriarch of Alexandria, who consecrated him. It was a worthwhile bargain because Synesius proved to be an effective bishop. He was generally a Neoplatonist in his philosophy, and his Christianity seems to have affected it little; he was also a courageous critic of the abuses of the imperial court.

SYZYGY

In *Gnostic teaching, a pair of opposites, often cosmological or metaphysical; the coming together of opposites was thought responsible for some aspects of creation; some Gnostic teachers put together tedious lists of these syzygies.

T

TALL BROTHERS

Name given to four brothers, Egyptian monks who supported *Origenism at the end of the fourth century, thus incurring the wrath of *Theophilus of Alexandria; in 399 they went to Constantinople via Alexandria to seek the help of the *patriarch of that city, *John Chrysostom, against Theophilus; John's reception of them provoked Theophilus' anger against him and was one of the factors that led to his eventual deposition. Their names were Ammonius, Dioscorus, Eusebius, and Euthymius.

TARSICIUS

According to tradition, a Roman *martyr of either the third or fourth century; Pope *Damasus I, who wrote verses about him, said he was carrying the *Eucharist to some Christians when a pagan mob accosted him, demanded to know what he was carrying, and stoned him to death when he refused to tell them; the tradition that he was an acolyte at the time has made him the patron saint of altar boys and now, presumably, of altar girls.

TATIAN (d. ca. 180)

A Syrian and a pagan by birth, he studied at first in the Eastern Mediterranean, next in Rome with *Justin Martyr and probably became a Christian there; he returned to the East around 172, where he founded the sect of the *Encratites, a strongly *ascetic group. Unlike Justin, Tatian loathed Greek culture, rejecting Greek philosophy out-of-hand as an aid to Christian theology; possibly his ascetic inclinations moved him to reject a culture so successful in understanding the material world. Only two of his works have survived, the first a *Discourse to the Greeks,* which is ostensibly a defense of Christianity, a new religion in an age that insisted on the antiquity of belief, but which is actually a sustained attack on all that is Greek; his second book is of enormous importance, the *Diatesseron* (literally, through the four), a harmony of the Gospels that later became canonical; this was the first gospel harmony, and it is important not only for being the first instance of a much-imitated form and a major source for New Testament textual critics but also because it became the gospel of the Syrian Church down to the fifth century. A fragment of the *Diatesseron* was discovered at *Dura Europos.

TELEMACHUS (d. 391)

According to *Theodoret of Cyrrhus, Telemachus was a monk who tried to separate two gladiators but was killed in the process; this caused the emperor Honorius (395–423) to abolish the gladiatorial contests; this is probably a legend.

TELESPHORUS (d. ca. 136)

Pope from about 125; like most early popes, he is only a name to later generations; his Greek name fits in with what is known of the early Roman community's strong foreign element; furthermore, *Irenaeus says that he was a *martyr, the only pope between Peter and *Pontian who was definitely a martyr. Later tradition claimed that Telesphorus introduced the song of the angels (*Gloria in excelsis Deo*) into Christmas Midnight Mass.

TERTULLIAN (ca. 160–ca. 220)

Quintus Septimius Florens Tertullianus was born a pagan at Carthage in North Africa; he was well educated in the law, rhetoric, and Greek; around 195 he was converted to Christianity, and he threw himself completely into his new calling. He was the first great Latin Christian writer, and he wrote extensively. Consequently, he created much Latin theological terminology, which in turn found its way into English, for example, from the words *tria* (three) and *unitas* (unity) he created *Trinitas* (Trinity). He also used words such as *substantia* and *persona,* terms with long theological futures. He had an uncompromising character, and almost all his writings were written against someone, whether *heretodox Christians such as *Marcion of Pontus or *persecuting pagan governors such as Scapula; he was a brilliant writer whose literary abilities sometimes outstripped his arguments. Although at first a Catholic, he soon let his *asceticism and rigorism get the better of him; around 206 he abandoned the Church for *Montanism, whose uncompromising strictness suited his temperament; now his former coreligionists felt the lash of his pen as he turned on them the skills with which he had attacked the pagans. Around 220 he decided that Montanism was no longer strict enough, and he founded his own group, the Tertullianists. Theologically he was a *Trinitarian, and he strongly opposed *modalism; in *Christology he was a *subordinationist; his ecclesiology was that of the gathered Church, not just cut off from society at large but actually opposed to it. His famous remark, "What has Athens to do with Jerusalem?" separating Christianity from pagan culture, did not really apply to him, since he had a formidable education, but many Christians after him saw this as an ideal. His legal background found its way into his theology; he was fond of arguing with *heretics from a legalistic viewpoint, which enabled him to score many points but did not bring much sophistication to his thought. He was excellent on the attack, but he was not a systematic thinker, and he did not really construct an extensive theology. But as the later history of African Christianity—with its *martyrdom, fanaticism, emphasis upon ritual purity—proved, Tertullian was very much the Father of the African Church.

TESTAMENT OF OUR LORD JESUS CHRIST

In Latin, *Testamentum Domini;* originally a Greek treatise of the fourth or fifth century, extant now only in Oriental languages; in two books, it purports to be instructions Jesus gave to his disciple before his ascension, especially about the Antichrist but also about church buildings (bk. 1) and instructions for Christian life (bk. 2).

THADDEUS, ACTS OF

This survives in two versions or recensions, one the story of *Abgar and the other the *Doctrine of *Addai.*

THECLA

According to the *Acts of *Paul and Thecla,* she was a pagan virgin of Iconium in Asia Minor who was converted by Paul; she broke off her engagement; her enraged fiance stirred up the local populace against Paul and Thecla. Condemned to the beasts, she was in the arena before she had been *baptized; seeing a large pit of water, she baptized herself; she later escaped and became a missionary. *Tertullian strongly denied that this episode proved that women were entitled to baptize, so apparently some were interpreting the story of Thecla that way.

THEMISTIANS

Also called Agnoetae; a *Monophysite splinter group, it took its name from an Alexandrian *deacon named Themistius and claimed that the human soul of Christ was ignorant.

THEODORA (ca. 500–547)

Roman empress and wife of *Justinian; the daughter of an animal trainer, she came from the lower classes of Byzantium, and her enemies, of whom there were many, claimed that as a young woman she had been a prostitute; whatever the truth of that, she was a loyal wife to Justinian and a great inspiration to him at crucial moments in his career. She was also a *Monophysite who did her best to promote the cause, sheltering refugee Monophysite *bishops, sending a mission to Nubia, and interfering in papal affairs, for example, the choice of *Vigilius to be pope. Her loyalty to the Monophysites probably influenced her husband's constant efforts to reconcile them to the supporters of *Chalcedon, even to the point of calling an *ecumenical council (*Constantinople II in 553).

THEODORE ASCIDAS

A Palestinian monk and by 543 *metropolitan of Caesarea in Cappadocia, he became the emperor *Justinian's theological and spiritual advisor. He was interested almost completely in Eastern affairs and eventually ousted the papal representative *Pelagius (later Pope Pelagius I) from any influence over Justinian, turning the emperor's attention to the Eastern province, where *Monophysitism continued to divide the empire. Theodore apparently formulated the condemnation of the *Three Chapters in an attempt to win back the Monophysites. It is likely that he also coauthored some of Justinian's theological writings.

THEODORE LECTOR
(fl. ca. 510–530)

Church historian who combined sections from *Socrates, *Sozomen, and *Theodoret to form his own *Historia Tripartita;* he also wrote an independent Church history down to the year 527 which survives in fragments and contains some valuable information about the reigns of the emperors *Zeno, Anastasius I, and *Justinian.

THEODORE OF MOPSUESTIA
(ca. 350–428)

A native of Antioch, he studied rhetoric in the school of the famous pagan teacher Libanius; there he became friends with *John Chrysostom, beginning a lifelong association; at John's urging, in 369 he joined him in the *monastic school of *Diodore of Tarsus, a famous *Antiochene exegete.

Theodore decided to leave, marry, and begin a legal career, but John convinced him to stay in religious life. He was ordained a *priest in 383 and by 392 was *bishop of Mopsuestia in southeastern Asia Minor. He had a quiet episcopate and built for himself a considerable reputation for scholarship and orthodoxy. He was a true Antiochene as an exegete and probably the greatest exegete of that school. He accepted little without questioning, for example, he challenged the Davidic authorship of some of the psalms, and he tried to understand many biblical passages and books by considering their historical background—now a staple of modern exegesis. He also used philology and literary criticism. Besides exegesis, he also wrote *ascetical tracts and treatises against *heretics, but he became notorious in antiquity for his *Christology. Theodore, like most Antiochenes, emphasized the independence of the human and divine in Christ, and he explained the unity of the two in terms that, not surprisingly, lacked the specificity of the First Council of *Ephesus and that of *Chalcedon. *Nestorius was his pupil, and the brush of heresy that tarred him was occasionally used to tar his teacher. In the sixth century, things went much futher when the emperor *Justinian (527–565) and his associates in an attempt to pacify the *Monophysites, who considered the Council of Chalcedon to be *Nestorian, decided to condemn Theodore and his writings in the notorious affair of the *Three Chapters. Theodore's reputation was still considerable a century after his death, and many Church leaders objected to the posthumous condemnation of someone who had died in the peace of the Church. Justinian, however, got his way at the Second Council of *Constantinople in 553, but the continued use of Theodore's exegesis in the Middle Ages proved that even this did not keep appreciative scholars from using his work, especially his commentary on the Psalms.

THEODORE OF RAITHU
(fl. ca. 537–553)

Monk from the Sinai peninsula who wrote a work on the incarnation in which he defended *Chalcedon and refuted many *heretics, from *Manes to his contemporary *Severus of Antioch.

THEODORE THE ABBOT
(fl. 350–368)

*Horsiesi, the second successor to *Pachomius, when faced with discontent in his communities, appointed Theodore to be his coadjutor. Theodore proved to be an effective administrator who settled the communal difficulties and went on to found several new Pachomian houses. Three letters of his survive.

THEODORET OF CYRRHUS
(ca. 393–ca. 468)

Born at Antioch and educated in *monastic schools, around 416 he decided to become a monk. In 423 he was elected *bishop of the Syrian town of Cyrrhus; he did not want the post but accepted it, and for more than thirty years he was an eager pastor and effective administrator. He battled against paganism and *heresy, but he also saw to the material well being not only of his congregations but also of the city as a whole; for example, he helped to finance an aqueduct. Like many *Antiochene theologians, he entered the *Nestorian controversy on the side of *Nestorius, fearful that *Cyril of Alexandria's *Christology emphasized the union of the divine and human in Christ to the extent that the human was practically swallowed up, that is, that Cyril was teaching a disguised *Apollinarianism. He criticized Cyril's position, and at the First Council of *Ephesus in 431, he sided with *John of Antioch. After the council, however, he made the magnanimous gesture of accepting the *Union of 433; indeed, many scholars believe Theodoret himself had drawn up the *creed, which both sides accepted. He returned to his diocese, but when another Alexandrian bishop, *Dioscorus, began his defense of *Eutyches, Theodoret found himself a center of controversy. The Second Council of *Ephesus deposed him, but he appealed to *Leo the Great of Rome, who condemned the council. At *Chalcedon he was rehabilitated, but only after he condemned Nestorius and all who did not acknowledge that the Blessed Virgin Mary can be called *Theotokos; he then returned to his diocese and lived in peace. Because he was widely considered to be a Nestorian, which he may have been early in his episcopal career, he was loathed by the *Monophysites, and in 553 the emperor *Justinian (527–565) arranged for the Second Council of *Constantinople to condemn his teaching as one of the *Three Chapters. Although best known for his role in the Christological controversies, Theodoret was also a prominent exegete, especially of the Old Testament, as well as an *apologist and Church historian—his *Church History* and *History of the Monks* combine to form one of the most valuable accounts of early Eastern Christian life and preserve important information not found in other sources.

THEODOSIAN CODE

Law code promulgated by *Theodosius II in 438; it outlawed paganism and established guidelines for Church and state relations in the Roman Empire.

THEODOSIUS I (ca. 346–395)

Son of a general who was executed in 376 and a distinguished soldier himself, he was appointed head of the armies of the East by the emperor Gratian in 378 when the emperor Valens was killed battling the Goths; in 379 Gratian proclaimed Theodosius emperor of the East. The new emperor was a strong adherent of the *creed of *Nicea, and in 380 he defined the Catholic faith as that professed by *Damasus I of Rome and Peter of Alexandria; in 381 he made Christianity the official religion of the Eastern empire. In that same year he called the First Council of *Constantinople, which put an end to *Arianism in the East. In 388 he defeated the usurping emperor Maximus to keep the emperor Valentinian II on the throne, but, in 394, he deposed by war Valentinian's successor, Eugenius, a nominal Christian with strong pagan support, and

for one year he ruled the empire alone, the last emperor to do so. He was always severe against Christian *heretics; he was more tolerant of pagans, at least until 391, when he outlawed paganism and closed the temples. His rigorous approach usually met with the approval of the leading *bishop of the age, *Ambrose of Milan, but on two occasions, the ordering of the rebuilding of a synagogue burned by a Christian mob in 388 and the massacre of civilians in Thessalonica in 390, Ambrose disagreed with Theodosius and forced the emperor to make amends and do public *penance.

THEODOSIUS II (401–450)

Grandson of *Theodosius I, he acceded to the throne of the Eastern Roman Empire in 408. At first his elder sister *Pulcheria influenced him, but in 421 he married *Eudoxia, an equally strong influence; in the 440s the imperial minister Chysaphius replaced the women as his chief advisor, although the emperor also listened to the *ascetic *Simeon Stylites. In spite of his having invited *Nestorius to be *bishop of Constantinople, Theodosius, at the urging of Pulcheria, deserted him at the First Council of *Ephesus in 431, favoring *Cyril of Alexandria; astonishingly, he did the same thing to another bishop of Constantinople, *Flavian, at the Second Council of *Ephesus in 449, favoring yet another bishop of Alexandria, *Dioscorus, and his *Monophysite theology. Possibly Theodosius cannily considered that the best interests of the empire lay in support of Alexandrian *Christology, which was widely accepted in the Eastern provinces. In 450 Theodosius fell from his horse and was killed, to be succeeded by Pulcheria and her husband, who immediately reversed his policies.

THEODOSIUS ARCHIDIACONUS
(fl. ca. 520–530)

North African who wrote about the Holy Land.

THEODOTION

Either a Jew or a Jewish convert to Christianity; sometime in the second century he made a translation of the Old Testament into Greek or a revision of the *Septuagint (scholars are uncertain which); *Origen used it in preparing the *Hexapla; *Jerome placed Theodotion among the *Ebionites while *Epiphanius of Salamis placed him among the *Marcionites.

THEODOTUS

Second-century *Gnostic from the Levant and a disciple of *Valentinus, he is known from excerpts of his work made by *Clement of Alexandria in his *Excerpta ex scriptis Theodoti;* the excerpts deal with *baptism and the *Eucharist as well as standard Valentinian themes about cosmology and the various states of humanity.

THEODOTUS OF ANCYRA
(d. ca. 444)

*Bishop of Ancyra and opponent of *Nestorius.

THEODOTUS THE BANKER
(fl. ca. 190–200)

A member of the Roman community and an ally of his namesake, the Shoemaker; he favored an *Adoptionist *Christology and apparently made some speculations about the Old Testament figure Melchizedek (Gen 14:18-20).

THEODOTUS THE SHOEMAKER
(fl. ca. 190–200)

He was active in Rome during the pontificate of *Victor I, who excommunicated him; Theodotus taught an *Adoptionist *Monarchianism, which claimed that Jesus was just a man, although a very virtuous one, who became the Christ when he received the Holy Spirit—or, rather, was adopted by him—at his *baptism, after which he had the power to work miracles; Theodotus and his followers mixed biblical exegesis with the study of logic.

THEOGNOSTUS OF ALEXANDRIA (d. 280)

Head of the *catechetical school of Alexandria from about 265; he wrote seven books of theology based on *Origen's teachings, but these are now lost; they appear, from surviving fragments, to have been *subordinationist in character.

THEOPASCHITES

Sixth-century *Monophysite group that claimed that "one of the Trinity suffered in the flesh" (*Unus ex Trinitate carne passus est*). The leader of the group was a Scythian monk named

*John Maxentius, who preached his doctrine in Rome and Constantinople in 519 and 520. The formula was well received in some parts of the East and was for a time acceptable to the emperor *Justinian, while the see of Rome maintained a careful neutrality because neither the emperor nor the popes considered the formula to have compromised *Chalcedon; eventually, however, the sees of Constantinople and Rome both refused to accept it.

THEOPHILUS OF ALEXANDRIA
(d. 412)

*Patriarch of Alexandria from 385; he was a respected theologian and got on well with the monks of the Egyptian desert, but he is rightly remembered for his ruthlessness in ecclesiastical politics. A determined foe of paganism, he arranged for the destruction of many important pagan monuments, including the famous temple of the Serapeum; the loss to culture and art was significant. Theophilus had theologically been a follower of *Origen, but when, in 399, some desert monks began to question Origen's and thus his own orthodoxy, Theophilus quickly changed his mind and even presided over a *heresy hunt for Origen's followers, including the *Tall Brothers. This brought him into the *Origenist controversy then raging in Palestine, thanks to *Epiphanius of Salamis, but when the Tall Brothers received support and refuge from *John Chrysostom at Constantinople, Theophilus began his most famous and most insidious intrigue. He was a true Alexandrian, proud of the long and distinguished history of his see; he resented the rise of Constantinople, the imperial see, and he equally resented the rival theological school of *Antioch. John Chrysostom was from Antioch and *bishop of Constantinople, and Theophilus seized the opportunity to attack and embarrass both rival sees. John's careless offending of important imperial personages made things easier. In 402 John called Theophilus to come to Constantinople to answer charges made by the refugee monks, but, collaborating with the empress *Eudoxia and accompanied by his nephew and successor, *Cyril, and thirty-five other bishops, Theophilus organized the Synod of the Oak in 403, where John was convicted of several trumped-up charges, deposed, and sent into exile (although John soon returned, only to be soon sent into a second, fatal exile by the empress). The rest of Theophilus' episcopate was quiet.

THEOPHILUS OF ANTIOCH
(fl. ca. 160–180)

An *apologist, he was born a pagan, received a good Greek education, and after his conversion (date unknown) became the sixth *bishop of Antioch; only one work of his survives, To Autolycus, a defense of Christianity against the criticisms of the pagan Autolycus; in this book is the first Christian use of the word triad, the Greek equivalent of the Latin Trinitas, for the three persons in God. There is also a more developed *Logos theology than that of *Justin Martyr, since Theophilus distinguished between the Logos internal to God and the Logos emitted by God for the purposes of creation.

THEOTOKOS

Greek for "God-bearer," that is, Mother of God; this term was used theologically as early as *Origen as a title for Mary, and it soon became a widely popular devotion among the uneducated, logically so, since most ancient pagan religions included some mother goddess and Mary filled that old role. The term became most important in the early fifth century, when *Nestorius of Constantinople rejected it as *heretical and claimed that Mary could rightly be called *Christotokos,* that is, Mother of Christ. This went contrary to the theology of *Cyril of Alexandria, who claimed that the divine and human in Christ was so united that Mary could indeed bear that title. The First Council of *Ephesus in 431 settled the matter in favor of Cyril, a decision ratified at the Council of *Chalcedon in 451, and the title *Theotokos* has been in use ever since.

THOMAS, ACTS OF

An *apocryphon, probably from Edessa and from the third century; it tells of the Apostle Thomas' journey to India, where he converts a king named Gundophorus; he works elsewhere in India until an angry husband, whose wife had given up sexual relations with him after becoming a Christian, has Thomas killed. This mildly *Gnostic work contains the *Hymn of the Pearl,* an account of a journey a young prince took to Egypt, where he recovered a great pearl and then abandoned the soiled clothes that the local people had given him, the clothes symbolizing the body and the pearl the soul. Although this apocryphon is throughout a work of fiction, it may reflect an actual historical situation, that is, an early Christian mission to India.

THOMAS, APOCALYPSE OF

*Manichean work written in Latin around 400; it speaks of the end of the world; it was popular in *Priscillianist circles.

THOMAS, GOSPEL OF

An *Encratite *apocryphon from Edessa, dating about 140, and widely used by various *Gnostic groups; it contains 114 sayings, or *logia,* of Jesus; Thomas is the guardian of these sayings; this work stresses the importance of knowledge for salvation, a view reflected in its interest in Jesus' words, not his deeds. The current form of the gospel is of the second century, but many scholars would date it to the late first century, especially since its form, a collection of sayings, reflects the likely mode of transmission of Jesus' words before the canonical Gospels were written.

THOMAS, INFANCY GOSPEL OF

Many famous and notorious stories about Jesus' childhood appear in this second-century work, probably of Syrian provenance; these stories include Jesus making clay birds come to life; they also include portraits of him as a detestable little brat who shows off his powers and often uses them vindictively, for example, Jesus strikes dead a child who bumps into him. This surprisingly popular work clearly reflects the importation of folklore in narratives about Jesus.

THREE CHAPTERS

Name given to passages in the works of three theologians, *Ibas of Edessa, *Theodore of Mopsuestia, and *Theodoret of Cyrrhus, which were singled out for condemnation at the emperor *Justinian's Second Council of *Constantinople in 553 in order to pacify the *Monophysites, who were resisting imperial authority; actually all the works of Theodore and even his person were condemned at the council.

THUNDERING LEGION

Several Christian writers, including *Tertullian and *Eusebius of Caesarea, testify that during a campaign on the Danube when the emperor Marcus Aurelius (161–180) and his army were facing drought, Christian soldiers prayed and a great thunderstorm broke out, saving the Romans. The legion was known as the *Legio fulminata* (Thundering Legion), but the title dates to the time of Augustus (d. 14), so it is unconnected to the event described; several pagan writers tell the story but do not attribute the rainstorm to Christian prayers, and Marcus Aurelius commemorated the event on a column in Rome that portrays the god Jupiter as the savior of his army.

TIMOTHY OF CONSTANTINOPLE (d. 518)

*Patriarch of Constantinople from 511; a somewhat vacillating man, he gave in to *Monophysite pressure in order to forestall the appointment of *Severus of Antioch as his replacement. The Monophysites never trusted him, and he outraged the *Chalcedonians by permitting a Monophysite addition to the *Trisagion; by 515 he was working with Severus to promote the Monophysite cause.

TIMOTHY OF JERUSALEM

Sixth-century Greek homilist whose work raised the question of the assumption of Mary; a very obscure figure.

TIMOTHY THE CAT (d. 477)

A *Monophysite and supporter of *Dioscorus of Alexandria; although Alexandria had a *Chalcedonian *bishop after Dioscorus' deposition, his followers continued to resist and in 457 chose the *priest Timothy, nicknamed "the Cat" (presumably because of his small size), to be their *patriarch; the governor arrested him, but his supporters revolted, killed the Chalcedonian patriarch, Proterius, and forced his release. Timothy ruled for three years before being banished by the emperor Leo I (457–474); his supporters maintained his cause, and in 474 the usurping emperor, Basiliscus, permitted him to return. *Zeno recaptured the throne in 476 and wished to exile Timothy again, but, as he was an old man, he was allowed to remain in Alexandria, where he died the following year. Timothy was neither a great theologian nor a great leader, but he maintained the Monophysite cause in Egypt in the quarter century after Chalcedon, no easy feat, and the strength of that movement in

Egypt in the following century owes much to him. Some theological works, only recently discovered, survive.

TITUS, EPISTLE TO

An *apocryphon in Latin from the fifth century; it is apparently *Priscillianist; it stresses *asceticism and cites other apocrypha.

TITUS OF BOSTRA (d. 371)

*Bishop of Bostra in Roman Arabia; the emperor *Julian the Apostate in 362 urged his people to depose him for sedition, a suggestion the people did not take. Titus' extant writings include a commentary on Luke and a sermon on the Epiphany, but his reputation rests on a detailed and skillful refutation of the *Manicheans, including a strong defense of the Old Testament.

TOME

Title given to the book (in Latin, *tomus*) written by *Leo I and sent to the Council of *Chalcedon expressing the classic Roman view of *Christology; although unimaginative by Greek standards, it is clear in its emphasis upon the one person of Christ with two natures, united but unmixed.

TRADITION

From the Latin *traditio,* literally, "a handing down"; although it occasionally meant the handing over of the Scriptures in time of *persecution (one who did so was a *traditor*), it almost always meant what had been handed down from earlier generations. Although the term did not have the binding notion it possessed for Roman Catholics after the Council of Trent (1545–1563), ecclesiastical tradition was clearly authoritative; for example, *Irenaeus uses tradition against the *Gnostics to demonstrate the novelty of their teaching. *Vincent of Lérins enshrined tradition in his famous *Commonitorium.*

TRADITOR

One who handed over the Scriptures during a *persecution; this accusation was widely bandied about in Africa after the persecution of Diocletian (303–305), and the *Donatist Church grew out of a *schism with what the Donatists considered to be a Church of *traditores* in Carthage; the English word "traitor" comes from this.

TRADUCIANISM

The notion that in conception the human soul is passed along from parents to children, as distinguished from *creationism, the notion that God created each soul individually. Coarse as traducianism sounds, it had a distinct appeal, especially to *Augustine, since it could explain how original sin was passed from Adam and Eve to generation after generation. *Fathers who favored this theory feared that the notion of separate creation of souls would make it impossible for the sin to be passed along; moderate traducianists would say that God used the souls of parents as the substance from which the new souls were created, thus allowing for individual creation of souls while retaining the ancestral link; those opposing it said the passing on of the sin was spiritual.

TRINITARIAN THEOLOGY

Name for that theology that dealt with Christian teaching on the Father, Son, and Holy Spirit; the Greek term *triad* was first used by *Theophilus of Antioch; *Tertullian of Carthage was first to use *Trinitas.* The Trinity was always a central feature of Christian theology, but the *Arian controversy of the fourth century brought the question of the Trinity onto center stage. The *ecumenical Council of *Nicea in 325 affirmed the oneness of God as well as the full divinity and equality of Father and Son in the Trinity; the ecumenical Council of *Constantinople in 381 defined the full divinity and equality of the Father, Son, and Spirit. After the fourth century, the focus of theology shifted to *Christology in the East and, thanks to *Augustine and *Pelagius, to grace and free will in the West.

TRISAGION

The *doxological chant "Holy God, holy and mighty, holy and immortal, have mercy upon us," was introduced into the Greek liturgy by *Proclus of Constantinople (d. 446), and it made its way eventually into the Roman liturgy for Good Friday. The *Monophysites added the phrase "who was crucified for us" to this doxology, and this was a point of controversy in the sixth-century Eastern Church.

TRITHEISM

A *Monophysite teaching that denied the actual unity of nature of the three persons in the Trinity; *John Philoponus taught this, but since he had a strong interest in philosophy, scholars believe that he may have been speculating, since he could not have been unaware of the consequences of this teaching for the Faith.

TYCONIUS (fl. ca. 370-390)

A *Donatist, he saw through the narrow ecclesiology of his coreligionists, who condemned him in 380, but since he considered the Catholics *traditores,* he could not join them; he remained a Donatist layman and put up with the criticism. He recognized that the Donatist insistence upon ritural purity was not only impractical but unscriptural, since the Bible speaks of the wheat and the tares, of redeemed sinners, and the like. The books he wrote critical of the Donatists are now lost; he is known as a writer through an Apocalypse commentary that was widely used in the early Middle Ages but mostly for his *Liber regularum* (Book of Rules), a guide to the exegesis of Scripture; it is marked by moderation and lucidity, urging the reader to follow seven rules to understand the text. One of his readers was *Augustine, who cited Tyconius in his enormously influential book on Christian education, *De doctrina Christiana,* thus guaranteeing by his authority that the most talented of his Donatist opponents would influence Latin exegesis for centuries.

U

ULPHILAS (ca. 311–383)

A Christian from Asia Minor whose family was kidnapped by the Goths, Ulphilas grew up in Gothic captivity as a Christian; he was part of the Gothic embassies sent to Contantinople; while there, he came under the influence of the *Arian *Eusebius of Nicomedia, who recognized the young man's talents and had him consecrated *bishop of the Goths; Ulphilas was a very successful missionary, so successful that for centuries to come the Goths were Arians and their brand of Christianity spread to other tribes, such as the Vandals, who settled in Spain. Ulphilas also prepared a translation of the Bible into Gothic (deliberately omitting the books of Kings, since he thought the Goths did not really need scriptural encouragement to go to war), an enormously valuable work for philologists; around 350 he had to flee from his missionary area in the face of growing Gothic hostility to Rome and to those perceived as its representatives. He led a group of Goths into Roman territory south of the Danube to an area set aside for them by *Constantius II. Because of his Arian beliefs, Ulphilas has not figured prominently in Church histories, but he must rank as one of Christianity's great missionaries.

UNION OF 433, FORMULA OF

After the First Council of *Ephesus in 431, there was a serious split between the sees of Alexandria and Antioch, with the latter convinced that *Cyril, *bishop of the former, had imposed an *Apollinarian *Christology on the council and had engineered the condemnation of *Nestorius, bishop of Constantinople and an *Antiochene as well. The emperor *Theodosius II (408–450) intervened, both diplomatically and with threats, and in 433 the Antiochenes offered Cyril a *creed, probably drawn up by Cyril's theological rival *Theodoret of Cyrrhus, which asked Cyril to withdraw some anathemas he had prepared against Nestorius and to clarify some of his theological terminology; the Antiochenes for their part abandoned the cause of Nestorius and accepted the Council of Ephesus. Cyril accepted the document and peace was restored, although some of his supporters felt he had compromised too much; they surfaced two decades later as *Monophysites.

URBAN I (d. 230)

Pope from 222; virtually nothing is known of this pope; he was a Roman and apparently a supporter of *Callistus, since *Hippolytus and his group remained in *schism; during Urban's pontificate the Roman emperor was Alexander Severus (222–235), who had a positive interest in Christianity. The Christian scholar Sextus *Julius Africanus designed a library for the emperor, *Origen spoke before him and his mother, and Hippolytus dedicated a treatise to her; a later tradition claimed that the emperor, a religious eclectic, kept statues of Abraham and Jesus in his private chapel along with those of several pagan gods. Urban's pontificate thus saw no difficulties with the Roman state.

URSACIUS

See **Valens.**

URSINUS (d. ca. 385)

*Antipope from 366; the losing candidate in the (literal) battle to be successor to Pope *Liberius, he remained a nuisance but not a threat to *Damasus I; Ursinus maintained himself in Rome during 366–367 but was then exiled; he was released to go to Milan but ordered not to go to Rome; at Milan he worked to discredit Damasus, inducing a converted Jew named Isaac to accuse him of a crime, apparently adultery, but the pope was exonerated by the emperor Gratian (375–383); the emperor exiled Ursinus to Cologne and Isaac to Spain; in 381 Ursinus' followers convinced the prefect of the city of Rome to look into Damasus' conduct once again, but led by *Ambrose of Milan, the northern Italian *bishops protested this action to the emperor and the matter was dropped. Ursinus caused Damasus no more trouble after that.

URSULA

According to legend, she was a British Christian princess who was *martyred along with eleven thousand companions by the Huns at Cologne around 400; the actual Saint Ursula was probably a German virgin-martyr who was venerated locally along with some companions; indeed, the number eleven thousand results from the misreading of an inscription! But she was a very popular saint in the Middle Ages and beyond.

V

VALENS AND URSACIUS

Balkan *bishops and pupils of *Arius who worked together to destroy *Athanasius and to advance the *Arian cause; they were highly politicized, changing their views to meet the opinions of the emperor *Constantius II (337–361); for example, they were at first *Anomoeans, then *Homoians. They were literally anathema in the West, having been excommunicated at several synods, but they maintained their influence in the East; their careers lasted from 335, when they attacked Athanasius at the *Council of Tyre, to 359 at the Synod of *Ariminum in 359. Valens was bishop of Mursia; Ursacius, of Singidunum.

VALENTINE

The man venerated on February 14 as Saint Valentine is a combination or, more accurately, a confusion of two Valentines, a Roman *priest traditionally said to have been *martyred under the emperor Claudius (41–54), an unlikely event, and a *bishop who was martyred at Rome on an uncertain date; indeed, it is possible that the traditions about the two are in fact about one person; the link between Valentine and lovers is difficult to explain, one explanation being that the Roman pagan feast of the Lupercalia, a fertility rite, was observed on February 15 and Valentine became connected with that.

VALENTINUS (fl. ca. 135–165)

Possibly an Alexandrian and the most prominent *Gnostic teacher, he came to Rome during the bishopric of *Hyginus and became a prominent figure in the community, even to the point of hoping to be elected *bishop; possibly he left Rome after realizing this was not to be. Valentinus taught primarily a cosmology, speaking of a spiritual world filled with aeons, one of whom, Christ, united himself with the man Jesus to redeem some humans by gnosis, that is, saving knowledge, from the material world, which was created by the *Demiurge, an offspring of the fallen aeon Sophia (Wisdom); this Demiurge was to be identified with the God of the Old Testament. The humans who received this gnosis were pneumatics, or spiritual persons, although these were limited to the followers of Valentinus; other groups were psychics, who could attain a limited form of enlightenment, while the vast majority of people were primarily corporeal in orientation and would be forever trapped in matter. In spite of, or possibly because of, this spiritual aristocracy, Valentinianism flourished, at least into the fourth century. Valentinus also had several prominent disciples, the most important of whom was *Ptolemy. Clearly he was a great speculative theologian and a man open to diverse influences but unsympathetic to Jewish thought patterns.

VENANTIUS FORTUNATUS
(ca. 530–d. after 600)

Northern Italian who studied at Ravenna. He went on a pilgrimage to the shrine of *Martin of Tours (566), met the Frankish saint *Radegunde, was ordained a *priest, and became chaplain of Radegunde's convent; sometime after 590 he was elected *bishop of Poitiers. He wrote more than three hundred poems, most in the style of the great Latin classical poets although with a Christian spirit and emotion; his two greatest poems, *Vexilla regis* and *Pange lingua* became part of the Western Latin Passion liturgy and traversed the boundary between Roman and medieval poetry. He also wrote some *hagiography.

VERECUNDUS OF JUNCA (d. 552)

An African opponent of the *Three Chapters, he wrote some Old Testament exegesis and also edited excerpts of the Council of *Chalcedon.

VETUS LATINA

Literally, "Old Latin," that is, of the Bible; this is something of a catchall term to label all Latin versions of the Bible before and besides the *Vulgate; *Augustine labeled one of the versions as the *Itala, but scholars have not been able to isolate this version.

VICTOR I (d. 198)

Pope from 189; an African, he was the first Latin-speaking pope; like most Africans, he was rigorous on religious matters; when the *Quartodeciman controversy arose again, Victor claimed that Rome followed the correct method for calculating the date of Easter, and at his initiative, synods of *bishops met to discuss the question. Most agreed with him, but those of Asia Minor, led by *Polycrates of Ephesus, disagreed. Victor overreacted to this challenge to his views; he wanted to excommunicate all the Asian bishops, and he wrote to other bishops for support. They, however, were shocked at his bellicose attitude and told him that peace and unity were more important than uniformity; *Irenaeus wrote from Gaul to cite the example of *Anicetus and *Polycarp. The controversy died down, but it is unknown if Victor changed his mind. This pope also condemned the *Monarchian teaching of *Theodotus the Shoemaker, and he deposed the

*Gnostic Florinus from the *priesthood. Victor was also the first pope to have a connection, albeit questionable, with the imperial court. The emperor Commodus (180–192) had a Christian concubine named *Marcia who asked Victor to prepare a list of the Christians condemned to the mines of Sardinia; he obliged, and Marcia arranged to have them freed. The prisoners included the future pope *Callistus, whom, says *Hippolytus, Victor did not want freed.

VICTORINUS, MARIUS
(d. after 362)

African pagan rhetorician who converted to Christianity around 355; his study of Neoplatonic philosophy brought him to that point; before his conversion he had written several philosophical works, and after his conversion he used philosophy more than the Scriptures to explain his new faith; in 362 the emperor *Julian the Apostate ordered Christians to cease teaching the classics, and Marius abandoned his position; he turned to writing against the *Arians. Indeed, he even anticipated the eventual recognition of the divinity of the Holy Spirit, accomplished at the First Council of *Constantinople. His conversion was considered a remarkable feat; thirty years after the event *Augustine still marveled at it.

VICTORINUS OF PETTAU
(d. ca. 304)

*Bishop of Pettau on the Danube, one of the few Christians from that region to leave any writings behind; he was the first Christian to write formal biblical commentaries in Latin, mostly on the Old Testament, but he also prepared an important commentary on the Apocalypse. He was, however, a *millenarianist, which caused his works to fall into disuse after his death, although *Jerome revised the Apocalypse commentary. Victorinus died as a *martyr during the *persecution of Diocletian (303–305).

VICTORIUS, CLAUDIUS MARIUS
(fl. 425–450)

Gallic poet and rhetorician from Marseilles who wrote a verse commentary on Genesis down to Abraham; theologically weak, it draws from pagan as well as Christian writers, and it introduces legendary material into the discussion.

VICTOR OF ANTIOCH
(fl. fifth century)

Compiler of a commentary on the Gospel of Mark that drew from several earlier Greek *Fathers, including *Origen, *John Chrysostom, and *Cyril of Alexandria.

VICTOR OF CAPUA (d. 554)

Italian *bishop who prepared a harmony of the four Gospels reflecting the *Diatesseron of *Tatian; it was enormously popular in the Middle Ages; it survives in the *manuscript called the Codex Fuldensis, which was once in the hands of the great Anglo-Saxon missionary Boniface (d. 754).

VICTOR OF VITA (fl. ca. 480–490)

African *bishop and author of *A History of the Persecution of the Province of Africa,* an account of the *persecution of the Catholics by the *Arian Vandals from 428 to 484; it gives a picture of Africa in the period after *Augustine.

VICTRICIUS OF ROUEN (ca. 340–ca. 410)

What is known of his life comes from two letters of *Paulinus of Nola; Victricius entered the Roman army at age seventeen but left when he became a Christian; he became a *priest and evangelized in what is now the Flanders region; in 385 he became *bishop of Rouen in Gaul, where he built churches and encouraged *monasticism; around 396 he traveled to Britain to strengthen the Churches there, and he visited Rome in 403; his one literary remain is a well-written work, *On the Praise of Saints.*

VIGILIUS (d. 555)

Pope from 537; of a noble Roman family, he was a *deacon of *Boniface I, who tried to designate Vigilius his successor but backed down when this engendered fierce opposition; Vigilius was then ambassador to Constantinople, where he got to know the future emperor and empress, *Justinian and *Theodora, who befriended him and offered him the papacy if he would compromise with the *Monophysites, Theodora herself being a Monophysite. Vigilius agreed, but on the death of *Agapitus in 536, he was unable to return to Rome in time to prevent the election of *Silverius, whom, however, the Byzantine commander in Italy, Belisarius, deposed; in 537, with Silverius in prison, Vigilius became pope. Although Vigilius had a good record in his dealings with the West, his relations with Justinian dominated his reign. The emperor followed *Chalcedon, so Vigilius went back on his pledge to Theodora to compromise with the Monophysites. Ironically, the emperor himself had also made a decision to compromise because the continuing religious division was weakening the empire's eastern frontiers. The emperor decided to condemn both the persons and teachings of three dead theologians whom the Monophysites loathed; the portions of their works singled out as *heretical were known as the *Tria Capitula,* hence the name of the controversy, "the *Three Chapters." The West was strongly against this for two reasons: all three had died in the peace of the Church, and it was blatantly unjust for later generations to condemn them; furthermore, this was a poorly disguised attack on the Council of Chalcedon. Vigilius resisted at first, but Justinian had him arrested in 545, kept in Sicily for two years, and then brought to Constantinople. In 548, after a year of imperial pressure, Vigilius agreed to condemn the Three Chapters. Western reaction was immediate and harsh; in 550 the African *bishops excommunicated Vigilius, who, in his turn, had to excommunicate members of his own household and eventually of his own family (*see* **Rusticus**). To protect the pope, Justinian allowed him publicly to withdraw his agreement but forced him to write a secret agreement for condemnation. By 551 Justinian had decided again to demand a public condemnation, but Vigilius refused and was again imprisoned, although he managed to escape and flee to Chalcedon. He worked out another compromise with Justinian in 552, but in 553 the emperor decided that the Three Chapters should be condemned by an *ecumenical council, which he called in 553 (the Second Council of *Constantinople) and which he forced the pope to attend. The emperor made public the pope's secret agreement to condemn the Three Chapters and finally got Vigilius to agree to the condemnation; in 554 he forced Vigilius to accept the decisions of the council. Vigilius remained in Constantinople for another year, and then died in Sicily on his voyage home to a very uncertain reception. The *schism his actions provoked in Italy and Africa lasted into the next century, and the divisions spilled over into the civil realm, facilitating the Lombard conquest of northern Italy.

VIGILIUS OF THAPSUS (fl. ca. 500)

African *bishop during the Vandal occupation; he wrote two anti*heretical works, a dialogue against the *Arians, and an attack on *Eutyches, an anti-*Monophysite work.

VINCENTIAN CANON

See **Vincent of Lérins.**

VINCENT OF LÉRINS (d. ca. 450)

A Gaul who began life as a soldier but became a *priest and was attached to the monastery of *Lérins; apparently he joined with *Salvian in educating *Salonius and Veranus, the two sons of *Eucherius of Lyons, apparently with some success, since both became *bishops. Vincent is known for one work, the *Commonitorium* (Memorandum), and he is actually known mostly for one phrase in the work. This is a treatise on methodology, an attempt to define for theologians and others where Christian truth is to be found; it derives from another Gallic work, the *Against Heresies* of *Irenaeus of Lyons. Vincent demonstrates where orthodox teaching is to be found, and he, perhaps inadvertently, summed it up in the phrase, *quod ubique, quod semper, quod ab omnibus creditum est,* ([we believe] what has been believed everywhere, always, and by everyone). This phrase became enormously influential and popular, and it is known as the Vincentian Canon.

VINCENT OF SARAGOSSA (d. ca. 304)

*Deacon and the proto*martyr of Spain; while his martyrdom is historically validated, virtually nothing reliable is known of his life.

VITA

Latin for "life," it means in early Christianity the biography of a saint but one written primarily to edify rather than to inform; a vita usually contains biographical information but also elements not historically verifiable, such as miracles; by the end of the *patristic period a vita had predictable elements, such as a marvelous childhood, for the subject.

VITALIS

Third-century Italian *martyr who died at Bologna; his cult was widespread in the West, and a beautiful fifth-century church was built in his honor in Ravenna.

VITUS (d. ca. 303)

Originally he was venerated along with two other *martyrs, Modestus and Crescentia, but by the end of Christian antiquity, he was venerated separately as the patron of those afflicted with nervous diseases, including St. Vitus' dance (Sydenham's chorea), as well as those who have been bitten by animals.

VULGATE

From the Latin *Vulgata Latina,* that is, the common Latin version, a name given in the Middle Ages to the translation of the Bible made mostly by *Jerome, who undertook the work on his own and not with official sanction. Many contemporaries, such as *Augustine, give witness to the poor state of the *Vetus Latina,* and this new translation should have been welcome. Liturgical conservatism, however, hindered its acceptance, although its use by *Gregory the Great (590–604) secured its place in the West. By the end of the Middle Ages its use was taken for granted, hence the name *Vulgata.* The Vulgate is enormously important in Christian history, since it was the Bible of all medieval scholars, such as Bede and Thomas Aquinas; it also influenced much medieval liturgical writing as well. It provided medieval scholars not only with their knowledge of the Bible but also with much of their theological terminology. The Vulgate is likewise an important witness to the Greek and Hebrew biblical texts of around 400 as well as literary monument on its own.

X

XYSTUS

Greek spelling of the Latin name "*Sixtus," borne by three popes of this period; indeed, it is likely that all three popes originally had this Greek name.

Z

ZACHARIAS OF MYTILENE (d. ca. 550)

Also called Zacharias Rhetor and Zacharias Scholasticus; a Palestinian by birth, he was originally a *Monophysite who converted to the *Chalcedonian cause; he wrote a church history in Greek which is now preserved in a *Chronicle of the World* in Syriac; it has valuable information about the period from 450 to 491 in the East; Zacharias also wrote biographies of such Monophysite luminaries as *Severus of Antioch and *Peter the Iberian.

ZENO (ca. 450–491)

Byzantine emperor from 474; a soldier who had himself proclaimed emperor by the widow of the emperor Leo I (d. 474), he had to flee Constantinople in 475 but returned successfully in 476 and ruled securely after that. Although personally a follower of *Chalcedon, he was concerned to bring the *Monophysites back into the empire, so he published the *Henoticon* in 482 with the aid of *Acacius of Constantinople and *Peter Mongos of Alexandria; the *Henoticon* avoided repudiating Chalcedon but made some concessions to the Monophysites; it failed, and Zeno was unable to pacify the West or the East.

ZENO OF VERONA (d. ca. 380)

*Bishop of Verona from 363; probably an African by birth, he used his position to combat *heresy and paganism in the Verona region; he was also a famous homilist who drew from his fellow Africans *Tertullian and *Lactantius; scholars debate how many of the many homilies attributed to him are authentic.

ZEPHYRINUS (d. 217)

Pope from 198; despite his long reign (the longest of the first thirty-five successors of Peter) he remains an obscure man, known largely from what his later enemy *Hippolytus tells us; Zephyrinus, clearly a weak-willed man, succeeded the strong-willed *Victor, so possibly the community wanted a quieter pontificate; this was not to be the case. The pope relied heavily on his strong-willed arch-*deacon *Callistus, who actually governed the lower clergy. Zephyrinus was no theologian, and he was tolerant of the *modalists, but he condemned *Theodotus the Shoemaker and the other *Adoptionists along with their *bishop, Natalius, whom the pope commendably readmitted into communion after rigorous *penance. It was during Zephyrinus' pontificate that *Origen visited Rome, proof of Rome's continuing attraction to foreign, especially Eastern, scholars.

ZOSIMUS (d. 418)

Pope from 417; a Greek by birth, he stirred up difficulties with the African *bishops by agreeing to reopen his predecessor's (*Innocent I) condemnation of *Pelagius and *Celestius; the Africans, led by *Augustine, massed against him and even went above his head to the emperor Honorius (395–423); Zosimus soon gave in, although his letter to the Africans saying that he would not reopen the case asserts papal primacy. The pope also fought with the Africans about the *priest *Apiarius, whose appeal from an African excommunication he had agreed to hear; Zosimus asserted the right of the bishop of Rome to hear appeals from Africa; the matter was not settled until after the pope's death. In Gaul, Zosimus promoted the career of Patroclus of Arles, raising his see to *metropolitan status and thus laying the seeds for another problem that came to fruition after his death, specifically in the reign of *Leo I.

A Brief History of the Early Church

(an asterisk indicates that there is an article
about this person or movement in the text)

The history of the Christian Church began at Pentecost, when the frightened, intimate disciples of Jesus received the gift of the Holy Spirit and thus had the faith and courage to preach the gospel. They preached at first only to Jews and even limited themselves to the city of Jerusalem, but, inevitably, they came into contact with Gentiles, and the Church then had to face its first great problem— for whom was the message of Jesus intended?

The answer, of course, was everyone. In Acts 15 Luke portrays the decision as having been made in a council by representatives of the Twelve and by James, leader of the Jerusalem community, but he—and Paul's letters—make it clear that Paul was the moving figure here. The Apostle to the Gentiles brought Christianity out of a Jewish environment and into the larger Roman world.

The career of Paul, as told in the New Testament, probably began around 35 and lasted until his death in Rome. Paul evangelized largely in Asia Minor, although Luke hints of missions to Cyprus (Acts 15:39) and also to Italy, since there were Christians there to greet Paul (Acts 28:14-16). Paul said that he hoped to go to Spain (Rom 15:28), but there is no way to determine if he ever got there.

In the 60s of the first century, two events changed Christian history. The first was the Great Fire of Rome in 64, an event for which the emperor Nero used the Christians as scapegoats. For the first time, the Roman state persecuted the Christians, but it was not to be the last. Peter and Paul both died about this time, probably as victims of the *persecution. The other event was the Roman-Jewish War of 66-70. It ended in defeat for the Jews, and after this the Jerusalem Christian community no longer played a major role in the Church at large.

The rest of the first century is rather obscure. Much literature survives, including the Synoptic Gospels, the Catholic Epistles and those of the Pauline school, and the Book of Revelation, but scholars cannot be certain of the time and place of their composition. Clearly, the Christians were organizing and finding their place in the world.

Finding their place in the world was no easy thing to do because many Christians such as Paul (1 Thess 4:13-18) expected the imminent end of the world. But as the years passed and it became clear that the end was further off than previously anticipated, the Christians looked more and more to living in this world rather than longing for its end.

The Christians were also finding that their originally Jewish movement was changing rapidly in the cultural world of the Greeks and Romans. Although Jewish influence continued to be strong into the second century, more and more the influence of the Gentile civilization was felt. Around 95 *Clement of Rome could praise the organization of the Roman army and speak of God's ordering of the world in Stoic terms. These new Christians also asked different questions. The *Docetists wanted to know how a divine being such as the Son of God could be immersed in the flesh, concluded that he could not, and proclaimed that Jesus did not really have a body but only seemed to have one.

With diversity of teaching, threat of persecution, and just the simple physical growth of the Church, the need for more effective organization became obvious. In what turned out to be a sure sign for the future, *Ignatius of Antioch spoke of a community revolving around and headed by a monarchical *bishop. But not all Christians favored such organization. The *Gnostics considered the teacher, not the bishop, the most important person in the community, and the various Gnostic sects, often disagreeing with one another, agreed that knowledge, not Christ's redemptive death, would save people, although not everyone was capable of salvation.

The Gnostics did not have much use for the Old Testament, except for Genesis, which provoked their cosmological speculations, and their outlook was heavily Greco-Roman. *Marcion of Pontus (fl. ca. 140–160) went so far as to dismiss the Old Testament and to create Christianity's first formal New Testament, something that provoked other Christians to further what had been till then a slow process, namely, the recognition of inspired Christian books.

Another group of Christians, the *apologists, produced the first Christian literature for those outside the community, a sure sign that the belief in an imminent end had largely faded. The apologists tried to convince the authorities to stop the persecutions, and they, especially *Justin Martyr (d. ca. 165) with his spermatic *Logos theory, argued that Christianity was not antithetical to Greek learning but could be reconciled to it.

While Gnostics and apologists were debating the role of Greek culture in Christianity, still another group of Christians saw things in a very different light. The prophet *Montanus, probably around 160, claimed that the Holy Spirit was speaking through him and his associates, and many Christians responded to this message, perceived to be a revival of Old Testament prophecy. The Montanist movement failed, but it raised the crucial question, what could the Church do about prophecy?

In the last quarter of the second century, things were seriously confused for the Christians; the central question had become authority. To which authorities could one refer? the Spirit? a Gnostic teacher? Greco-Roman philosophy? Scripture? The person who answered the question was *Irenaeus of Lyons, who, around 180, argued that authority rested in the teaching of the apostles and their co-workers, who had transmitted their teachings in the Scriptures, especially the four Gospels, and in a succession of bishops (Irenaeus singled out the see of Rome as an example of this succession), thus establishing the basic theological method for all the Church *Fathers, namely, Scripture and Tradition. All writers after him would claim scriptural support and consonance with the Fathers for their teaching.

Irenaeus was a Greek from Asia Minor who was part of the foreign community in Lyons, but by the end of the second century the Latin element in Christianity was growing, with its earliest manifestations in Roman North Africa. The martyrs of *Scilli showed the firm character of the African Church, and in the person of *Tertullian (fl. ca. 200–220) this Church produced the first great Latin theologian, a man whose many works established Latin theological terminology and whose rigorist approach to moral questions both reflected and determined the narrow African ecclesiology. His successor *Cyprian (d. 258) furthered his views and helped to make the African episcopate a strong, vital organization.

In Alexandria, however, a far different type of Christianity emerged. In that cosmopolitan center, a meeting place for people of so many cultures of the Mediterranean, of Africa, of the Middle East, and even of Asia, an educated, liberal Christianity took shape. *Clement of Alexandria (fl. ca. 190–202) welcomed Greek learning into Christianity, calling it a school to prepare the Gentiles for Christ, the role the Old Testament had played for the Jews. His great successor, *Origen (d. ca. 253), although professing little sympathy for pagan culture, knew it well, and many of his greatest achievements reflected his contacts with the non-Christian world, such as his *Hexapla, a monumental work of textual criticism to aid his debates with the Jews, and his Against *Celsus, a response to a pagan critic. Origen also wrote copiously on the Bible, establishing exegesis as a major theological discipline, and his On First Principles tried to unify several theological themes into a system.

Little is known about Roman Christianity at this time. No great theologians emerged from the Roman Church; those we do know of had migrated there, for example, *Valentinus the Gnostic or Justin Martyr. The second-century popes before *Victor I (189–198) are little more than names, although Victor was not unwilling to assert Roman authority in the *Quartodeciman controversy with the bishops of Asia Minor. In the person of *Callistus I (217–222) Rome produced a rather unusual but strong leader, one who abandoned the Church of saints for the Church of sinners, relaxing requirements for *penance and simply taking a more humane approach to human behavior. By the middle of the century, however, with Pope *Stephen I (254–257), the papacy was asserting its primacy and basing it on Saint Peter, a theme with a long future.

The internal development of the Church was largely uninhibited by persecutions. There were fierce local persecutions, such as one in Gaul in 177 and in Africa and Egypt in 202, and in 235 the emperor Maximinus Thrax exiled both Pope *Pontian and the *antipope *Hippolytus to Sardinia, but it was not until 250 that the emperor Decius launched the first empire-wide persecution, an example followed by later emperors. Decius' death in 251 saved the Christians from a drawn-out struggle, although it also precipitated the controversy over what to do with those Christians who had *lapsed during the persecution, a controversy especially bitter between Cyprian of Carthage and Stephen of Rome.

The history of the Church in the latter half of the third century remains obscure. It is clear that in this time at least two important Roman provinces had become largely Christian, North Africa and Asia Minor. It is also clear that a Church governed by bishops had become the order of the day and that, led by the Africans' example, the bishops of particular regions would meet in *council to discuss matters of more than local interest. For example, the bishops of Syria met to get the disreputable *Paul of Samosata deposed from the see of Antioch in 268.

There were no serious persecutions against the Christians in the late third century, and the Church continued to grow both geographically and materially. The Faith had definitely reached Spain and Britain by the third century, and the Christians had begun to build churches for themselves and to purchase cemeteries, the Roman *catacombs being the most famous. To many Christians a peace with Rome had finally been established, and Christians began to move up in the ranks of Roman society.

This peace came to an end in 303 when the emperor Diocletian, urged on by his associate Galerius, decided to persecute the Christians, blaming them for the considerable economic woes of the empire. Known as the Great Persecution for its duration (two years) and the number of victims, this assault on the Church proved as unfruitful as the earlier ones, and Diocletian called a halt to it. Two accounts about the beginnings of the persecution illustrate the Christians' social ascent by 303. When the emperor's priests found the entrails of some sacrificial animals to be unfavorable, some Christians who had been there and who had made the sign of the cross were blamed. Also, Diocletian could see a Christian church from his palace in Nicomedia. With a church within view of the palace and Christians present at imperial sacrifices, it is clear that the Christians had benefited from the years of peace and had become trusted, even at the highest levels of Roman society.

Although rightly remembered as a persecutor, Diocletian was also a government reformer. In the third century Roman generals and politicians routinely plotted to overthrow the emperor, and the constant turnover at the top guaranteed that the government could no longer work on behalf of its citizens. Economic woes and, increasingly, barbarian invasions threatened the Roman world. Diocletian tried to reform the system, dividing the empire in two, the general division being the Latin-speaking Western provinces and the Greek-speaking

Eastern provinces, and arranging for each emperor to have an associate to succeed him in 305, the year agreed upon for Diocletian's retirement. But his carefully structured system did not work for long, and in 306 the several claimants for the throne began a vast and confusing civil war. The two victors were *Constantine I and Licinius, the former becoming ruler of the West and the latter of the East in 313.

Because of a (now famous) vision, Constantine believed that the Christian God had aided him in an important battle. Although he did not become a Christian right away, in 313 he issued jointly with Licinius the Edict of *Milan, which gave the Christians freedom of worship and also restored much of their confiscated property. By 319 Constantine had become a Christian, and, like any emperor, he thought it his right and obligation to intervene in religious affairs. When Licinius initiated a senseless persecution of some Christians in the East, Constantine marched against him and, with Licinius' execution in 324, he became the sole emperor of Rome, to the delight of many Christians and the chagrin of pagans.

If Constantine thought that a Christian emperor would enjoy peace with his coreligionists, he was soon disabused of that notion. In Africa the *Donatist *schism broke out over whether bishop *Caecilian of Carthage had been ordained by *traditores or was even one himself. Constantine arranged for Western councils to settle this matter, but the Donatists defied emperor and councils and the schism continued down to the Muslim invasion.

More important was the *Arian controversy, in which bishops of the East divided over how to explain the relation of the Father to the Son in the Trinity. The emperor had an imperial idea and called the first *ecumenical council at *Nicea in 325, where *Arius and his *subordinationist theology were condemned and the equality and divinity of Father and Son were affirmed. But now that the Roman court had become Christian, Christianity became involved in political intrigues. After the council, supporters of Arius, led by *Eusebius of Nicomedia, worked to change Constantine's mind, and they very much influenced his sons, especially the emperor *Constantius II (337–361), who was a convinced Arian.

For the Nicene cause, *Athanasius of Alexandria labored against considerable odds, although he always enjoyed the support of the Westerners, especially the papacy. The Eastern bishops who had reservations about Nicea feared that it taught a form of *Sabellianism, which did not really distinguish Father and Son in the Trinity; they did not, however, favor radical Arianism. Led by the three *Cappadocians, the Nicenes won over these moderates to their cause. In 381 the second ecumenical council, held at *Constantinople, reaffirmed Nicea and also affirmed the divinity of the Holy Spirit.

After Constantine became a Christian, the Church made great progress in converting Roman society. During the reign of Emperor *Theodosius I (379–395) Christianity became the official religion of the empire. Many large churches were built, especially in Rome, and the Christians, led by *Ambrose of Milan, began to work out a theory of Church and state.

But not all Christians were pleased with these developments. A surprising number left society and went into the deserts of Egypt, Syria, and Palestine to lead lives of frightful *asceticism. The *monastic movement was the great spiritual movement of the fourth century, and when monastic literature reached the outside world, it had an enormous impact. After the Bible, the two most popular Christian books were Athanasius' life of *Antony of Egypt and *Sulpicius Severus' life of *Martin of Tours, an Eastern monk who had migrated to the West. Bishops lived with their clergy in community, and monastic values such as mortification became widespread.

Latin Christian intellectuals had for a long time been pale contrasts to their Greek brethren, but Ambrose, *Jerome, *Pelagius, and especially *Augustine showed the maturity of this branch of Christianity. Augustine and Pelagius struggled to shape the Christian understanding of free will and original sin, and the African went on to treat of many more topics, such as history, religious education, and spiritual life. But, ironically, all this was happening when the Western empire was passing into the hands of the invading Germanic barbarians, one tribe of which had actually captured the city of Rome in 410.

As Rome fell, the Christian Church became the only institution to survive intact. The bishops of Rome had, since the middle of the second century, claimed the primacy of the Western Church, based upon their see's having been traditionally founded by Saint Peter, leader of the apostles. This argument was never very successful in the East or in Africa, but by the middle of the fourth century most Western Churches went along. When Africa fell to the Vandals in the fifth century, the popes emerged as the unquestioned leaders of the Latin-speaking world. *Leo I the Great (440–461) ruled as no pope before him.

The invading barbarians provided the Western Church with a significant challenge. Although Bishop *Patrick worked successfully among the barbarian Irish outside the Roman Empire, most barbarians within the imperial borders were either hostile pagans or Arians—thanks to the work of *Ulphilas—and they were rarely amenable to the religion of the Romans. But in the fifth and especially the sixth centuries, many of these barbarians, such as the Anglo-Saxons and Franks, received missions and converted. The heroes of this struggle were hundreds of local missionaries and one pope, *Gregory I the Great (590–604), who turned the Church's eyes away from the Mediterranean and into northern Europe. Yet in the sixth century the most influential man for the future was not a pope or a missionary but a monk, *Benedict of Nursia, whose monastic rule was to guide the spiritual and intellectual leaders of the West for almost six hundred years.

While some were converting the barbarians, others, such as *Boethius and *Cassiodorus and *Isidore of Seville, were laboring to preserve as much of ancient knowledge as they could, lest the culture of Greece and Rome disappear.

While the Western empire was falling, the Eastern empire remained secure, urban, and literate. With the great *Trinitarian questions of the fourth century now settled, it was almost inevitable that the theologians would turn to the person of Christ. Unfortunately, what should have been a theological discussion was marred by vicious ecclesiastical rivalries, as the bishops of Alexandria tried to maintain their leadership of the East against their old antagonists from Antioch and the new bishopric of Constantinople, revelling in the status of imperial see.

When in 403 *Theophilus of Alexandria successfully worked for the deposition and exile of *John Chrysostom, an Antiochene who had become bishop of Constantinople, the pattern for the next half century was set. In 431 *Cyril of Alexandria triumphed over another Antiochene bishop of Constantinople, *Nestorius, at the ecumenical Council of *Ephesus, a triumph not only of politics but of theology. The council agreed with Cyril that the Blessed Virgin Mary could indeed be called *Theotokos, the Mother of God, because the human and divine in Christ were so united, against Nestorius and the Antiochenes, who usually emphasized the distinction between human and divine. When the monk *Eutyches began to teach that the union was so close that the divine had swallowed up the human and that after the incarnation Christ had only one nature, *Flavian of Constantinople condemned him, but *Dioscorus of Alexandria used the controversy Eutyches had begun to work the deposition of Flavian at the Second Council of *Ephesus in 449. But Eutyches' teaching, the basis of *Monophysitism, was rejected by Leo I of Rome, who strongly influenced the ecumenical Council of *Chalcedon in 451, at which Dioscorus was deposed and Christ was affirmed to be one person having two natures, one human and one divine.

Chalcedon was a watershed. Monophysitism became virtually the national religion of Egypt, and, thanks to *Severus of Antioch and others, it soon spread to Syria. Byzantine emperors—for the Eastern empire was now known as Byzantium—tried to put a stop to the split this dispute caused, but they always failed because the supporters of Chalcedon feared a betrayal. The most zealous effort was made by *Justinian (527–565), who had managed to reconquer much of Italy from the barbarians and now wished to secure the Eastern part of the empire. He called the second ecumenical council at *Constantinople, at which he contrived the condemnation of three theologians, called the *Three Chapters, whom the Monophysites detested, but even this did not end the schism. The Chalcedonian-Monophysite split endured until the seventh century, when much of the Monophysite territory passed into the hands of the Muslims.

After the year 600, the history of the Church becomes the history of medieval Christianity. Many ancient attitudes and customs held on, and scholars like John Damascene (d. ca. 749) in the East and the Venerable Bede (d. 735) in the West read more like Fathers of the Church than medieval writers; but, their achievement notwithstanding, the world of the early Church had passed into history.

The Popes of the Early Church

(an asterisk denotes an antipope)

Peter (d. ca. 64)

Linus (ca. 66–ca. 78)

Anacletus (ca. 79–ca. 91)

Clement (ca. 91–ca. 100)

Evaristus (ca. 100–ca. 109)

Alexander I (ca. 109–ca. 116)

Sixtus I (ca. 116–ca. 125)

Telesphorus (ca. 125–ca. 136)

Hyginus (ca. 136–ca. 142)

Pius I (ca. 142–ca. 155)

Anicetus (ca. 155–ca. 166)

Soter (ca. 166–ca. 174)

Eleutherius (ca. 174–189)

Victor I (189–198)

Zephyrinus (198–217)

Callistus I (217–222)

Hippolytus* (217–235)

Urban I (222–230)

Pontian (230–235)

Anterus (235–236)

Fabian (236–250)

Cornelius (251–253)

Novatian* (251–258)

Lucius I (253–254)

Stephen I (254–257)

Sixtus II (257–258)

Dionysius (260–268)

Felix I (269–274)

Eutychian (275–283)

Gaius (283–296)

Marcellinus (296–304)

Marcellus I (306–308)

Eusebius (309)

Heraclius* (309)

Miltiades (311–314)

Sylvester (314–335)

Mark (336)

Julius I (337–352)

Liberius (352–366)

Felix* II (355–365)

Damasus I (366–384)

Ursinus* (366–367)

Siricius (384–399)

Anastasius (399–401)

Innocent I (401–417)

Zosimus (417–418)

Boniface (418–422)

Eulalius* (418–419)

Celestine I (422–432)

Sixtus III (432–440)

Leo I (440–461)

Hilarus (461–468)

Simplicius (468–483)

Felix II (III) (483–492)

Gelasius I (492–496)

Anastasius II (496–498)

Symmachus (498–514)

Laurence* (498–499, 501–506)

Hormisdas (514–523)

John I (523–526)

Felix III (IV) (526–530)

Boniface II (530–532)

Dioscorus* (530)

John II (533–535)

Agapetus I (535–536)

Silverius (536–537)

Vigilius (537–555)

Pelagius I (556–561)

John III (561–574)

Benedict I (575–579)

Pelagius II (579–590)

Gregory I (590–604)

The Roman Emperors

I. The Pagan Emperors

Augustus 27 B.C.–A.D. 14
Tiberius 14–37
Gaius Caligula 37–41
Claudius 41–54
Nero 54–68
Galba 68
Otho 69
Vitellius 69
Vespasian 69–79
Titus 79–81
Domitian 81–96
Nerva 96–98
Trajan 98–117
Hadrian 117–138
Antoninus Pius 139–161
Marcus Aurelius 161–180
Lucius Verus 161–169
Commodus 180–192
Pertinax 193
Didius Julianus 193
Septimius Severus 193–211
Caracalla 211–217
Macrinus 217–218

Elagabalus 218–222
Severus Alexander 222–235
Maximinus 235–238
Gordian I, Gordian II,
    Balbinus, Pupienus 238
Gordian III 238–244
Philip the Arab 244–249
Decius 249–251
Gallus 251–253
Aemilianus 253
Valerian 253–260
Gallienus 253–268
Claudius Gothicus 268–270
Quintillus 270
Aurelian 270–275
Tacitus 275–276
Florianus 276
Probus 276–282
Carus 282–283
Numerianus 283–284
Carinus 283–285
Diocletian 284–305
Maximian 286–305
Constantius I 305–306

Galerius 305–311
Maxentius 306–312
Severus 306–307
Licinius 308–324
Maximinus Daia 310–313

II. The Christian Emperors
(before the division of the empire)

Constantine I 306–337
Constantine II 337–340
Constans 337–350
Magnentius 350–353
Constantius II 337–361
Julian* 361–363 (pagan)
Jovian 363–364

(after the division of the empire)

East:
Valens 364–378
Theodosius I 379–395
(West also after 394)
Arcadius 395–408
Theodosius II 408–450
Marcian 450–457
Leo I 457–474
Leo II 474
Zeno 474–475
Basiliscus 476–476

West:
Valentinian I 364–375
Gratian 367–383
Valentinian II 383–392
Eugenius 392–394
Honorius 395–423
Valentinian III 425–455
Maximus 455
Avitus 455–457
Majorian 457–461
Severus 461–467
Anthemius 467–472
Olybrius 472–473
Glycerius 473–474
Julius Nepos 474–475
Romulus Augustulus
   475–476

III. The Byzantine Emperors

Zeno (again) 476–491
Anastasius I 491–518
Justin I 518–527
Justinian 527–565
Justin II 565–578
Tiberius II 578–582
Maurice 582–602
Phocas 602–610

*born a Christian but became a pagan

Bibliography

The best reference book for this period is *The Encyclopedia of Early Christianity,* edited by Everett Ferguson, Frederick Norris, and Michael McHugh (New York, 1990). This is a large, well-illustrated work with entries prepared by leading scholars in the field.

The Oxford Dictionary of the Christian Church, second edition, edited by F. M. Cross and Elizabeth Livingstone (Oxford, 1978) is a standard reference work for Church history in general, but it has many entries on the early Church. The same can be said for *The Westminster Dictionary of Church History,* edited by Jerald Brauer (Philadelphia, 1971). Multivolume reference works such as *The New Catholic Encyclopedia* (New York, 1967–) also carries articles on early Christianity.

Two other general reference books with much application to early Christianity are *The Oxford Dictionary of Saints* by David H. Farmer (Oxford, 1978) and *The Oxford Dictionary of Popes* by J. N. D. Kelly (Oxford, 1986).

Two good surveys of early Christianity are *The Early Church* by Henry Chadwick (New York, 1967) and the larger and more recent *The Rise of Christianity* by W. H. C. Frend (Philadelphia, 1984). The multivolume *History of the Church,* edited by Hubert Jedin, has as its first two volumes *From the Apostolic Community to Constantine* by Karl Baus (New York, 1965) and *The Imperial Church from Constantine to the Early Middle Ages* by Karl Baus and others (New York, 1980).

Superb supplements to these are two collections of documents from the period, both edited by James Stevenson and recently revised by W. H. C. Frend, *A New Eusebius* (London, 1987) and *Creeds, Councils, and Controversies* (London, 1988). A much shorter collection which extends only to Constantine is *The Fathers of the Primitive Church* by Herbert Musurillo (New York, 1966).

Much of the study of early Christianity deals with the Fathers of the Church. A good introduction to them is *Beginning to Read the Fathers* by Boniface Ramsey

(Mahwah, N.J., 1985). Two basic guides to the Fathers are *Patrology* by Bernhard Altaner (New York, 1960) and *Patrology*, four volumes, by Johannes Quasten; the first three volumes were published between 1950 and 1960 but have been republished (Westminster, Md., 1983). In 1986 Angelo di Berardino headed a team of contributors who published *Patrology*, volume 4, with the approval of Quasten, as a continuation of his work. Altaner and Quasten both provide a brief life of the writer in question, a list of his or her writings, and an analysis of the writer's theology. For the Greeks in the great age of theological controversy, see Frances Young's *From Nicea to Chalcedon* (Philadelphia, 1983).

Many patristic works are available in English translation, often in multivolume series of entire works and often in topical selections. The basic modern multivolume series are *Ancient Christian Writers* (Westminster, Md., 1946–) and *Fathers of the Church* (Washington, 1947–). There are also older sets of translations, such as *The Ante-Nicene Fathers* (New York, 1926) and *A Select Library of the Nicene and Post-Nicene Fathers of the Christian Church,* first and second series (New York, 1886, 1890).

Many readers may find the books of topical selections more accessible. *Documents in Early Christian Thought,* edited by Mark Santer and Maurice Wiles (Cambridge, England, 1975) contains selections on several theological themes by many Fathers, although Irenaeus is the earliest representative; the selections are both representative and of reasonable length. Henry Bettenson has edited two volumes, *The Early Christian Fathers* and *The Later Christian Fathers* (Oxford, 1969, 1972) in which the material is divided according to the Fathers, whose work in then divided topically; the selections are well chosen, clearly divided, and begin with the Apostolic Fathers.

Increasingly common is the practice of devoting an entire book to a topic and then excerpting from various early Christian works on the topic. The series *Sources of Early Christian Thought* (Philadelphia, 1980–) edited by William Rusch, includes volumes on biblical interpretation, military service, and Christology among other things; the volumes are published irregularly. They include brief and helpful bibliographies. The series *The Library of Christian Classics* also has several patristic volumes, such as Owen Chadwick's *Western Asceticism* and S. L. Greenslade's *Early Latin Theology,* but the series as a whole covers a much wider chronological range.

The best introduction to patristic thought with excerpts on particular issues is *Message of the Fathers of the Church* (MFC) edited by Thomas Halton for Michael Glazier Books of The Liturgical Press (Wilmington and Collegeville, 1983–). It includes volumes on diverse topics: *Ministry* by Joseph Lienhard (vol. 8), *Women in the Early Church* by Elizabeth Clark (vol. 13), *Teaching Authority in the Early Church* by Robert Eno (vol. 14), *Grace and the Human Condition* by Peter Phan (vol. 15), and *The Early Fathers on War and Military Service* by Louis Swift (vol. 18). Inevitably in a series, not all the volumes are of the same quality, but the series as a whole is well done and will introduce the reader to patristic thought on many issues. The books also contain up-to-date bibliographies.

Recent study of early Christianity has dealt not only with the traditional Fathers but also with writers formerly considered outside the orthodox pale. The best collection of Gnostic writings is by James Robinson, *The Nag Hammadi Library,* second edition (New York, 1988). As for the many apocryphal scriptures, the standard collection is *New Testament Apocrypha,* two volumes, edited by Edgar Hennecke and Wilhelm Schneemelcher (London, 1963, 1965).

Many patristic works have been translated separately, for example, *The Confessions of Saint Augustine* in many editions; only the series and basic one-volume works are included here.

The early Christian period saw the shaping of most basic Christian doctrines, such as those of the Trinity and the person of Christ. Two standard general treatments of patristic theology and doctrine are J. N. D. Kelly, *Early Christian Doctrines* (New York, 1978) and Jaroslav Pelikan, *The Christian Tradition, a History of the Development of Doctrine, I: The Emergence of the Catholic Tradition (100–600)* (Chicago, 1971). Also, the volumes containing excerpts from the Fathers will usually discuss the development of patristic theology related to the excerpts, for example, *The Holy Spirit* (MFC, vol. 3) by J. Patout Burns and Gerald Fagin.

There is an enormous amount of literature on the Fathers—on individual persons, events, doctrines, attitudes—and many of the volumes listed here will guide the reader to those. I do, however, wish to mention three volumes which have appeared too recently to be included in the books listed above and which deal with topics that appear very frequently in this dictionary. First, Leo Donald David, S.J., has produced a clear, useful, and reliable guide, *The First Seven Ecumenical Councils (325–787): Their History and Theology* (Wilmington, Del., 1987); this book is the best introduction to the councils in English, and it offers handy chronologies and bibliographies. Second, Robert Eno's *The Rise of the Papacy* (Wilmington, Del., 1990) provides a learned, readable, and well-documented account of the early papacy and of the individuals and forces that conspired to make the bishops of Rome the leaders of the Western Church. Third, R. P. C. Hanson's *The Search for the Christian Doctrine of God* (Edinburgh, 1988), the *magnum opus* of a distinguished scholar, traces the Arian controversy and the establishment of Trinitarian doctrine from 318 to 381.

Finally, for those wishing to keep abreast of what is happening in early Christian studies, the journal *Patristics,* published twice annually by the North American Patristic Society, carries reviews of new books in the field.